91 - another essay

HOW DO STORIES SAVE US?

LOUVAIN THEOLOGICAL & PASTORAL MONOGRAPHS
—————————— 35 ——————————

HOW DO STORIES SAVE US?

An Essay on the Question with the
Theological Hermeneutics of David Tracy in View

by

Scott Holland

PEETERS
LOUVAIN – PARIS – DUDLEY, MA

W.B. EERDMANS

2006

Library of Congress Cataloging-in-Publication Data

Holland, Scott, 1954-
  How do stories save us? : an essay on the question with the theological hermeneutics of
David Tracy in view / by Scott Holland.
    p. cm. -- (Louvain theological & pastoral monographs ; 35)
  "Bibliography for David Tracy": P.
  Includes bibliographical references (p.   ) and index.
  ISBN 90-429-1786-5 (alk. paper)
    1. Narrative theology. 2. Tracy, David. I. Title. II. Series.

BT83.78.H65 2006
230'2092--dc22   2006043998

© 2006, Peeters, Bondgenotenlaan 153, 3000 Leuven, Belgium

ISBN-10 0-8028-2470-6 (W.B. Eerdmans)
ISBN-13 978-0-8028-2470-7
ISBN-10 90-429-1786-5 (Peeters Leuven)
ISBN-13 978-90-429-1786-6
D. 2006/0602/76

TABLE OF CONTENTS

For David Tracy: Public Theologian

PART ONE

INTRODUCTION

The truth of religion, like the truth of its nearest analogue,
art, is primordially a truth of manifestation.
David Tracy

Over a decade ago I met Father Andrew Greeley in the city of New
Orleans. The storyteller and sociologist claimed that David Tracy's
theology of the analogical imagination greatly informed his own
work as a novelist of popular fiction, a sociologist of religion and
a Roman Catholic priest. So appreciative was Greeley of Tracy's
theology that he used the royalties from his novels to endow a chair
for him at the University of Chicago Divinity School in memory
of his parents. Thus, Tracy now holds the Andrew Thomas and
Grace McNichols Greeley Distinguished Service Professor of Theology chair at Chicago. I was most intrigued by a comment Greeley made about Tracy, story and theology. A decade ago narrative
theology was the rage in the academy. Andrew Greeley suggested
that Tracy understood story in religion much differently than
Protestant narrative theologians because of his Catholic imagination, which is an analogical imagination rather than a dialectical
imagination. I agreed with Greeley. He promised to someday write
a book on the topic.

In fact, Greeley had traveled to New Orleans to present his sociological findings validating David Tracy's theology of the analogical imagination at the Annual Meeting of the American Academy of
Religion. To accomplish this he first presented his sociological theory of religion as imagination, which he argued paralleled Tracy's
theological theory. He contended that religion is imaginative before

it is propositional and that in the Catholic imagination, if there is any conflict between sacramental imagery and propositional teaching, the former will almost always win the hearts and minds of the faithful. Religion, according to Greeley, begins in (1) experiences which renew hope, is encoded in (2) images or symbols which become templates for action, is shared with others through (3) stories which are told in (4) communities and celebrated in (5) rituals. Greeley explained that this model is a circle not a straight line, and hence permits the creative, mutual interaction of experience, image, symbols, story, community and ritual.[1]

Drawing from David Tracy's *Analogical Imagination* as well as his own empirical sociological surveys and studies, Greeley argued that the classic works of Catholic theologians and artists tend to emphasize the presence of God in the world, while the classic works of Protestant theologians tend to emphasize the absence of God from the world. The Catholic writers stress the nearness of God to creation while Protestant writers mark the distance between God and creation. Protestants emphasize the risk of superstition and idolatry, Catholics the dangers of a creation where God is only marginally present. In story, symbol and sacrament, Catholics tend to emphasize the immanence of God while Protestants accent the transcendence of God. Greeley was careful to remind the audience of academics that these different moods and models of religious imagination were not mutually exclusive and that David Tracy believed that both imaginations — analogical and dialectical — were necessary in theological conversation and construction.

Father Greeley used his skills as a preacher and storyteller to declare that the Catholic spiritual sensibility easily imagines the Holy "lurking" in all creation. He suggested rather freely in a public forum

---

[1] Andrew M. Greeley, "Theology and Sociology: Validating David Tracy," *Journal of the American Academy of Religion* 59 (1991) 643-652.

text v. universe

what most polite and theologically-correct Catholic theologians only dare utter in tavern table-talks over beer: *the Protestant dialectical imagination envisions life within a sacred text while the Catholic analogical imagination imagines life in a sacramental universe.* Greeley gave this lecture in New Orleans, the city where, as Tennessee Williams reminded us, the line of the streetcar named Desire intersects with the line of the streetcar called Cemeteries. Yet as one would expect from such a passionate Irish priest, always aware of the inevitable sting of death, Greeley, in his fascinating remarks, hailed Desire and rode far from the century's dark dialectics of human destruction and death.

David Tracy's earlier work, although more carefully nuanced than Greeley's, shared his optimism and enthusiasm about the presence of God in a world of grace. Consider Tracy on the Catholic analogical imagination:

> Do you believe, with Albert Camus, that there is more to admire in human beings than to despise? Do you find that with Erasmus and Francis of Assisi that in spite of all folly, stupidity, illusion and even sin, reality in its final moment is trustworthy? Do you find within yourself a belief with Aquinas and Thomas More that reason is to be trusted for finding the order of things; that faith transforms but does not destroy our reason? Is your final image of God one like John's gospel of love, not fear; of Christ as fundamentally a community of hope, not a ghetto of escape and fear? Does your image of society include a trust that can somehow be ordered short of radical disjunction? Does your image of the cosmos itself include a trust that it too is somehow ordered by relationships established by God for all reality; and that reality itself — in spite of all serious, sometimes overwhelming evidence to the contrary — is finally benign? Then you possess, I believe, a Catholic analogical imagination.[2]

---

[2] David Tracy, "Presidential Address: The Catholic Analogical Imagination," *Catholic Theological Society Proceedings* 32 (1977) 234-244.

Andrew Greeley published his long-promised book on this topic in 2000 under the title, *The Catholic Imagination*.[3] Father Greeley's optimism and enthusiasm have not waned since New Orleans. Indeed, this work expands and extends that earlier study by blending sociological research with spiritual and artistic reflection on the promise of the analogical imagination, which is always, according to Greeley, a creation-centered, metaphorical and sacramental imagination. By this assertion Greeley means that ordinary phenomenological slices of life hint at the nature of God and indeed make God in some way present to us. He contends that "God is sufficiently like creation that creation not only tells us something about God but, by so doing, also makes God present to us." God lurks in all creation and thus creation itself discloses God's grace and makes it present among us. Greeley uses his voice as a writer to celebrate this vision of the world:

> Catholics live in an enchanted world, a world of statues and holy water, stained glass and votive candles, saints and religious medals, rosary beads and holy pictures. But these Catholic paraphernalia are mere hints of a deeper and more pervasive religious sensibility which inclines Catholics to see the Holy lurking in creation. As Catholics, we find our houses and our world haunted by a sense that the objects, events, and persons of daily life are revelations of grace.[4]

Despite all folly, failure, stupidity, illusion and even sin, for Greeley, the stories of life reveal the stories of God and are in the end revelations of grace in an enchanted universe. The Catholic Christian can make such a claim, Greeley suggests, because the early Church, unlike prophetic Judaism, implicitly and occasionally explicitly made peace with the pagan nature-religions and absorbed whatever seemed good from those religions, cultures and traditions.

---

[3] Andrew Greeley, *The Catholic Imagination* (Berkeley, CA: University of Calfornia Press, 2000).

[4] *Ibid.*, 1.

This became part of the Catholic sacramental sensibility.

The thoughtful work of David Tracy has never been as wildly optimistic as Greeley's Catholic imagination. He has understood with Walter Benjamin that even the greatest works of creativity and civilization can also become expressions of barbarism. Although his analogical imagination has affirmed the eros toward God and the world manifested in the life and work of so many inspired mystics and poets through the centuries, he has likewise known how to proclaim a thunderous, dialectical "No!" in the company of visionary prophets. Despite Greeley's reminder, carefully citing Tracy, that an intelligent faith is informed by both the analogical and dialectical movements of the imagination, his work seems only haunted, at least in the end, by the Holy.

The recent work of David Tracy, however, is often more haunted by the tragic and terrifying ghosts of this century of the Holocaust and continuing holocausts of genocide, ethnic cleansings, violence and massive global suffering. Some have even noted a persistent somber and gloomy tone in his current writing as he turns more towards a negative dialectics and an engagement with postmodernism. He has delayed publication of volume three of a projected trilogy for several years because he has been "stuck," by his own admission, on some rather profound God-questions. He has been at work on a substantial "God-book" for most of the past decade. Two essays he released to the journal *Cross Currents* give some indication of the direction of that work. One piece, "The Hidden God," turns to Luther's hidden God and to the apophatic mystical traditions to explore a question which Tracy argues transcends the teleological schema of modernity: "Does God lead history or disrupt it? — appear at its center or at its margins?"[5]

---

[5] David Tracy, "The Hidden God: The Divine Other of Liberation," *Cross Currents* 46 (1996) 5-16.

Tracy continues this line of inquiry in the second essay, "The Post-Modern Re-naming of God as Incomprehensible and Hidden."[6] This piece, which Tracy wrote as a theological continuation of the "The Hidden God," brings the postmodern deconstruction of presence and masternarratives into constructive conversation with historic and current prophetic, apophatic and apocalyptic theologies, including the disruptive political theology of Johann Baptist Metz. Metz, of course, grounds his political theology in both the prophetic cries and mystical realities of human suffering. After all, the embodied analogical imagination knows suffering and absence as well as presence and bliss in this blessed fallen world. Tracy's more recent attention to the shadows of the postmodern condition and to the hidden God does not mark an abandonment of hope. On the contrary, one might contend that we see a more profound if sobered hope which reads the contemporary human and historical condition as carefully and critically as ancient, sacred texts, always resisting any ideological, dogmatic or narrative closure. Let me explain.

A few years after meeting Andrew Greeley in New Orleans I was at work researching narrative theology with the theological hermeneutics of David Tracy in view. Through the generosity of a grant from Duquesne University's Theology Department, I was able to accept an invitation to present a paper on narrative theology at the annual meeting of The Society for the Study of Narrative Literature. The meeting was held in the lovely setting of Robert Redford's Sun Dance Film Festival town, Park City, Utah. After I read my paper, David Tracy's University of Chicago colleague and conversation partner, Wayne Booth, invited me to join him for breakfast the next morning.

---

[6] David Tracy, "The Post-Modern Re-Naming of God as Incomprehensible and Hidden," *Cross Currents* 50 (2000) 240-247.

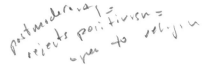

Booth spoke with me about the dissenting, disruptive stories of his sectarian Protestant roots and then moved on in the conversation to his thoughts about [the possibility for a great revival of religious rhetoric because of — not in spite of! — the postmodern turn in the academy and society] Booth, Chicago's towering rhetorician, suggested that in its rejection of scientism, positivism, rationalism and any inherited universalism, postmodern discourse functions like some of the best classical religious or theological rhetorics and thus this genre of inquiry invites theology back into serious philosophical and public conversations. Booth reported that when Jacques Derrida lectured at Chicago his language about the a "gift beyond the economy of exchange, forgiveness, spirit, the other, human obligation and responsibility ('one ought, one must'), absence/presence, the trace, difference and death" sounded to this master of rhetoric "theological."[7]

He asked Derrida about this and at first the famous French deconstructionist quickly responded that he represented no particular religious or theological tradition. Yet when Booth pushed him further about his rhetoric Derrida conceded, "Yes, my inquiry is essentially religious — or if you prefer theological."[8]

That morning over breakfast Wayne Booth, speaking from a rather dialectical religious imagination, outlined five points that he believed all major religions as well as many postmodernists hold in common, at least rhetorically:

One: Insistence that the world is somewhat flawed.

Two: Insistence that the flaws be seen in light of the Unflawed.

---

[7] Booth later published these reflections under the title, "Deconstruction as a Religious Revival," *Christianity and Culture in the Crossfire*, ed. David A. Hoekema and Bobby Fong (Grand Rapids, MI: Eerdmans, 1997) 131-154.

[8] *Ibid.*, 150. For the best treatment of Derrida in light of religious rhetoric see John D. Caputo, *The Prayers and Tears of Jacques Derrida: Religion Without Religion* (Bloomington, IN: Indiana University Press, 1997).

In this context Booth recounted one of his favorite David Tracy anecdotes. It was not a story about God lurking in an enchanted creation but rather about the problem of naming and knowing God in a broken creation. Tracy had been meeting for several years with leaders of the "major world religions' in an inter-religious dialogue with the goal of identifying some clear, substantive common ground among the religions. Meeting annually with Buddhists, Jews, Muslims, Hindus and Christians, Tracy would return to Chicago looking discouraged. Over coffee he would tell Booth, "We found little or nothing this year." Then, one year, as Booth reported it, David returned from the meetings much buoyed up. They had finally found something important they had all agreed on. Tracy said with enthusiasm, "We all agreed that something went radically wrong with creation."

Booth noted that the agreement was not that something was wrong with the world but that "something *went wrong* with *creation.*" Something *became* dis-ordered or dis-connected. This agreement was not merely a personal lament that creation is flawed and that I would *like* to see it otherwise but rather that it *ought* to be different and otherwise. In this affirmation there is a sense not only of an acute awareness of brokenness but an implicit vision of how it ought to be; it is a vision not of an alternative creation but of the need and possibility for what the Jewish tradition calls *tikkun,* a mandate to mend or heal the world.

Three, emerging from the first two: All whom I'm calling genuinely religious will somehow see themselves as in some inescapable sense a part of the brokenness. Not only is creation or the cosmos flawed or broken, Booth explained, but if the genuinely religious person at times feels connected to the goodness and grace of creation, he or she will also feel part of its fall. Not because of some sacred text or dogmatic decree about original sin but because of the nature of life itself, the religious person will know brokenness,

absence, and a sense of being personally, socially and spiritually
disconnected or de-centered.

Four, following inescapably from the first three: The cosmos I
believe in, the cosmos in which I feel gratitude towards its gift of
my existence and its implied ideals, the cosmos that is in some
degree broken — my cosmos calls upon me to do something about
the brokenness. Booth believes that the religiously awake person
has an awareness of both the need and responsibility to repair the
brokenness without and within.

Five, a corollary of the other four: Whenever my notion of what
the cosmos requires of me conflicts with my immediate wishes or
impulses, I ought to surrender to its commandments. Booth suggests that there is a sense within the religious consciousness that
one *ought* to allow cosmic commandments to override mere personal wishes for all have *obligations* not just to others but to the
Other.

As Wayne Booth sees it, the often strange discourse of postmodernism, from its deconstruction of presence, through its interest in the trace, to its emphasis on difference and the otherness of
the other, has dimensions that are rhetorically parallel to theological discourse, especially the traditions of dialectical prophetic religion and apophatic mysticism. Booth later published the substance
of our breakfast conversation in an article with the surprising title,
"Deconstruction as a Religious Revival."

David Tracy's earlier work charted the analogical and dialectical movements of the religious imagination under the categories of
"manifestation and proclamation." His more recent work uses the
paradigm of the "mystical-prophetic." He shares Booth's conviction that there is indeed common ground for productive conversation between postmodern theorists and Christian theologians and
that the way into this conversion is often *via negativa.* Thus, he
has turned his attention to the Protestant hidden God and to the

unknowable, un-nameable God of the apophatic mystics, the God beyond God. Yet as we shall see in this study, Tracy has not abandoned his passion for the great hopes of the analogical imagination. His critical turn to negative dialectics in the conversation has only made his project more phenomenologically *and* analogically honest to the embodied, storied realities of this blessed *and* fallen world.

This study began as a constructive investigation into the varieties of narrative theology — how do stories save us? — with the hermeneutics of David Tracy in view, since Tracy had entered the theoretical and theological conversation around narrative. Thus, it *was* not and *is* not merely a study of David Tracy's work. However, like Tracy, in the process of writing, thinking and living, I became stuck in several theological and philosophical problems, although my problems were undoubtedly somewhat different than Tracy's dialectical broodings.

Believing Tracy's claim that "the truth of religion, like the truth of its nearest analogue, art, is primordially a truth of manifestation," I became more ponderous about the limits of language in general and the limits of the grammar of narrative in particular.[9] If indeed, as many phenomenologists have insisted, *the tongue is an organ of both language and taste, is not the human person performatively as well as narratively constituted?* This question, which really has its beginnings in the primordial origins of art and religion, led me through the many hermeneutical turns of narrative theology and ethics to an unexpected consideration of sacramental theology and aesthetics as I, using the incomparable work of David Tracy as a conversation partner, attempted to offer a constructive answer to the question, "How Do Stories Save Us?" This study records the theological exploration of that question.

---

[9] David Tracy, "The Uneasy Alliance Reconceived: Catholic Theological Method, Modernity, and Postmodernity," *Theological Studies* 50 (1989) 548-570.

POSTMODERN AND PUBLIC STORIES BEYOND CATHEDRALS AND CAGES?

To see the similar in the dissimilar is the mark of poetic genius
Aristotle

INTRODUCTION

One afternoon Ernst Bloch and Johann Baptist Metz were walking the streets of the city of Munster. As their conversation turned to political theology, Bloch pointed to the three iron cages that still hang outside the Saint Lamberti Church. Heretics of the Radical Reformation were executed in those cages and their bodies and bones remained on public display as a warning to dissenters and witness to the triumph of imperial Christendom. "One must do theology from there," Bloch said to the Baptist.[1]

Although Bloch's declaration was driven by important political concerns, pragmatic and pastoral considerations would also lead one to conclude that if Christian theology is to continue as a mode of reflection at the beginning of a new century, it must be conceived after Christendom in surprising spaces outside the cathedral. Both modern statisticians and postmodern theorists agree: the grand temple of Western Christendom can no longer seduce and satisfy the religious imagination nor can its old Constantinian

---

[1] I learned about this exchange between Bloch and Metz from Jürgen Manemann during a personal conversation with him in the summer of 1997 at Columbia University, where we were both doing research under an ARIL Coolidge Fellowship. Manemann is a member of Metz's circle of political theologians on the Roman Catholic faculty at Munster.

heresy provide an interesting or instructive vision of God in the world. To many, God is dead or eclipsed or exiled. Yet as Bloch's prophetic gesture implied, if God is to indeed return, it will be from the cages, from the margins, from life's liminal spaces, from somewhere *other*, from somewhere *beyond*.

Literary theorists Gilles Deleuze and Felix Guattari write of the importance of "minor literatures." A minor literature, according to Deleuze, makes intensive and transgressive use of a major language as a witness to the representational incompleteness in all discourse. It accents other stories within the story. It invites repressed, silenced or exiled voices within the text, voices that were once rendered merely minor or disturbingly other, to speak. As such, it points to something other, to the possibility of an Other beyond the master-narrative.[2]

I need not rehearse for my readers the story of the postmodern collapse of the master-narrative and the late modern or postmodern emergence of minor literatures. Jean-Francois Lyotard has demonstrated rather convincingly in his famous work, *The Postmodern Condition*, that the one grand, modern narrative in which all could hope to find their plots and places has been deconstructed under the hermeneutics of suspicion, leaving us with a plurality of little stories or minor literatures.[3] This is a well-known and now even a rather tired story. I will return to Johann Baptist Metz and his theological response to Bloch's prophetic gesture, but first I want to turn to a question raised by David Tracy. It is a question I find far more interesting than the old story of the end of the master-story. The question is at once postmodern, modern and classical:

[2] Gilles Deleuze and Felix Guattari, *Kafka: Toward a Minor Literature* (Minneapolis, MN: University of Minnesota Press, 1986).

[3] Jean-Francois Lyotard, *The Postmodern Condition: A Report on Knowledge* (Minneapolis, MN: University of Minnesota Press, 1984).

"Do particular traditions bear public resources?"[4] Stated another way, can minor literatures become part of the public conversation in quest of a common weal, a common good? Can they open one to a human connection, compassion, and even spiritual presence beyond cathedrals, creeds, bounded communities and tribal gods? Our postmodern condition has contributed to a new rise of fundamentalisms, sectarianisms, orthodoxies and communitarianisms, all in the name of particularities in resistance to the imperialism and colonialism of the modern project, a "universalism" which is little more than the universalizing of Western values as these communitarian critics often correctly charge. Yet these new cosmologies, theologies and cultures tend to isolate faith from the wider world and thus from a truly public quest for the shalom of the city. Can Christian theologies as minor literatures resist becoming sacred reservations of bounded texts and privileged communities and embody a sacred presence as well as recover an ecumenical spirit without becoming imperial?

In a recent lecture at the Graduate Theological Union in Berkeley, sociologist of religion Robert Bellah admitted that he and his co-authors were wrong about something in their celebrated book, *Habits of the Heart.*[5] Their book quoted a famous passage in Tocqueville's *Democracy in America*: "I think I see the whole destiny of America contained in the first Puritan who landed on those shores." *Habits* then went on to name John Winthrop, following the lead of Tocqueville, as the best candidate for being that first

---

[4] David Tracy, "Particular Classics, Public Religion and the American Tradition," *Religion and American Public Life*, ed. Robin W. Lovin (New York: Paulist Press, 1986) 115-131.

[5] Bellah's lecture or paper has not been published; however, he begins to develop this idea in an earlier essay. See Robert N. Bellah, "Is There a Common American Culture?," *Journal of the American Academy of Religion* 66 (1998) 613-625.

Puritan, that representative of the new world. At Berkeley Bellah confessed that this was likely wrong. The first "Puritan," Bellah now speculates, who contained our whole destiny — the destiny of the new world — was one banished from the Massachusetts Bay Colony by Winthrop, Roger Williams, or perhaps even Ann Hutchinson — religious dissenters, indeed, heretics! Contemporary theologians must never forget the destinies of Williams, Hutchinson, or Mary Dyer, a Quaker thinker who was hanged by the Puritan fathers, because of her religious dissent, on Boston Commons in 1660.

Roger Williams, a Baptist, established the Rhode Island Colony and made hospitable space there for Baptists, Quakers, Jews, Catholics, Native Americans, and a variety of saints and sinners dissenting from the Puritan story. Those dissenters stressed the centrality of religious freedom and the sacredness of individual conscience in matters of faith and practice. They recognized that truth, divine presence and humane connection were at times present in the exception and not simply in the rule. That minority culture of religious dissent evolved into a majority in American religious culture from the early nineteenth century. Robert Bellah's lecture cited Seymour Martin Lipset who has recently pointed out that America is the only North Atlantic society whose predominant religious tradition is sectarian or dissenting or even "heretical" rather than established church.

Indeed, Jean-Francois Lyotard and Jean Baudrillard, in the discourse of postmodern excess and exaggeration, have declared that America is a prototypical Anabaptist nation![6] This radically democratic model or method of religious reflection is now becoming a truly global hope for ending tribal wars, sectarian violence and

---

[6] Jean Baudrillard, *America* (London: Verso, 1989) 41. Also see Jean-François Lyotard, *Toward the Postmodern* (New Jersey: Humanities Press) 115-124.

ideological oppression. This says much about the possibilities of religion and intellectual life or theology and culture as we enter a new millennium. Finally, in the late modern or postmodern world, God no longer dwells only in temples or texts made with magisterial hands. Yet this makes David Tracy's question even more urgent: *How do particular traditions or stories bear public resources in an age of radical plurality and ambiguity?*

Theology written in the shadow of postmodernism has produced many interesting minor literatures of God without being, identity politics, multiculturalisms, bodies, sex, aesthetics and poetry. However, often the reader of these texts discovers a God without wonder, subject positions without souls, multiculturalisms without analogies of being, bodies without passion and sex without real bodies, aesthetics without art, and poetry without strong poets. Indeed, postmodernism celebrates "the death of the author." The author was indeed killed in Paris, embalmed at Yale and pronounced dead again and again in many distinguished European and American English departments and divinity schools.

I have learned much from postmodernism. In fact, I have contributed to postmodern books, journals and conferences. Yet, following the incomparable work of David Tracy, I remain intrigued by what Louis Dupre has called "the unfinished project of modernism," not the hardened, reified Enlightenment version, but a pluralistic modernism marked by transgression of national, ethnic and generic boundaries.[7] With Tracy, I remain attracted to the spirit of that great modern but neglected book, *The Varieties of Religious*

---

[7] Peter Cassarella and George P. Schner, S.J. (eds.), *The Thought of Louis Dupre: Christian Spirituality and the Culture of Modernity* (Grand Rapids, MI: Eerdmans, 1988). David Tracy has the first chapter in this collection of essays on the work of Dupre's broad understanding of modernity, in which he includes fifteenth-sixteenth century expressions and not merely the standard postmodern equating of modernity with the Enlightenment.

Experience by William James. We now know that James was inspired by Walt Whitman's democratic vistas and poetic vision in his own understanding of religious and cultural pluralism, a pluralism not merely in society, but in the soul. We contain a multitude.

Although postmodern, post-liberal and the newer communitarian theologies do in fact present important correctives to the modern project's iron cage of reason and its colonization of life worlds, many have abandoned the best hopes embodied in the unfinished project of modernism: a protest against the dehumanization of the human through truly analogical links or principles of correlation in a graced but fallen world. In many ways David Tracy extends and expands this kind of modern hope by bringing it into productive conversations with the best of postmodern thought. The question of how particular traditions might bear public resources continues to accent the concerns that the great modern author, Paul Tillich, began in his work toward a theology of culture.

PROTESTANT PRINCIPLE AND CATHOLIC SUBSTANCE

The very posthumous publication of Paul Tillich's 1963 Berkeley lectures on *The Relevance and Irrelevance of the Christian Message* went largely unnoticed outside the circle of Tillich specialists.[8] Tillich's modernism seems terribly out of fashion to many in the contemporary guild of academic theology. However, when the New York Public Library recently listed its *Books of the Century* only one theologian made the cut: Tillich and his profoundly existential book, *The Courage to Be*. Tillich came to New York in 1933 to

---

[8] Paul Tillich, *The Relevance and Irrelevance of the Christian Message* (Cleveland, OH: The Pilgrim Press, 1996).

not merely a
churchly theologian

teach at Union Theological Seminary after his dismissal from the
University of Frankfurt for his opposition to the Nazis. Always a
theologian in public view, he told a reporter for the *New York Post*,
"I had the great honor and luck to be about the first non-Jewish professor dismissed from a German University."[9]
Tillich's writing remains interesting and at times inspiring
because he was not merely a churchly theologian. He viewed his
calling as a theologian of culture *and* an interpreter of the Christian message. For Tillich, the God-question could not be pried apart
from "the human question." I'm very fond of his comment, "To
be a theologian one has to be a non-theologian." When the old
New York intellectuals in the *Partisan Review* circle gathered the
likes of Hannah Arendt, W.H. Auden, Alfred Kazin and John
Dewey together in 1950 for a major symposium on "Religion and
the Intellectuals," one Christian theologian was warmly welcomed
into the conversation. It was of course Paul Tillich, who understood well the religious dimensions of art, literature and philosophy and who remained committed to the life of the mind and spirit
throughout his career as an intellectual preacher of the Christian
Gospel and theologian of culture. This was of course the same year
that several "non-theologians" interested in religion, theatre, fiction
and poetry established *Cross Currents* as an alternative to academic journals that feared engaging the full range of intellectual passions under the editorial direction of Catholic intellectual, Joe Cun-
neen.
Perhaps most interesting about *The Relevance and Irrelevance of
the Christian Message* is the way Tillich revisits the classic conversation around Protestant Principle and Catholic Substance
addressed in his earlier works under the theme of "theologians of
offense and theologians of mediation." According to Tillich, the

---

[9] *Ibid.*, 8.

theologians of offense echo Tertullian's, Kierkegaard's and Karl Barth's infamous "No!" to the invitation to mediate between the Christian message and the particular cultural situation. Theologians of mediation, on the other hand, attempt some mediation, analogy, correlation or conversation between the Christian message and every particular cultural expression. In the history of Christian theology this has led to sharp contrasts and conflicts between the theological models of Bernard of Clairvaux and Abelard, Luther and Erasmus, and Barth and Tillich. Nevertheless, Tillich respected the message-centered (kerygmatic) witness of Barth and other theologians of offense and insisted that this model was a necessary movement in theology reminding all of the Otherness — *Ganz Anders* in German — of God. Biblical religion must retain a prophetic edge. His own work, however, was given to what he termed an "answering theology," a theology of mediation.

One can learn much from Tillich's model and mood of engaging cultural questions and responding to human concerns. At a time when so much contemporary Christian theology — whether postmodern, communitarian or radical orthodox — seems to celebrate "the Word made strange" and thus offensive and in sharp opposition to every modern passion, thought or situation, the correlational, conversational style of Tillich is again welcome. How can a theology which negates the cultural history of how we have come to think about ourselves and how we view the world ever hope to connect with our contemporary loves, longings and losses? Can a word that falls strangely like a stone from heaven hope to be incarnational and truthful to those living and loving in the fleshly texts of dreams and bones? How can there be genuine dialogue and compassion in communities of discourse that almost bless the category of the incommensurable? No matter how textually and rhetorically rigorous, is not such a message irrelevant to our ultimate human concerns?

Tillich reminds us through his mediating theology of the hopes and possibilities of some simultaneous engagement of the same and the different, the general and the particular, in all realms of church, culture and creation. This is what David Tracy, who has done much to expand and extend the style of Tillich's conversational thinking through his own theology of the analogical imagination, calls the possibility of "similarity-in-difference." We seek to know ourselves, others, God and the world through analogy. Indeed, to do theology with an analogical imagination is a theopoetics. According to Aristotle, "To spot the similar in the dissimilar is the mark of poetic genius." Poet James Tate has taught theologians such as Tracy much about the rule of metaphor:[10]

When I think no thing is like any other thing
I become speechless, cold, my body turns silver
and water runs off me. There I am
ten feet from myself, possessor of nothing,
uncomprehending of even the simplest particle of dust.

But when I say, you are *like*
a swamp animal during an eclipse,
I am happy, full of wisdom, loved by children
and old men alike. I am sorry if this confuses you.

During an eclipse the swamp animal
Acts as though day were night,
Drinking when he should be sleeping, etc.
This is why men stay up all night
writing to you.

Modernity's self-doubt along with the recent postmodern turn in academic circles are creating a growing suspicion as to whether theological discussions about God or human values can hope to

[10] Tate's poem is used in David Tracy's *The Analogical Imagination* as a poetic and metaphorical expression of the classical attention to the rule of analogy in human consciousness and cognition. See *The Analogical Imagination*, 446.

make both public and specifically Christian sense. "Let the church be the church!" is the new rallying cry for those in the church and theological academy who are becoming convinced that theological discourse must inhabit its own semiotic world if it hopes not only to be faithful, but intelligible.[11] The ancient formula, *extra ecclesiam nulla salus*, is being articulated with a new postmodern, postliberal understanding and sophistication.[12]

There is an increasing anticorrelational mood in contemporary theology that informs thinkers who do their work far from the

[11] The postmodern condition has produced a variety of theological responses to its intellectual and ethical challenges from the "eliminative postmodern" a/theology of Mark Taylor's Derridian project to neo-conservative or post-liberal theological proposals and responses. For a helpful typological study see David Ray Griffin, William A. Beardslee and Joe Holland, *Varieties of Postmodern Theology* (Albany, NY: SUNY Press, 1989). George Lindbeck's intratextual, post-liberal theology has indeed become for many a coherent response to a postmodern, pluralistic world as we shall see in the next chapter. See especially his "The Church's Mission to a Postmodern Culture," *Postmodern Theology: Faith in a Pluralistic World*, ed. Frederich B. Burnham (San Francisco, CA: Harper and Row, 1989) 37-55.

[12] I am thinking here especially of the continuing influence of Stanley Hauerwas in both Protestant and Catholic circles. See "The Politics of Salvation: Why There is No Salvation Outside the Church," in his *After Christendom: How the Church is to Behave if Freedom, Justice, and a Christian Nation are Bad Ideas* (Nashville, TN: Abingdon Press, 1991) 23-44. For his unapologetic advocacy of a non-public or anticorrelational theology and ecclesiology see his *Resident Aliens: Life in the Christian Colony* (Co-authored with William Willimon, Nashville, TN: Abingdon Press, 1989); *Unleashing the Scriptures: Freeing the Bible from Captivity to America* (Nashville, TN: Abingdon Press, 1993). Hauerwas was trained at Yale. For an examination of the Yale-Hauerwas connection, see my "The Problems and Prospects of a Sectarian Ethic: A Critique of the Hauerwas Reading of the Jesus Story," *Conrad Grebel Review* 10 (1992) 157-168. For a critique of the narrowly communitarian approaches to theological method advocated by Hauerwas and other pure narrative theologians in light of my understanding of Christian theology's demand for "publicness" (influenced greatly by David Tracy's hermeneutics), see my "Dialogue with the Other?," *Conrad Grebel Review* 11 (Spring 1993) 175-179.

formal postmodern circles. Many Protestants have grown increasingly uneasy with the Schleiermacher-Tillich method of correlation and have found that the theology of Karl Barth speaks more convincingly to the challenges presented by the postmodern critique of modernity.[13] Likewise, some Roman Catholics are moving from the correlational theologies of Rahner, Lonergan and Tracy to the thought of more conservative theologians like Balthasar and Ratzinger, following their argument that Bonaventure rather than Aquinas provides the superior classical model for theology because of his noncorrelational methodology.[14]

Although there is a growing interest in the communal character of theology and a renewed emphasis on the confessing community as the privileged and proper location for all theological reflection and construction, David Tracy's theology remains sharply critical of these retreats from the public square into separate "reservations of spirit." His theological program is committed to breaking through the "swamp of privateness" that afflicts much of contemporary theology and religion.[15] Even as Tracy writes theology in the

---

[13] There is currently a great revival of interest in Karl Barth's thought in both the church and academy. This renewed interest has been inspired largely by the work of theologians associated with Yale. They are presenting through their work what David Tracy has described as a "methodologically sophisticated version of Barthian confessionalism." Concerning George Lindbeck's project, Tracy observes, "The hands may be the hands of Wittgenstein and Geertz but the voice is the voice of Karl Barth." David Tracy, "Lindbeck's New Program for Theology," *The Thomist* 49 (1985) 465.

[14] For David Tracy's discussion of this trend, see his "The Uneasy Alliance Reconceived: Catholic Theological Method, Modernity, and Postmodernity," *Theological Studies* 50 (1989) 554-556. Tracy does not share this reading of Bonaventure. The current "re-presentation" of Bonaventure as a noncorrelational thinker by Ratzinger and other neo-conservatives is challenged by Ewert Cousins, *Bonaventure and the Coincidence of Opposites* (Chicago, IL: Franciscan Herald, 1978).

[15] See David Tracy's "Defending the Public Character of Theology," *Theologians in Transition*, ed. James M. Wall (New York: Crossroad, 1981) 114-124.

shadow of postmodernism, he remains convinced that "the very nature of the claim of theology demands public, indeed transcendental or metaphysical explication."[16] This chapter will explore David Tracy's understanding of the truly public vocation of the theologian through an overview of some of the major themes evolving in his theological program.[17]

There is a resurgence of neo-conservative, neo-orthodox or postliberal/postmodern methodologies in the contemporary theological guild, emphasizing the particular, unique or special character of Christian language. Yet David Tracy insists that while the contextual and thus particular nature of all theological utterances must be acknowledged and respected, "God" is universal, thus the public demands of God-talk must be recognized or else the theologian is "either speaking nonsense or Zeus-talk, not Yahweh-talk."[18] His theology is quite attentive to the fact that all theologians

---

[16] David Tracy, *Dialogue with the Other: The Inter-Religious Dialogue*, Louvain Theological and Pastoral Monographs, 1 (Louvain/Grand Rapids, MI: Peeters Press/Eerdmans Publishing Company, 1990) 1.

[17] Although a book-length study of Tracy's theology has not yet been written, there are some helpful summaries or overviews of his thought. His former student at Chicago, Werner G. Jeanrond is becoming a well-recognized interpreter of his former mentor. See his treatment of Tracy's theology and hermeneutics in *Text and Interpretation as Categories of Theological Thinking* (New York: Crossroad, 1988) 129-149. Also see his "Theology in the Context of Pluralism and Postmodernity: David Tracy's Theological Method," *Postmodernism, Literature and the Future of Theology*, ed. David Jasper (New York: St. Martin's Press, 1993) 143-163. Two other fine studies of Tracy's thought are: T. Howland Sanks, S.J., "David Tracy's Theological Project: An Overview and Some Implications," *Theological Studies* 54 (1993) 698-727; and S. Alen Ray, *The Modern Soul: Michel Foucault and the Theological Discourse of Gordon Kaufman and David Tracy*, Harvard Dissertations in Religion (Philadelphia, PA: Fortress Press, 1987). A Tracy *Festschrift* includes several essays in conversation with his thought: Werner G. Jeanrond and Jennifer L. Rike (eds.), *Radical Pluralism and Truth: David Tracy and the Hermeneutics of Religion* (New York: Crossroad, 1991).

[18] David Tracy, "God, Dialogue and Solidarity: A Theologian's Refrain," *The Christian Century* (October 10, 1990) 901.

think and write in particular, historical contexts. These contextual realities do make the public or universal claims of God-language exceedingly difficult to justify and explicate in a world of increasing plurality and ambiguity. Yet doing theology in light of this profound historical consciousness has driven Tracy not into the safe and clearly defined boundaries of sacred reservations but into a more rigorous and demanding exploration of methodological questions and criteria, not only in theology, but across the modern disciplines which he consults freely in the challenge of doing theology.

DAVID TRACY AND THE PUBLIC VOCATION OF THE THEOLOGIAN

Born in 1939 in Yonkers, New York, David Tracy began his theological training in seminaries in New York and Rome in the stimulating and engaging climate of Vatican II, which in his words solidified his conviction that, "there can be no return to a pre-ecumenical, pre-pluralistic, ahistorical theology."[19] His first major and really formative mentor in theology was Bernard Lonergan, who devoted much of his intellectual and professional career to questions of method in theology. Tracy studied with Lonergan at Rome and eventually wrote his doctoral dissertation on the development of Lonergan's theological method. He was most attracted to Lonergan's post-1957 work in which categories of historical consciousness became his primary methodological concerns. His first book emerged from this study: *The Achievement of Bernard Lonergan.*[20]

---

[19] Tracy, "Defending the Public Character of Theology," 114.

[20] David Tracy, *The Achievement of Bernard Lonergan* (New York: Herder and Herder, 1970). Tracy received the Licentiate in 1964 and Doctorate in Sacred theology in 1969 from the Gregorian University in Rome. His dissertation was entitled, "Lonergan's Interpretation of St. Thomas Aquinas: The Intellectual Nature of Speculative Theology."

Tracy often quotes what he learned from Lonergan about the calling of the theologian: "Be attentive, be intelligent, be reflective, be responsible, and if necessary, change!"[21] Tracy has followed that advice in his conversational approach to theological investigation, and although he has moved beyond the critical realism of Lonergan's transcendental neo-Thomism to a more hermeneutically nuanced project, he remains indebted to Lonergan and his passion for careful and creative theological method.[22]

Although David Tracy had a short pastoral stint in a rather conservative parish in Stamford, Connecticut and a faculty appointment at Catholic University of America — where he was one of twenty faculty members put on trial in 1968 by the university for criticizing *Humane Vitae* — he has spent most of his professional career at the University of Chicago Divinity School, a school noted for its concern for method in religious studies, theology and philosophy. In 1969 he was the first Roman Catholic priest ever appointed to the Chicago faculty where he joined internationally-recognized scholars such as Paul Ricœur and Mircea Eliade.[23]

In addition to being a Distinguished Service Professor and the Andrew Thomas Greeley and Grace McNichols Greeley Professor of Roman Catholic Studies at the University of Chicago, Tracy was the first theologian of any denomination to be invited on the university's prestigious Committee on the Analysis of Ideas and

[21] David Tracy, *Blessed Rage for Order* (New York: Seabury Press, 1975) 12.

[22] Bernard Lonergan, *Method in Theology* (New York: Seabury Press, 1972) 55. David Tracy, *Blessed Rage for Order: The New Pluralism in Theology* (New York: Seabury Press, 1975) 12.

[23] For two somewhat biographical looks at Tracy see: Eugene Kennedy, "A Dissenting Voice: Catholic Theologian David Tracy," *New York Times Magazine* (Nov. 9, 1986); and Kenneth L. Woodard, "David Tracy, Theologian," *Newsweek* (Aug. 24, 1981). In addition to his demanding academic schedule, Father Tracy presides and preaches regularly at the Newman Center at the University of Chicago.

Methods. He is also one of the few theologian members of the American Academy of Arts and Sciences. Martin E. Marty, the dean of modern American church historians, has said of Tracy: "[He is] the most original of today's Catholic theologians, and one with whom other theologians, Catholic and Protestant, have to reckon."[24] Indeed, David Tracy's work and life embody a public theological vision.

Tracy joins the company of many contemporary theologians in defending public theology. Yet some critics ask: "Is not all Christian theology in some sense public?" The advocacy of the public character of all good theology is not merely claiming that all theology must actively express love and justice to all God's creatures and creation in this graced but fallen world. Most theologians would agree that their faith communities have some responsibility to "publics" — individuals, communities, societies, governments and ecosystems — beyond their sanctuary doors. Tracy and other public theologians are arguing for much more than ethical and evangelical compassion in the public square; indeed they are suggesting that the public square itself — the world in all its plurality and ambiguity — must be viewed not merely as an *object* of theological description, prophetic critique and action, but rather as a rich *source* for imaginative and revisionary theological construction.[25] Not Barca or Wilking

---

[24] *New York Times Magazine* (cited above), 23.

[25] The University of Chicago Divinity School has had an historic interest in and commitment to "public" styles of theological reflection. For a representative expression see Martin E. Marty, *The Public Church* (New York: Crossroad, 1981). Tracy's advocacy of "publicness" in theology bears "family resemblances" with thinkers as diverse as Kaufman, Ogden, Pannenberg, Ebeling, Harvey, Küng, Gilkey, Metz, et al. For one of the best general treatments of "public theology" and ethics from a Catholic perspective see: Michael J. Himes and Kenneth R. Himes, O.F.M., *Fullness of Faith: The Public Significance of Theology* (New York: Paulist Press, 1993).

The emphasis on the worldly as well as churchly sources of theological production is the major hermeneutical emphasis separating public and revisionary theologians like Tracy from the more communal, postliberal "narrative" programs like those of Hans Frei and George Lindbeck.[26] To do theology in a public rather than in a provincial voice, according to Tracy, is to "speak in a manner that can be disclosive and transformative for any intelligent, reasonable, responsible human being."[27] This disclosive and transformative discourse is in Tracy's view conversational or dialogical. Hence, the theologian not only speaks in public but is spoken to by public agents who inhabit other texts, other traditions, and other experiences of what it means to live authentically; thus the theologian opens himself or herself to the possibility of transformation through genuine encounter with the other. As Lonergan suggested, intelligent, reflective attention may demand "change." Public theological discourse is always marked by a correlational methodology in which some interpretation of the theological and religious tradition is critically correlated with some interpretation of the contemporary situation.

We have noted the similarities between Paul Tillich's existential theology of correlation and David Tracy's analogical imagination. In the tradition of Schleiermacher, von Drey, Blondel, and other modern theologians, Tillich is credited with translating classical

---

[26] It must be recognized, however, that some younger scholars from the Yale circle of Frei and Lindbeck have been making some modest moves beyond their teachers' rather strict anticorrelational tendencies. See William C. Placher's fine work, *Unapologetic Theology: A Christian Voice in a Pluralistic Conversation* (Louisville, KY: John Knox Press, 1989). Also see Ronald F. Thiemann, *Constructing a Public Theology: The Church in a Pluralistic Culture* (Louisville, KY: Westminster/John Knox Press, 1991); and Kathryn Tanner, *The Politics of God: Christian Theologies and Social Justice* (Minneapolis, MN: Fortress Press, 1992).

[27] Tracy, "Defending the Public Character of Theology," 114.

theology's apologetic concerns into a methodological strategy he termed the "principle of correlation."[28] Tillich considered the correlational method the backbone of his systematic theology. Tillich distinguished his method from the "kerygmatic theology" of Protestant orthodoxy, neo-orthodoxy and fundamentalism.

According to Tillich, kerygmatic theologies emphasize the unchangeable truth of the message (kerygma) over against the changing demands of the situation. In this model the proclamation of the kerygma mutes the existential questions of the human situation with the thunder of the Word. The message is "thrown at the situation like a stone." For Tillich, the situation — "the interpretation of existence ... the totality of man's creative self-interpretation in a special period" — and the Gospel are interdependent and correlated. The Christian message did not fall out of heaven but emerged and evolved in the context of existential questions and answers which mark and constitute what it means to be human. One cannot hope to understand the kerygma without also understanding the human situation.[29]

Tillich often referred to his method as "answering" or apologetic theology in contrast to a kerygmatic theology. Theology for Tillich is about both divine and human concerns: God as the ground of being addresses the human's ultimate questions and concerns. Yet for a theologian to offer answers to humanity's probing questions he or she must have something in common with those who ask and seek. Tillich criticized kerygmatic theologians for their tendency to deny any common ground with those outside their theological circle. His apologetic theology presupposes some common

---

[28] Paul Tillich, *Systematic Theology*, vol. I (Chicago, IL: University of Chicago Press, 1951) 59-66. For a splendid treatment of Tillich's theology of culture and correlation, see Langdon Gilkey, *Gilkey on Tillich* (New York: Crossroad, 1990).
[29] Tillich, *Systematic Theology*, vol. I. See "Message and Situation," 3-6.

ground with even "cultured despisers of religion."[30] In this sense
Tillich's theology attempts to be genuinely public.

Postliberal theologies like those advocated by Hans Frei and
George Lindbeck have appropriately been termed "unapologetic
theologies" because of their rejection of public and correlational
criteria for their truth claims. They fear that the search for common
ground in theological discourse risks denying and destroying the
uniqueness of the Christian message. "What has Athens to do with
Jerusalem?"[31] Methodologically very little, according to these
postliberals.

Whether considering the early Christian apologists who found
common ground with various philosophies of the Logos, the
Alexandrian school's use of Platonism, Aquinas's appropriation of
Aristotle, or various modern theological attempts to demonstrate
critical and creative links with the Enlightenment, Romanticism,
Idealism, Kantianism, humanism, naturalism or existentialism,
these postliberal critics charge that the common ground is nothing
more than the shifting sands of the historical situation. Thus, it is
argued, in correlational or public hermeneutics, theology surren-
ders its holy ground and constructs its house on foreign territory
that while seductive, is really inhospitable to the true household of
faith.

Paul Tillich remained critical of hard kerygmatic theologies and
committed to his correlational method through his last lecture at the
University of Chicago where death ended his impressive career.
Tillich was one of the twentieth century's finest theologians of culture. Theology for Tillich was not merely about God, Christ and the

[30] Concerning the issue of common ground with those beyond the theological
or ecclesiastical circle see Tillich, *Systematic Theology*, vol. I, 6. (The phrase,
"cultured despisers of religion," is of course Schleiermacher's).

[31] Tertullian's ancient question is indeed relevant to the contemporary corre-
lational-anticorrelational, pure narrative-impure narrative debate.

church, but about this blessed fallen world. Although he had many admiring students, Tillich specialists have noted that none has really explicitly developed and carried forward his method of correlation.[32] Although David Tracy never studied under Tillich, he has perhaps done more than any other theologian to critique, revise and recover Tillich's method of correlation for his own theology and hermeneutics.

Tracy is appreciative yet not uncritical of Tillich's correlational style. He finds Tillich's method important yet inadequate since it does not explore the full hermeneutical range between questions and answers or the situation and the message. Tracy suggests that Tillich's method tends to affirm the need for a correlation of the "questions" expressed in the situation and the "answers" provided by the Christian message. Even though Tillich wished to demonstrate the interdependence of the situation and message, Tracy complains that in practice his correlation is really between questions of one source and the answers of another. Tracy argues that if the "situation" is to be taken seriously, then its answers to its own questions independent of the Christian message must be critically investigated. For example, Tracy asks, why does Tillich assume the Christian message provides a better or more truthful answer to ✓ the questions of existential angst than the philosophy of Jean Paul Sartre or Karl Jaspers?[33]

Further, Tracy believes a critical hermeneutics must be brought to bear on the message itself if the theologian is to develop rigorous critical criteria that successfully correlate the questions and answers which are always found in *both* the situation and the message. Tracy's program seeks to practice a critical correlation

---

[32] Wilhelm and Marion Pauck, *Paul Tillich: His Life and Thought*, vol. I (New York: Harper and Row, 1976) 172.

[33] Tracy, *Blessed Rage for Order*, 45-46.

between what for him are the two principal sources of theology: Christian texts and common experience and language.[34]

He understands these two principal sources for theology to be the "two constants" guiding all theological discussion and work. He thinks Hans Küng offers well formulated general descriptions of these two constants. Küng suggests that all Christian theological interpretation must involve the constant of "our present world of experience in all its ambivalence, contingency and change" in active dialogue with the constant of the "Judaeo-Christian tradition which is ultimately based on the Christian message, the Gospel of Jesus Christ."[35] Yet while Küng's work, inspired as it is by Karl Barth's kerygmatic theology, tends to emphasize "confrontation" over "correlation" between the two constants, Tracy is convinced that a close reading of both the religious tradition and the present world in all its tragedy, wonder, despair and hope will disclose connections (as well as conflicts and confrontations) as the religious dimension of common human experience is uncovered and manifested.

Following the lead of Edward Schillebeeckx, Tracy's more recent work has added the qualifier, "mutually" to the principle of correlation, thus, "mutually critical correlation."[36] This qualifier signals the need to consider a fuller range of possible correlation

[34] *Ibid.*, 43. Also see David Tracy and John B. Cobb, Jr. *Talking About God: Doing Theology in the Context of Modern Pluralism* (New York: Seabury Press, 1983) 5-7.

[35] David Tracy, "Hermeneutical Reflections on the New Paradigm," *Paradigm Change in Theology*, ed. Hans Küng and David Tracy (New York: Crossroad, 1989) 55-58. Hans Küng, "Toward a New Consensus in Catholic (and Ecumenical) Theology," *Consensus in Theology: A Dialogue with Hans Küng and Edward Schillebeeckx*, ed. Leonard Swidler (Philadelphia, PA: Westminster Press, 1980) 1-17.

[36] David Tracy, "Hermeneutics and the Tradition," *Proceedings of the American Catholic Philosophical Association* 62 (1990) 46.

between the situation and the language of text and tradition. Neo-orthodox, postliberal, and several revisionist critics have noted that the Tillichian correlational model tended to assume the possibility of a harmonious relationship between Christian texts and the conforming demands of contemporary culture. Hence, it is charged, the theologian forces the text and tradition to comfortably accommodate modernity's agendas and thus the Bible can no longer be heard as a wholly other, oppositional or prophetic voice. Tracy intends his qualifier to indicate that correlation is not always harmonious or "liberal." Tracy's method wants to critically explore the full range of possibilities between tradition and situation — from confrontation or nonidentity through analogy to connection or identity.[37]

By the method of mutually critical correlation between theologically informed interpretations of both situation and message, Tracy takes seriously both manifestation and proclamation, or what Tillich termed "Protestant principle and Catholic substance."[38] Within the tradition of Catholic theology, David Tracy's program links the classic strengths of analogical traditions represented by thinkers like Rahner and Lonergan with the concerns more attuned to negative dialectics such as Metz's political theology or Küng's Barth-inspired

---

[37] Tracy discusses his addition of the qualifier "mutually" to the principle of correlation to signal that correlation of the two sources is not always harmonious or liberal in the *Christian Century* series, "How My Mind Has Changed." See Tracy, "God, Dialogue and Solidarity."

[38] David Tracy, *The Analogical Imagination: Christian Theology and the Culture of Pluralism* (New York: Crossroad, 1981) 419. Paul Tillich, *Systematic Theology*, vol. III, 11-30. An interesting collection of essays on Tillich's thought by a number of Roman Catholic theologians is quite relevant to Tracy's interpretation of Tillich's Protestant principle and Catholic substance as analogous to his own "proclamation and manifestation." See Thomas A. O'Meara O.P. and Celestin D. Weisser, O.P. (eds.), *Paul Tillich in Catholic Thought* (Dubuque, IA: The Priory Press, 1964).

kerygmatic voice. Thus, Tracy's catholic or public theology employs
a hermeneutics of suspicion and a hermeneutics of connection (or
retrieval) as it seeks to understand and interpret similarities-in-difference, named analogies, throughout all reality.

Francis Schüssler Fiorenza has written critically about the problem of a hermeneutical circularity in modern correlational theologies. He observes that correlational methodologies do not *simply*
correlate contemporary human experience with divine revelation
and the Christian tradition. Rather, they correlate human experience as transcendentally and phenomenologically analyzed to
uncover its religious dimension, while "the content of Christian
faith is interpreted to show its disclosive meaning and its coherence
with the religious dimension of human experience."[39]

As we have seen, Paul Tillich's principle of correlation failed to
acknowledge the possibility that the present existential situation
contained answers as well as questions. He also failed to critically
articulate how and in what possible ways the message of the gospel
arose in response to deep existential questions. Likewise, Fiorenza
reminds us that Bernard Lonergan's correlational theology assumes
a religiously-converted subject as theological hermeneut and Karl
Rahner's theology of experience assumes that humanity exists in
the presence of divine grace and therefore has a pre-apprehension
of the transcendent which becomes thematized in the formal task
of doing theology. Fiorenza's criticism is that these methods are in
fact circular and not really critically correlational. He argues that
they tend to neglect the historical and hermeneutical dimension of
all human experience. He charges that they are not attentive enough
to how the "present experience" of the theologian and its theological interpretation are inescapably situated within the cultural

---

[39] Francis Schussler Fiorenza, *Foundational Theology: Jesus and the Church* (New York, 1985) 277.

tradition of Christianity and Western civilization.[40] Since there can-
be no raw or unmediated experience, Fiorenza calls theologians to
interrogate how both experience and interpretation are already pre-
determined by Christian beliefs, narratives, symbols and rituals.

Fiorenza fears that even David Tracy's rigorous correlational
theology fails to escape this hermeneutically circularity, at least in
his earlier work. Tracy is aware of this difficulty and his developing hermeneutical project seeks to be attentive to the intellectual
and theological challenges presented by criticisms like those of
Fiorenza. He conceded that while it is methodologically helpful to
distinguish the correlation principle's two distinct acts of interpretation — the situation and the message — the interpreter cannot
existentially separate the two acts. He writes: "Whenever Christian theologians interpret contemporary experience theologically,
the history of the effects of the Christian tradition is already present in the interpretation itself. Whenever theologians interpret the
Christian message theologically, we are inevitably also applying it
to our contemporary experience precisely to understand it."[41]

We shall see in the following chapters of this study how David
Tracy's quest for a public theology attempts to overcome the problem of circularity through attention to the particular subject matter
of theology and by conversation with the other. In any concrete
case of interpretation he wants the particular subject matter itself
and not the theologian's methodological rules to reign in questions
of both truth and meaning. His developing work seeks to accomplish this through committed conversation with the other, the
stranger, the different. "Conversation is our only hope," he insists.
We will examine what he sees as the emerging two self-corrective
foci of his theology: a hermeneutics in which the "other" not the

[40] *Ibid.*, 281.
[41] Tracy, "Hermeneutics and the Tradition," 50.

"self" is the dominant focus; and a theological insistence that only
a mystical-prophetic model of theology can save us.

David Tracy is very deliberate in his choice of the word "public" to describe his theology. Theology for Tracy is always
involved in complex and interesting relationships with diverse historical and social realities: publics. A central thesis of Tracy's theology and hermeneutics is stated in his claim: "If any human being,
if any religious thinker or theologian, produces some classic expression of the human spirit on a particular journey in a particular tradition, that person discloses permanent possibilities for human existence both personal and communal. Any classic ... is always public,
never private."[42] Thus, serious theological reflection and construction much touch all of life. Tracy identifies the three publics of the
theologian: society, academy, and church.

David Tracy assumes that most Euro-American theologians are
involved in three distinct communities, social realities or publics:
society, academy and church. His public theological model identifies three subdisciplines constituting theology proper: foundational,
systematic and practical theologies. In terms of publics or social
realities, fundamental theology is related primarily but not exclusively to the academy; systematic theology finds its primary home
in the church; and practical theology addresses the reality of some
particular social, political, cultural, or pastoral movement or problem within the sphere of society.[43]

Most theologians will choose one of these subdisciplines as his
or her primary intellectual focus and will be most attentive to the
discipline's companion public or social reality. For example, the
systematic theologian will focus primarily on the representation,
interpretation and reinterpretation of the specific religious tradition
to which the theologian belongs. Nevertheless, Tracy contends,

[42] Tracy, *The Analogical Imagination*, 14.
[43] *Ibid.*, 3-46.

because these subdisciplines are interrelated and because the truth of religious manifestations is worldly as well as churchly— we are living in a sacramental universe — all theology, even systematics, concerns itself with public and not merely confessional criteria for all truth claims. Indeed, Tracy believes a coaffirmation of church and world is intrinsic to all serious theology.[44] Let us consider Tracy's understanding of the three publics of society, academy and church and their corresponding theological disciplines.

SOCIETY AND THE DISCIPLINE OF PRACTICAL THEOLOGY

David Tracy has projected a theological trilogy to address the theologian's publics and their companion theological disciplines. His *Blessed Rage for Order*, published in 1975, is his book on fundamental theology and expresses his hope for modern revisionist theology. According to Tracy, fundamental theology is concerned with the discovery of the religious dimensions of human experience and with public and philosophically-oriented discussions about God. The second volume of his trilogy, *The Analogical Imagination*, published in 1981, is devoted to the discipline of systematic theology. Tracy's systematic theology is concerned with specific confessions of faith which are expressed and interpreted through classic texts, symbols, rituals and traditions. In writing these two books Tracy remembered the words of Karl Rahner on the problem of the theologian's preoccupation with methodological issues and questions. Rahner, although committed to careful theological method cautioned, "But we cannot spend all our time sharpening the knife; at some point we must cut."[45] Thus, Tracy devoted about half of each book to method. The other half is given to the testing the

---

[44] *Ibid.*, 56.
[45] Tracy, "God, Dialogue and Solidarity," 901.

method with substantive theological issues — God, revelation, Christ.

Tracy has published three books since *The Analogical Imagina-tion*, but none is book three of the trilogy, which promises to treat practical theology. His *Plurality and Ambiguity*, published in 1986, addresses methodological and hermeneutical concerns in light of the challenges of postmodern plurality and ambiguity and proposes his model of "conversation" for theology in the shadow of post-modernism. His *Dialogue with the Other*, first presented as a series of lectures at Louvain and published in 1990, applies his hermeneu-tical theory to the inter-religious dialogue and also enters into con-versation with a host of thinkers including Sigmund Freud, Jaques Lacan and William James. *On Naming the Present: God, Hermeneutics, and Church*, published in 1994, is a collection of essays which Tracy originally wrote for the international theolog-ical journal, *Concilium*.[46]

Tracy confesses he is not yet ready to attempt writing a third volume of the projected trilogy. That work promises to address the relationship of theory and praxis in both personal and social terms. The principle theological topics will be Spirit and church. He feels he must gain more insight and understanding about four issues cen-tral to practical theology before he writes: contemporary social the-ory, ethics, ecclesiology and the history of spirituality. He concedes

---

[46] David Tracy, *Plurality and Ambiguity: Hermeneutics, Religion, Hope* (San Francisco, CA: Harper and Row, 1987); *Dialogue With the Other*; *On Naming the Present: God, Hermeneutics and the Church* (Maryknoll, NY: Orbis, 1994). In addition, Tracy has joined three other theologians in joint projects as a con-tributing co-author: With John Cobb in *Talking About God: Doing Theology in the Context of Modern Pluralism* (New York: Crossroad, 1981). With Robert Grant in *A Short History of the Interpretation of the Bible* (Philadelphia, PA: Fortress Press, 1984). With Stephen Happel in *A Catholic Vision* (Philadelphia, PA: Fortress Press, 1984). He has also worked on several book series and acad-emic journal projects with others as a co-editor.

that because of a change of focus in his theological research and personal thinking — the problem of naming God — he may never be prepared to attempt volume three of the trilogy. He is currently at work on the problem of God. It is certain that this massive "God book" will precede a volume on practical theology.

Nevertheless, David Tracy has done some writing on practical theology and society.[47] Tracy's program identifies the public of society as consisting of three realms: the technocratic realm, the realm of polity and the realm of culture.[48] The technocratic realm is given to the successful organization and allocation of goods and services. The realm of polity is concerned with the legitimate meanings of social justice and the use of power. The realm of culture is largely but not exclusively concerned with art and religion — "classical symbolic expressions" — and how those expressions of art, music, literature, religion, theology and philosophy inform society's ethos and worldview and thus explore and articulate meaning and values for individual, group and communal existence. These classic expressions are critically recovered by religions and humanistic disciplines for the general good and enrichment of society.

Although the realms of technoeconomics and polity demand the theologian's interest and attention, he or she works primarily in the realm of culture, where major religious traditions, texts and symbols

[47] In addition to the "anticipatory" work on practical theology in the first two books of Tracy's projected trilogy, see: David Tracy, "The Foundations of Practical Theology," *Practical Theology: The Emerging Field in Theology, Church and World*, ed. D. F. Browning (New York: Harper and Row, 1983) 62-82; and David Tracy, "Practical Theology in the Situations of Global Pluralism," *Formation and Reflection: The Promise of Practical Theology*, ed. L. S. Mudge and J. N. Poling (Philadelphia, PA: Fortress, 1987) 139-154. Also relevant to a consideration of Tracy's developing practical theology is his "Theology, Critical Social Theory and the Public Realm," *Habermas, Modernity, and Public Theology*, ed. D. S. Browning and F. S. Fiorenza (New York: Crossroad, 1992) 19-42.

[48] Tracy, *The Analogical Imagination*, 6-14.

have appeared and received their classic interpretations. David Tracy insists that religion "is a key cultural index." Tracy is happy with Clifford Geertz's well-known definition of the cultural function of religion as: "a system of symbols which acts to establish powerful, pervasive, and long-standing moods and motivations ... by formulating conceptions of a general order of existence and clothing those conceptions with such an aura of factuality that the moods and motivations seem uniquely realistic."[49]

According to Tracy, the good society does indeed employ the resources of the realm of culture for value questions in the realm of polity, technology and economics. Thus, the public theologian must handle her culture's classic symbols and narratives carefully and creatively in doing both theology and cultural criticism. He sees the theory of Paul Ricœur as relevant to this dynamic of the symbolic construction of reality or culture's power to shape politics: "The symbol gives rise to thought, but thought always returns to and is informed by the symbol."[50] Thus, a society's classic symbols, root metaphors and originating narratives are not to be taken lightly. They are not mere cultural ornaments; they give rise to both theoretical and practical thought which informs society's perception of reality, meaning and truth. They are constitutive; they can form and transform the social order.

Tracy reminds his readers of this important relationship between symbol and society in American culture and politics by calling our attention to the role of the Calvinist understandings of the covenant in its contributions to the American Constitution, Martin Luther King's appropriation of the biblical imagery of freedom and justice in the civil rights movement to remind American citizens of their country's most noble and hopeful dreams, Reinhold Niebuhr's

---

[49] *Ibid.*, 7.

[50] *Ibid.*, 13; Paul Ricœur, *The Symbolism of Evil* (Boston, MA: Beacon, 1967) 347-357.

dialectical use of the Christian symbols of "grace" and "sin" in discussing difficult political realities, and John Courtney Murray's correlation of "natural law" theory with complementary theories informing the principles of the American democratic tradition. He argues that King, Niebuhr, or Murray could never accept a privatization of religion for they understood that every classic expression of human culture is by its very nature public.[51]

In Tracy's evolving practical theology, he is careful to stress the transformative character of religious symbols and narratives. He is sympathetic with the reappropriation of Marx's observation in theological circles which argues that the task of philosophy, now theology, is not to simply interpret the world but to change it. He believes that together fundamental and systematic theology create a *theoria* which becomes a basis for the practical theologian's work in the area of praxis. In good theology, theory must move on to praxis. But Tracy emphasizes that praxis is not to be identified with mere practice. Instead, praxis must be understood as "the critical relationship between theory and practice whereby each is dialectically influenced and transformed by the other."[52] Tracy suggests that since the Enlightenment, theology has been concerned too exclusively with "the crisis of cognitive claims." He is convinced that the shift to praxis can help theologians realize "that the major question of our situation is not the crisis of cognitive claims, but the social-ethical crisis of massive suffering and widespread oppression and alienation in an emerging global culture."[53]

Tracy's developing practical theology shows a deep awareness of the important contributions of liberation theology.[54] Yet is his

---

[51] Tracy, *The Analogical Imagination*, 13.

[52] Tracy, *Blessed Rage for Order*, 243.

[53] Tracy, *The Analogical Imagination*, 78.

[54] See Tracy's "Introduction," *The Challenge of Liberation Theology: A First World Perspective*, ed. B. Mahan and L.D. Richesin (Maryknoll, NY: Orbis Books, 1981) 1-3.

emphasis on praxis the same as that of the liberation theologian's? In their concerns to address the crisis of massive suffering and widespread oppression and alienation, do Tracy and the liberationists share the same theological point of departure?

Dermont Lane addresses this question well in "The Debate About Praxis."[55] He suggests that in spite of Tracy's abiding interest in and commitment to praxis, the theologians of liberation and Tracy have very different methodological points of departure. Tracy's practical theology emerges from a deep commitment to *theoria* derived from philosophical reflection on the religious dimension of human experience (fundamental theology) and through the hermeneutics of classic texts (systematic theology). In contrast, Lane reminds us, for liberation theology the point of departure is the personal commitment of the theologian to social and political transformation of the status quo of suffering, oppression, injustice, and poverty. The actual experience of liberating praxis is the primary source for knowledge and understanding. It emphasizes "knowing by doing" over "knowing by reflection." According to Lane, its pre-reflective commitment to the praxis of liberation is something which "preceded theological reflection, becomes the object of theological reflection and judges theological reflection."[56]

Tracy, however, contends that the praxis of liberation, like all praxis, is theory-laden and thus emerges from reflective interpretation. Therefore, Tracy argues, "These liberation theologies of praxis are not faithful to the full demands of praxis."[57] For example, he

---

[55] Dermont A. Lane, "The Debate About Praxis," *Radical Pluralism and Truth*, ed. W. Jeanrond and J. Rike (cited above) 18-37.

[56] *Ibid.*, 32-36.

[57] Tracy, *Blessed Rage for Order*, 244. In this sense, according to Tracy, liberation theology displays methodological problems not unlike those of neo-orthodoxy. They do not bring a hermeneutics of suspicion to bear on their grounding narratives, symbols and dogmas.

notes that Gustavo Gutierrez in his *A Theology of Liberation* applies critical reflection on praxis to the concept of "development" in favor of the concept of "liberation" but fails to apply the same critical method to any of the major doctrines, narratives or symbols which inform his work. While Tracy admires and respects liberation theology's commitment to justice and solidarity with the poor and oppressed, he is troubled by their "lack of critical-theoretical rigor," and thus their tendency to not be adequately self-critical.

The work on practical theology by David Tracy is at this point, in his words, "merely anticipatory."[58] Yet he has given us a good sense of his methodological direction. He believes that the development of a practical theology must be collaborative and conversational, involving four steps: (1) the development of models of human transformation informed by the human sciences including theology; (2) the analysis of the public claims to human transformation; (3) the employment of a critical hermeneutics for the working out of steps 1 and 2; (4) the mutually critical correlation of secular models of praxis with faith-informed models of praxis. This fourth step is to be guided by a faith working through love and justice grounded in an eschatological hope.[59] A public practical theology, according to Tracy, must be especially attentive to three global issues: the inter-religious dialogue, the nuclear threat and the ecological crisis.[60]

Although critics have charged that Tracy's work to date is too fascinated with the problem of *understanding*, offering only occasional

---

[58] *Ibid.*, 240.

[59] Tracy, "The Foundations of Practical Theology," 76-78. Also see Dermont Lane's discussion of Tracy's developing practical theology in "The Debate About Praxis," 26-27.

[60] Tracy, "Practical Theology in the Situation of Global Pluralism," 140. Also see Lane's summary in "The Debate About Praxis," 26-27.

qualified references to political programs and liberating praxis, there is good reason to believe that the heart of his fundamental theology does indeed demand a practical theology of liberating action. He writes: "There is no manifestation disclosure that is not also a call to transformation. There is no revelation without salvation. There is no theological theory without praxis. There need be no hermeneutic without pragmatics."[61]

The Academy and the Discipline of Fundamental Theology

Friedrich Schleiermacher is known as the father of modern hermeneutics. Confronted by the intellectual challenges of the German Enlightenment and modernity's cultured despisers of religion, he attempted to demonstrate the public significance of religion and theology by redefining the nature of hermeneutics in a way which called theology to enter into serious dialogue with other scientific endeavors of the university. He wanted to free theology from the ecclesiological positivisms and ideologies of Protestant Orthodoxy and Roman Catholicism by grounding it in a philosophical or universal human understanding. In Schleiermacher's program, theology must develop its own questions and methods in critical relationship with other disciplines in the university, especially philosophy and the "philosophical dimensions" of other disciplines.[62]

David Tracy's theological vision shares Schleiermacher's enthusiasm for the university or academy, that public or social locus

---

[61] Tracy, "The Uneasy Alliance Reconceived: Catholic Theological Method, Modernity, and Postmodernity," 569.

[62] For an excellent discussion of Schleiermacher's hermeneutics within the context of the broader development of theological hermeneutics in this century see Werner G. Jeanrond, *Theological Hermeneutics: Development and Significance* (New York: Crossroad, 1991).

given to rigorous interdisciplinary and international research and conversation in quest of human understanding. In the academy the demands for publicness are quite explicitly imposed on all participants through the requirements for criteria of adequacy and evidence for all disciplinary assertions. Tracy is careful to note, however, that theology and religious studies, like psychology, sociology and anthropology, diverge from the "hard" sciences in significant ways and thus may be appropriately considered "diffuse" or "would-be" disciplines, in part because they are constituted by several disciplines and therefore lack uniform disciplinary standards. Academic theology, although a "diffuse" discipline, according to Tracy, must always be "apologetic" and must meet the highest standards of the contemporary academy. He argues, "Without such a demand for publicness — for criteria, evidence, warrants, disciplinary status — serious academic theology is dead."[63]

Whether in society, the church or the academy, for Tracy, theology must remain concerned with that elusive reality, "truth." Regarding this, Tracy reminds us that theology in the academy as a discipline is distinct from the field of religious studies. Scholars in religious studies may legitimately confine their interests and work to "meaning," while theologians must "by the intrinsic demands of their discipline face questions of both meaning and truth."[64] This demands a theological method which will investigate and correlate, through mutually critical correlation, questions and responses in *both* situation and tradition. Tracy calls this discipline fundamental theology.

He contends that the fundamental theologian (unlike the systematic theologian) must argue his or her position on strictly public grounds that are open to all persons. In doing fundamental theology, "personal faith or beliefs may not serve as warrants or

---

[63] Tracy, *The Analogical Imagination*, 21.
[64] *Ibid.*, 20.

quote

backings for publicly defended claims to truth."[65] The theologian must instead utilize some form of philosophical argument to investigate and explicate truth claims. Tracy identifies his own fundamental theology as "revisionist theology." He describes the vocation of the revisionist theologian as follows:

> In short, the revisionist theologian is committed to what seems clearly to be the central task of contemporary Christian theology: the dramatic confrontation, the mutual illuminations and corrections, the possible basic reconciliation between the principal values, cognitive claims, and existential faiths of both a reinterpreted post-modern consciousness and a reinterpreted Christianity.[66]

This method is of course radically different from the style and method of the neo-orthodox pure narrative or anticorrelational theologians since [it acknowledges the theological possibility of the disclosure of meaning and truth coming from outside the formally understood Christian tradition, and thus calls for revisions or reinterpretations of Christianity through philosophical reflection on the meanings past and present in common human experience and language.]

Yet true to his correlational aims, Tracy believes the Christian theologian's dual commitments to both the modern intellectual tradition and the God of Jesus Christ will "require a basic revision of traditional Christianity and traditional modernity alike."[67] A critical hermeneutics of suspicion and recovery must be applied to both traditions as evenly as possible.

As we have seen, in Tracy's program, the two principal sources for theology are Christian texts and common human experience and language. At times he substitutes "the Christian fact" or the Christian tradition for texts which includes not only texts but symbols,

---

[65] *Ibid.*, 64.

[66] Tracy, *Blessed Rage for Order*, 32.

[67] *Ibid.*, 4.

rituals, events, and witnesses. "Common human experience," for Tracy, is what in Tillich's theology is called "the situation." His linking of "language" with experience signals his hermeneutical understanding that all human experience is symbolically (or linguistically) mediated.[68] The theological task will always involve a mutually critical correlation of the results of these two sources of theology.

Methodologically, David Tracy's theology seeks to combine phenomenology, hermeneutics, and transcendental or metaphysical reflection. The investigation of human experience and language can be described as phenomenological; the investigation of the Christian tradition can be described as hermeneutical. To determine the truth-status of one's investigations into both common human experience and Christian texts, the theologian should employ the transcendental or metaphysical mode of reflection. Let us briefly consider how Tracy understands the operation of phenomenology, hermeneutics, and transcendental or metaphysical reflection in the task of fundamental theology.[69]

Phenomenology. Much of contemporary theology would assert that all theological statements involve an existential dimension which claims some form of general or universal existential relevance. In light of this, Tracy argues that the theologian is "obliged to explicate how and why the existential meanings proper to

[68] The way in which the postmodern "linguistic turn" in philosophy and criticism has attempted to correct modernity's "turn to the subject" is most fully developed in Tracy's *Plurality and Ambiguity.* A very fine examination of Tracy's thought relative to the linguistic turn and its implications for theology (especially moral theology) is found in Anne E. Patrick, "The Linguistic Turn and Moral Theology," *CTSA Proceedings* 42 (1987) 39-51.

[69] A very helpful summary and overview of the systematic movements and shifts in Tracy's method can be found in T. Howland Sanks, S.J., "David Tracy's Theological Project: An Overview and Some Implications."

✓ Christian self-understanding are present in common human experience."[70] Since experience for Tracy cannot be confined to the
realm of David Hume's sense-data but must also involve a recognition of the pre-reflective, pre-conceptual, pre-thematic realm of
the everyday, theology can help explicate a pre-conceptual dimension of our human experience which can be described as "both ultimate and religious."[71]

Tracy suggests that the phenomenological method is best suited
for explicating the "religious dimension" present in both everyday
and scientific experience and language. He is pleased that phenomenology has undergone significant transformations this century
from the "eidetic" thought of Husserl through the existential phenomenology of Sartre, Merleau-Ponty, Scheler and the early Heidegger to the hermeneutic phenomenology of the "later" Heidegger, Gadamer and Ricœur. Tracy has been very influenced by the
phenomenological hermeneutics of Paul Ricœur.[72]

He believes that the concept of "limit" can be used as "a key
(but not exhaustive category) for describing certain signal characteristics peculiar to any language or experience with a properly religious dimension."[73] This "limit" concept is very much like what
Langdon Gilkey, following his teacher Paul Tillich, calls "the
✓ dimension of ultimacy" in everyday secular experience.[74] Tracy

[70] Tracy, *Blessed Rage for Order*, 47.

[71] *Ibid.*

[72] Ricœur's movement from Husserl's phenomenology to the development of
his own hermeneutical phenomenology (from existentialism to a deepened emphasis on the philosophy of language) has been treated in many studies of Ricœur's
work. It is beyond the scope of this chapter to review the significance of that
development here. Tracy's deepening understanding of this hermeneutical "turn"
is reflected in his developing theological project.

[73] Tracy, *Blessed Rage for Order*, 93.

[74] Langdon Gilkey, *Naming the Whirlwind: The Renewal of God Language*
(New York: Bobbs-Merrill, 1969). See "The Dimension of Ultimacy in Secular
Experience," 305-364.

believes that all explicit religious experience and language and all implicit religious dimensions of common experience will witness to a limit-experience, a limit-language, or a limit-dimension. He identifies three areas in which limit-experiences or limit-languages are evident: science, morality, and everyday life.

In investigating limit languages and experiences in the sciences Tracy utilizes Lonergan's central category of "self-transcendence."[75] Lonergan's method taught Tracy that one lives authentically only as one allows oneself an expanding horizon. Thus, self-transcendence rather than self-fulfillment becomes the key to insight and understanding. According to Lonergan, on the most basic level, one transcends oneself first by sensitivity. Higher animals or sensitive beings like human persons have a sense of being related not only to themselves but to their surrounding realities. However, humans dwell not only in the life world of animals but in a world of profound meaning — "a universe." Humans ask questions about meaning, purpose and value in our life world and thus through reflection transcend the world of sensitive immediacy. Lonergan's work demonstrates that scientific questioning is an important example of this self-transcending dynamic. Scientific questioning drives the investigator beyond the life world of immediate experience to "an intelligently mediated and deliberately constituted world of meaning."[76]

In the course of normal scientific investigation, according to Tracy's reading of Lonergan, limit-questions follow scientific inquiry itself and are not simply imposed extrinsically by those

---

[75] In his theory of limit-experiences and limit-languages, Tracy combines and "reinterprets" Bernard Lonergan's concept of self-transcendence (in *Method in Theology*, 101-105) and Stephen Toulmin's notion of limit-questions (*An Examination of the Place of Reason in Ethics* [Cambridge: Cambridge University Press, 1950]).

[76] Tracy, *Blessed Rage for Order*, 96.

religious concerns and agendas. Limit-questions emerge within the scientist's or investigator's own discipline or horizon. What are examples of these limit questions? After the scientist reaches intellectually satisfying answers to his or her particular empirical research problems, he or she might be compelled to ask "limit-questions" such as: "Can these answers work if the world is not intelligible? Can the world be intelligible if it does not have an intelligible ground?"[77] Such questions, Tracy suggests, reveal a "religious dimension" of scientific inquiry. The ethical or value-based questions of the scientist also explore limits. For example, the investigator may ponder, "Is it worthwhile to ask whether our goals, purposes, and ideals are themselves worthwhile?"[78] Tracy uses these and other examples to assert that the scientist is often driven by his or her own critical intelligence to ask limit-questions which then point to a religious dimension of scientific inquiry.

These limit-questions are even more evident in the field of ethics and morality. Stephen Toulmin's work is attractive to Tracy in his analysis of the "religious" or "theological" character of limit-questions in the realm of morality. Since we cannot simply produce a moral argument for being moral, questions such as, "Why ought I keep my promise anyway?" can be described as limit-questions with a necessarily religious edge.[79]

Tracy turns his attention to existential analysis to discuss the limit-situations of everyday life. Here he sees both negative and positive limit-experiences. Karl Jaspers identified negative experiences such as sickness, guilt, anxiety, and the recognition of death as one's own destiny as "boundary-situations." These dark experiences demand serious reflection on the existential meaning and boundaries of our everyday existence. For example, when we

[77] *Ibid.*, 98.
[78] *Ibid.*
[79] *Ibid.*, 102.

receive a shocking announcement that our neighbor, a thirty-six year old mother of three, unexpectedly fell ill and died on Christmas day, we begin to experience the normal, everyday "real" world as terribly unreal — strange, foreign, and unexplainable — in light of the emotional and existential "realities" called forth by this intense awareness of the negative boundaries of human existence; an awareness that life is marked by tragedy and surrounded by death. These boundary situations shock us with an awareness that we too are vulnerable to the terrors of history and the tyranny of nature; we too will die. These haunting limit-experiences may "disclose to us either a faith or an unfaith in the meaningfulness of life."[80]

Abraham Maslow's theory of peak-experiences provides Tracy with reference for discussing life's positive limit situations. These peak-experiences, or "ecstatic" experiences as Tracy prefers — love, joy, the creative act, profound reassurance — "are authentically self-transcending moments in our lives."[81] These experiences

[80] *Ibid.*, 105. Tracy's more recent work expresses dissatisfaction with his earlier theology of suffering and negative limit-experiences as a route to a phenomenology of basic trust in God. That is, if the "limit-of" negative realities (like the limit-of positive experiences) is said to be God or an opening to God (the ground of the world's trustworthiness), do these negative experiences really reveal or disclose God? In discussing his change of perspective on this problem he confesses, "I no longer believe that the 'route' of negative realities is correctly described as an alternative route to the questions of religion and God." He is now becoming more at home with the language of "negative dialectics" when addressing the problem of suffering and oppression. He writes: "The classic theological language of analogy ... remains my real theological home. Yet now the analogies emerge more tentatively through (not in spite of) the various languages of negative dialectics. The recognition of the need for both the negative and the positive as already together in every religious journey has forced me onto a more unsteady route for every question of theology." Tracy, "Defending the Public Character of Theology," 355. For a commentary on this shift see S. Alen Ray, *The Modern Soul*, 133-135.

[81] Tracy, *Blessed Rage for Order*,105; Abraham H. Maslow, *Religions, Values and Peak Experiences* (New York: Viking, 1970).

tend to lift us from the mundane worlds and selves to touch a
dimension of experience which transcends everyday language and
experience. Tracy uses the experience of authentic love, both erotic
and agapic, to illustrate these peak-experiences which have such
undeniable power in our lives. He believes that however unique,
particular or different life's boundary-situations and ecstatic experiences may be, they are "common *human* experiences" and "signals of transcendence" which invite a response of "fundamental
trust" in the face of mystery.

Hermeneutics. After applying a general phenomenological analysis to the one constant source of theology, human language and
experience, Tracy turns to theology's other constant source, Christian texts, to explore how their explicit religious language might
correlate in a meaningful and truthful way with the limit-questions
and limit-experiences of the first source. For Tracy, the investigation of the Christian tradition can best be described as "an historical and hermeneutical investigation of classic Christian texts."[82]

I have already noted David Tracy's indebtedness to Paul Ricœur
in the development of his own theological hermeneutics. As biblical texts are skillfully and critically reconstructed by contemporary
historical scholarship, both thinkers insist that the question of the
meaning of the text for faith and life demands hermeneutical and
theological clarification. Like Ricœur, Tracy understands the task
of investigating classic Christian texts as involving at least four
related methods: history, semantics, literary criticism and
hermeneutics.[83]

Let us take, for example, New Testament texts about Jesus. The
historical method can critically reconstruct the christological texts.

[82] Tracy, *Blessed Rage for Order*, 49.
[83] *Ibid.*, 51.

Semantics can illuminate the linguistic structure and the play of images and symbols in the text. Literary criticism can aid the interpreter in "determining the particular character of literary genres by means of which the images, metaphors and symbols are structured, codified and transformed."[84] When applied to biblical studies these methods give us a historical reconstruction of the text and a good "sense" of the text, but the question of the text's meaning and "reference" must be advanced by hermeneutics. Tracy argues that a critical hermeneutics must formulate and investigate a question of great importance for the theologian: "What is the mode-of-being-in-the-world *referred to* by the text?"[85] This difference between the "sense" and "reference" of the text is important for the research concerns and goals of our study.

Tracy's understanding of this problem is informed by Ricœur. Ricœur's hermeneutical theories of linguistic "distanciation" and textual reference are relevant here.[86] Ricœur contends that a written text, as it is inscribed, is distanced from the original intention of its author and from its original reception in its first community of addressees or intended readers. Thus, the hermeneutical theologian must not, and indeed cannot, seek to understand the biblical text by simply attempting to grasp "the subjectivity either of the author's intentions or the original addressee's reception of its meaning." Further, Tracy argues, neither can a history-like, "plain sense" of the text" reading disclose the surplus of meaning in biblical writing, because christological texts refer both to Jesus *and* to a Christian mode-of-being-in-the-world.[87]

[84] *Ibid.*

[85] *Ibid.*, 52.

[86] Paul Ricœur, "The Hermeneutical Function of Distanciation," *From Text to Action: Essays in Hermeneutics, II* trans. Kathleen Blamey and John B. Thompson (Evanston, IL: Northwestern University Press, 1991) 75-88.

[87] Tracy, *Blessed Rage for Order*, 51.

Both Ricœur and Tracy are attentive to the important problem of textual reference, or the necessary distinction between sense and reference and the methods necessary to explicate each. A close reading can disclose the "sense" of the text — that "internal structure and meaning of the text as that structure can be determined through ordinary methods of semantic and literary inquiries."[88] The text's referents, however, are not confined to the world of the text or the world behind the text (the author's intention or the community's reception in its social-cultural context). According to both Ricœur and Tracy, the "referent" of the text becomes manifested as the disclosure of meaning in front of the text, in that existential reality and mode-of-being-in-the-world that the text opens for the committed, intelligent reader.

Tracy's reading and study of the New Testament lead him to conclude that its diverse linguistic forms — parables, narratives, proverbs, eschatological sayings — correlate with the limit-languages and limit-experiences of common human experience. Religious language is imaginative, analogical, mystical, metaphorical, mythical, symbolic, and poetic; indeed it is "logically odd." It has the characteristics of art. As such it "explodes our ordinary language forms," "disorients us," "redescribes our experience," and "discloses a limit-referent which projects and promises that one can in fact live a life of wholeness, total commitment or radical honesty and agapic love in the presence of the gracious God of Jesus Christ."[89] This language does in fact open the reader to the world of existential meaning in front of the text, but as a Christian theologian, Tracy remains clear about the text's ultimate referent: "The objective ground or referent of all limit-experience and limit-language is what in reality Christians name God."[90]

---

[88] *Ibid.*

[89] *Ibid.*, 136.

[90] *Ibid.*

Christian language, therefore, is not limited to expressions of existential meaningfulness. It does indeed make claims that are cognitive. Thus, to be meaningful, theological language must display some internal coherence; and to be true it must be adequate to experience. To interrogate the truth-status of the theologian's investigations of the critical correlation between common human experience and Christian texts, she or he must turn to a transcendental or metaphysical mode of reflection.

Transcendental or Metaphysical Reflection. Although Tracy was trained in Bernard Lonergan's transcendental Thomism, he does not employ Lonergan's (or Rahner's) transcendental method in his program of fundamental theology since Lonergan (like Rahner) was "unwilling to break with the classical theistic concepts of Aquinas."[91] While Tracy remains very appreciative of his former mentor's general metaphysical and transcendental methodological aims, intentions and sympathies, he complains that Lonergan too easily assumed the truth claims of the Christian dogmatic tradition without providing critical grounds for interrogating the theological enterprise and its received tradition. As a revisionist theologian Tracy concludes that classical Christian theism "is neither internally coherent nor adequate as a full account of our common experience and of the scriptural understanding of the Christian God."[92] In the development of his own fundamental theology, finding his roots in transcendental Thomism inadequate, Tracy has been attracted to the categories of process metaphysics, especially the revisionist process theology of his former Chicago colleague, Schubert Ogden.[93] He endorses Ogden's metaphysical understanding of

---

[91] *Ibid.*, 172.

[92] *Ibid.*

[93] The most concise and systematic statement of Ogden's method is found in his *On Method* (San Francisco: Harper and Row, 1986) Like Tracy, Ogden is

God as "the ultimate creative ground of anything that is so much as even possible, and hence to be in the strictest sense necessary, not merely a being among others, but in some way 'being itself'. In fact, the God of theism in its most fully developed forms is the one metaphysical individual, the sole reality whose individuality is constitutive of reality as such; the sole being who is, therefore, the inclusive object of all our faith and understanding."[94] Connecting Ogden's understanding of God with his own "limit" categories, Tracy suggests that if God is indeed the object ground of reality itself for the limit-experiences and limit-language of the Christian religion, it seems logical to describe our concept of "God" as a "limit-concept." Therefore, God-talk must enter into conceptual and not merely symbolic categories.

The cognitive claims of such an assertion demand careful and creative metaphysical explication. Tracy recognizes that many modern and postmodern theologians have abandoned any hopes for metaphysics of religion. Yet he retains a chastened commitment to the possibility of a metaphysics. He is happy with Frederick Ferre's definition of metaphysics: "A metaphysical system is a construct of concepts designed to prove coherence for all 'the facts' on the basis of a theoretical model drawn from among the facts."[95] In Tracy's own work, he tends to use "metaphysical" and "transcendental" interchangeably, viewing transcendental reflection as the modern formulation of more traditional expressions of metaphysics. He explains: "As transcendental, such reflection attempts the explicit mediation of the basic presuppositions (or 'beliefs') that are the conditions of the possibility of our existing or understanding

---

interested in linking his cognitive, theoretical concerns with liberating praxis in the world. See Ogden, *Faith and Freedom: Toward a Theology of Liberation* (Nashville, TN: Abingdon, 1979).

[94] Tracy, *Blessed Rage for Order*, 155.

[95] *Ibid.*, 152.

at all. Metaphysical reflection means essentially the same thing: the philosophical validation of the concepts 'religion' and 'God' as necessarily affirmed or denied by our basic beliefs and understanding."[96] Later in this study we will see how Tracy's interest in metaphysics intersects with his classic Catholic understanding of "the sacramental nature of the universe."

As we have noted, such reflections must move from *symbolic* languages and categories to more *conceptual* languages and categories. [Following Ricœur's dictum, "The symbol gives rise to thought yet thought returns to and is informed by the symbol,"] Tracy's work seeks to maintain an imaginative dialectic between the symbolic and the conceptual. The rich symbolic language of classic Christian texts gives rise to critical thought and reflection; yet the conceptual thought experiments and proposals of the theologian must always return to the symbol, story, parable, poem, myth and metaphor for a re-presentation and redescription of "reality," because these symbolic expressions are not merely existential possibilities, "they are representative facts of a particular culture."[97]

Tracy concludes that all transcendental theological reflection and work must be faithful to at least three criteria of adequacy: First, it must find a necessary and sufficient ground in human experience; second, it must be internally coherent; and third, it must cohere with other essential categories of knowledge and belief.[98] Such reflection is therefore never merely communal, confessional or intratextual; *it is indeed public.*

---

[96] *Ibid.*, 56.
[97] *Ibid.*, 216.
[98] *Ibid.*, 55.

THE CHURCH AND THE DISCIPLINE OF SYSTEMATIC THEOLOGY

For theologians with strongly confessional or intratextual sympathies like George Lindbeck, Hans Frei, and other "pure narrative" (anticorrelational) theologians that we will consider in the next part of this study, the church seems to function as the sole reference of theology. There is a temptation to view the church as the proper theological reality and society and the academy as mere sociological realities. However, Tracy reminds us that "the world" (society and academy) is also a proper theological reality. As we have seen, for Tracy, the world must be viewed as a complex *source* for theology and not simply its *object*. The public world of both society and the academy is a theological as well as a sociological reality. Likewise, Tracy suggests, the church is both a theological and a sociological reality.

As a sociological reality or public, the church is a "community of religious and moral discourse," and "a voluntary association," and as such its members are joined to "a social institution and to an interpersonal community and tradition of shared meanings."[99] As a voluntary association, church can function as a mediating public or social space between individuals and the broader society.

Sociologically, the church is one of Tracy's three "publics" and thus one public of every theologian. Yet the Christian theological self-understanding of "church" does place it above society and academy as a unique "gift" of God "participating in the grace of God disclosed in the divine self-manifestation of Jesus Christ."[100] Though a social institution, theologically it cannot be reduced to the status of simply another organization or institution among many. Nevertheless, theologically, this "unique" status is also relativized

---

[99] Tracy, *The Analogical Imagination*, 21.
[100] *Ibid.*, 23.

by the general theological recognition and consensus that the
church is not identical with the kingdom of God. Hence, Tracy
reminds us, "the Christian church, in its own self-understanding,
stands under the judgement of God and God's eschatological kingdom revealed in Jesus Christ."[101] To uncritically identify the social
institution of the church with the kingdom of God risks falling into
idolatry. A critical hermeneutics can in fact guard the church from
idolatry and false consciousness of a narrative closure around ideological readings and finite models of God.

As one would expect, Tracy suggests that the principle of correlation can help clarify this dual dimension of the church in the
world. He writes: "The theologian should in principle use a correlation model for relating sociological and theological understandings of the reality of the church in the same way one uses a correlation model for the more familiar relationship between philosophy
and theology."[102] This correlation will critically explore the complex range of relationships between church and world from "identity through transformation to confrontation."

Tracy's theology asserts that the social reality of the theologian
is that of an intellectual related to three publics. Even though the
primary social location of the practical theologian is society, the primary social location of the fundamental theologian is the academy,
and the primary social location of the systematic theologian is the
church, these realms and roles are inescapably interrelated. For
example, the fundamental theologian who is also a practicing member of a particular faith-tradition in the Christian church must be a
responsible participant in that tradition — and thus be attentive to
the particular questions, concerns, truth claims and practices internal to the ecclesiastical tradition.

---

[101] *Ibid.*
[102] *Ibid.*, 24.

Similarly, even though the systematic theologian is concerned
with the interpretation and reinterpretation of a particular tradition's
understanding and construal of the divine reality, the divine reality
is nevertheless "that ultimate ground of everything," indeed, the
same God referred to in the metaphysical reflections of the fundamental theologian. Although the systematic theologian's major task
is finally a reinterpretation of a particular and "confessional"
expression of the Christian tradition for the present situation, his or
her work refers to a "God" beyond denominational and dogmatic
boundaries.

David Tracy's project recognizes that the church will remain the
primary reference group and mediator of the divine reality for the
systematic theologian. The systematic theologian must remain
engaged in his or her tradition's particularity, yet that focus does
not render the task of systematic theology private. When Tracy
wrote *Blessed Rage for Order*, he recognized that there was a
dimension of publicness in all systematic theologies, but he also
recognized that his theory and criteria for the public character of
fundamental theology could not determine the distinctive form of
publicness proper to systematic theology. He confesses, "I knew at
the time (1975) that there was a real difference between fundamental and systematic theology and, therefore, between the forms
of publicness proper to each. Yet I could not formulate exactly
what the difference was."[103]

This problem occupied his thought during the late seventies and
he began to think of systematic theology in terms of the paradox
of the classic. He formulated the problem in this way: "Why do
classic systematic theologies, like classic works of art, function so
disclosively, indeed so publicly, in spite of their particularity?"
He soon replaced the critical clause, "in spite of," with a more

---

[103] Tracy, "Defending the Public Character of Theology," 117.

affirming "because of," as his investigations lead him to believe
that "every classic in both art and religion achieves genuine publicness because of, not in spite of, an intensified particularity."[104]
He turned to art and aesthetics to develop a working theory of
"the classic." He was influenced by Hans-Georg Gadamer's aesthetics which posits that a piece of art "can be called a realized
experience of an event of truth."[105] Tracy's growing conviction that
a public disclosure of truth actually happens in the classic works
of art was soon applied to the religious classic. Later, he brought
this insight to bear on "the Christian classic: the person and event
of Jesus Christ."[106] This work on the classic became a central theme
in his systematics book, *The Analogical Imagination.*

Tracy's notion of the classic is not confirmed to classicist norms.
Every culture and religious tradition produces classics. This means
that "in naming certain texts, events, images, rituals, symbols and
persons 'classics' ... we recognize nothing less than the disclosure
of a reality we cannot but name as truth."[107] A classic will claim
the attention of its interpreter with its sheer force. However, the
"truth" of the classic will not always appear as a harmonious identity with the interpreter's subjectivity; indeed it may come as a sur-
prise or shock inviting transformation:

The subject may not know how or why that claim exercises its
power — those are tasks for later reflection and more informed
readings. But that the claim to attention is present — that something

[104] *Ibid.,* 118.

[105] Tracy, *the Analogical Imagination,* 111. Tracy is drawing heavily from
Gadamer's theory here. See Hans-Geog Gadamer, *Truth and Method* (New York:
Seabury Press, 1975), 73-91. A very well-researched study on "disclosure" is
James J. DiCenso, *Hermeneutics and the Disclosure of Truth: A Study in the Work
of Heidegger, Gadamer and Ricœur* (Charlottesville, VA: University Press of Vir-
ginia, 1990).

[106] Tracy, *The Analogical Imagination,* 233.

[107] *Ibid.,* 108.

like what we have called a realized experience, ranging from a haunting sense of resonance and import to a shock of recognition, that sheer event-like thatness — is what cannot be denied. My *doxai* are suddenly confronted with a *paradoxon* demanding attention. My finite status as this historical subject is now confronted with the classic and its claim on me: a claim that transcends any context from my preunderstanding that I try to impose upon it, a claim that can shock me with the insight into my finitude as finitude, a claim that will interpret me even as I struggle to interpret it.[108]

According to Tracy, the Christian theologian committed to exploring truth must be deeply interested in all classic expressions of the human spirit. He reminds us that religious classics, like classics of art, music and literature, are also cultural classics and thus carry "public" possibilities for the disclosure of truth far beyond their particular tradition's original cultural-linguistic boundaries.

However, the special task of the systematic theologian is to interpret the classics of her or his particular faith-tradition — in conversation with other classics and works to be sure — but nevertheless with closest attention given to the originating or foundational texts, events, images, persons, rituals and symbols of her or his primary community. Yet even as systematic theologians attend to their tradition's own classics, Tracy insists, "they perform a genuinely public function for both society and academy analogous to the philosopher's interpretation of philosophy or the literary critic's interpretation of the classics of literature."[109]

Tracy does, however, distinguish a classic work of literature or philosophy from the religious classic. He applies his categories of

---

[108] *Ibid.*, 119.
[109] *Ibid.*, 68.

limit-language and limit-experience to the religious classic to suggest that while classics in art, literature and philosophy speak to us truthfully about particular areas of lived experience and human existence, religious classics do indeed address the *whole* of existence: "Explicitly religious classic expressions will involve a claim to truth as one event of disclosure-concealment of the whole of reality *by the power of the whole* — as in some sense, a radical and finally gracious mystery."[110] As such they invite an explicit response of faith and commitment from their readers or addressees.

As we have observed, in Tracy's program the theocentric character of all theological statements, whether they are practical, fundamental or systematic, "drives the theologian to truth claims which demand publicness and at the limit, universality."[111] Yet in a world of increasing plurality and ambiguity, indeed, in a world of increasing tribalism and sectarian and ethnic violence, how can the theologian hope to speak of God in public with integrity? Tracy's more recent work responds to this dilemma by suggesting that all authentic theology must be "conversational."

PUBLIC THEOLOGY, PARTICULAR STORIES, AND DIALOGUE WITH THE OTHER

Werner Jeanrond, David Tracy's former student at Chicago, who now teaches theology and hermeneutics at Trinity College, Dublin, is becoming a leading interpreter of his thought. In an insightful essay he observes that Tracy's understanding of the normative character of the Christian classic does not depend on the authoritative decree or declaration of any church, religious community, official

---

[110] *Ibid.*, 163.
[111] *Ibid.*, 80.

spokesperson or magisterium. Instead, the classic claims an alert
interpreter, impressing on him or her a reality he or she "cannot but
name as truth." As such it escapes the obvious dangers of ecclesiastical positivism or sectarianism present in many anticorrelational
theologies. However, Jeanrond charges that while this understanding of the disclosive function of the classic is an interesting
hermeneutical response to both the problem of religious particularity and cultural pluralism, it "still is too individualistic and
smacks somewhat of nineteenth-century liberal theology."[112]

Jeanrond suggests that Tracy recognized this limitation and that
his theory of classic disclosure needed a complementary category
which "would protect the text against the ideologies of readings
and the reader against ideological features of texts."[113] This complementary category would need to situate both texts and reading
subjects within some context or form of communal inquiry. This led
Tracy to develop further his hermeneutical emphasis on "conversation." His *Plurality and Ambiguity* has appropriately been called
√ a "conversation about conversation" in theology and hermeneutics.
This theme of conversation is carried on and extended in his *Dialogue with the Other*.

From Gadamer's work Tracy first learned that hermeneutics is conversation.[114] From Eliade's creative work he learned that hermeneutics must be done in conversation with the "radically other" if one
hopes to transcend one's boundaries and adequately expose one's
hidden ideologies.[115] Tracy's model of conversation does indeed

---

[112] See Werner Jeanrond, "Theology in the Context of Pluralism and Postmodernity: David Tracy's Theological Method," 151.

[113] *Ibid.*

[114] Hans-Georg Gadamer, *Truth and Method*, 325-345. Tracy states that while
his model of interpretation-as-conversation is certainly indebted to Gadamer, his
program is less directed than Gadamer's work to an ontology of understanding and
more concerned with developing an empirical model for the interpretation of texts.

[115] Tracy, *Dialogue with the Other*, 48-67.

place classic texts and their interpreters within the context of a community of inquiry. However, this "community" is not the tight, churchly cultural-linguistic community of the anticorrelational or pure narrative theologian. This community is in fact the world with its many communities of difference. It is dialogue with the "other." Conversation in this model is profoundly interdisciplinary, intercommunal, intertextual and multicultural. It is worldly as well as churchly; it is public. Central to Tracy's theology of hermeneutics is his relentless insistence that to enter this conversation well, one must have an active analogical imagination.

This brings us back to Tracy's important question, "Do particular traditions bear public resources?" His answer is, of course, "Yes." However, his most recent work turns to thinkers like Johann Baptist Metz to bring a dialectical tension to this analogical affirmation. This brings us back to Metz and his ponderous and prophetic response to Bloch about a theology beyond cathedrals and cages.

The collected essays of Johann Baptist Metz, *A Passion of God: The Mystical-Political Dimension of Christianity*, follows the understanding of Friedrich von Hugel that religion is always a complex interaction of three elements or modalities: the historical-institutional, the intellectual, and the mystical.[116] This collection is a translation of the very best from Metz's recent German writings. Translator and editor J. Matthew Ashley introduces the volume with a very useful overview of the evolution of Metz's thought from founder of European political theology to his current attention to the "irruption" of the third world into the church's consciousness,

---

[116] Johann Baptist Metz, *A Passion for God: The Mystical-Political Dimension of Christianity*, trans. and ed. J. Matthew Ashley (New York: Paulist Press, 1998). Also see Johann Baptist Metz, "In the Pluralism of Religious and Cultural Worlds: Notes Toward a Theological and Political Program," *Cross Currents* 49 (1999) 227-236.

calling for a global, polycentric church. Ashley traces how Metz has held in productive tension the historical, the prophetic-intellectual and the mystical as he has attended to both classic texts and voices from the margins, the stories of others, minor literatures.

One feels the force of Metz's familiar prophetic edge, inspired by his mentors from the Frankfurt School, Ernst Bloch, and his political engagement with "the dangerous memory of Jesus." Some of these pieces are vintage Metz, brooding over Theodore Adorno's haunting declaration that "after Auschwitz there can no longer be any poetry." Yet in two essays Metz returns to his more priestly and poetic teacher and "father in the faith," Karl Rahner. Especially moving is, "Do We Still Miss Karl Rahner?" Metz answers, "Yes," and contends that contemporary theology has lost interest in listening to religious experience and thus has lost the ability of "articulating one's life story before God." Metz honors Rahner's truly intellectual and spiritual theology in its good work of rendering "a mystical biography of the ordinary, average person." He suggests that his beloved teacher was successful in this rendering because he refused to pour interpretations of religious experience "from above into bewildered souls;" instead, his theology was "an invitation to a journey of discovery into the virtually uncharted territory of one's own life."[117]

Although this modern turn to the subject is critically out of fashion in contemporary academic theory and theology, Metz believes that it remains necessary intellectual work for both spiritual and political understanding. Metz is not interested in a return to an easy metanarrative or a generic story of the soul. He concedes that we live in a time of fundamental pluralism of cultures, religions and worldviews in which traditional ethical approaches to the relationship of "universalism and particularism" have reached an *aporia*.

---

[117] Johann Baptist Metz, *A Passion for God*, 8.

No one needs to alert Metz to the imperialistic dangers in claims of universalism and universal obligation. However, he worries deeply about the postmodern triumph and celebration of disconnected little stories and the communities of discourse and practice underwritten by them. In such a story line he wonders how the important universalism of human rights and the cherished notion of inalienable and intrinsic human and cultural differences might be respected and protected from predictable conflicts that lead either to violence or sectarian withdrawal from the public sphere. Thus, he ponders if there is in fact anything in an emerging world of minor literatures that can speak genuinely as a universal word.

Indeed, can minor literatures, can the cages finally speak out of a particularity that rises to some universal significance? Metz thinks so. He turns to the classic *memoria passionis* as a root metaphor calling humanity to a very particular expression of universal responsibility in the face of suffering — the suffering of the other, the stranger, even the enemy. The particularity of the incarnation and passion of Christ reveals something profound about the universality of creation. One is moved from the dangerous memories of the sufferings of Christ to a participation in and responsibility for the universalism of suffering in the world. For Metz, the cry of suffering, when truly heard, can be a universal word uniting all creatures in the passion of God and compassion for the other. For Metz, the cry of suffering is a classic expression of the human body and soul. One must do theology from there.

Tracy would agree. The cry of suffering may indeed be the universal human story, but what about the narratives of love, beauty, goodness, bliss, desire and doxology? Tracy's large analogical imagination asserts that in this blessed fallen world there must be a poetry and thus theology capable of naming it all, for sun and moon, light and darkness, together make up a day. A poetic fragment from Czeslaw Milosz, the long-exiled Pole, who has seen

more than his share of the terrors and tragedies of history, wisely
and beautifully catches the mysteries of the human heart and mind:

> Pure beauty, benediction: you are all I gathered
> From a life that was bitter and confused,
> In which I learned about evil, my own and not my own.
> Wonder kept dazzling me, and I recall only wonder,
> The risings of the sun in boundless foliage,
> Flowers opening after the night, universe of grasses,
> A blue outline of the mountains and a shout of hosanna.
> How many times I thought: is this the truth of the Earth?
> How can laments and curses be turned into hymns?
> Why do I pretend to know so much?
> But the lips praised on their own, the feet on their own were running,
> The heart was beating strongly, and the tongue proclaimed adoration.[118]

Let us now turn to a consideration of how David Tracy's theology
of the public, analogical imagination enters the specific conversations and debates around narrative theology. The important question, "How Do Stories Save Us?" has been answered very differently in contemporary theology. Much of the difference is directly related to the productive tensions between correlational and anti-correlational methodologies, the analogical and dialectical movements of the imagination, and a sensibility as to whether, primarily, we allow ourselves to be inscribed by a sacred text or baptized in a sacramental universe.

---

[118] Czeslaw Milosz cited in William Sloane Coffin, *The Heart is a Little to the Left: Essays on Public Morality* (Hanover, NH: Dartmouth/University Press of New England, 1999) 11.

PART TWO

HOW DO STORIES SAVE US?
TWO CONTEMPORARY THEOLOGICAL RESPONSES*

We tell a story in order to find a story
Elie Wiesel

INTRODUCTION

Although reflection on the religious meanings and claims embodied in stories has always been a task of the theologian, the turn to the narrative genre as a privileged theological category became one of the most significant methodological emphases of late 20th-century theology, hermeneutics, and critical theory.[1] Yet despite hundreds of books, articles and conferences on the topic there is clearly no consensus concerning how stories are to be used theologically in the conversations and debates within the contemporary theological guild. In fact, there are sharp tensions within the company of those committed to narrative theological inquiry.

---

* A parallel version of this chapter appeared in *Louvain Studies* 22 (1997) 328-351.

[1] One of the best general introductions to the varieties of narrative theology is Michael Goldberg, *Theology and Narrative: A Critical Introduction* (Nashville, TN: Abingdon, 1981). Also, for the best collection of essays on narrative theology, see Stanley Hauerwas and Gregory Jones (eds.), *Why Narrative? Readings in Narrative Theology* (Grand Rapids, MI: Eerdmans, 1989). A useful analysis of the reasons for the rise of narrative theology can be found in Terrence W. Tilley, *Story Theology* (Wilmington, DE: Michael Glazier, 1985). Tilley identifies the emergence of feminist and liberation theologies, the challenge of linguistic philosophy, the narrative quality of human experience, biblical criticism, and the failure of Enlightenment myths and the challenge of postmodernity. A good treatment of the contemporary narrative turn in the humanities is Martin Kreiswirth, "Trusting the Tale: The Narrative Turn in the Human Sciences," *New Literary History* 23 (Summer 1992) 629-657.

In recent years two major schools of interpretation have emerged around the narrative and theology question: the so called "Yale school" and the "Chicago school."[2] Those who identify themselves with Yale are committed to a rather strict cultural-linguistic method of interpreting religious stories and doctrines. In contrast, so-called Chicagoans are more interested in a phenomenology of the sacred as they approach narrative texts and traditions. This chapter will examine the distance between Chicago and New Haven on the question of "how stories save us." To illustrate the contrasts between the two schools, Yale theologian George Lindbeck's theological use of Clifford Geertz's work will be brought into conversation with Chicago theologian, David Tracy, and his appropriation of the creative hermeneutics of his late colleague, Mircea Eliade.

---

[2] Gary L. Comstock, "Two Types of Narrative Theology," *Journal of the American Academy of Religion* 55 (Winter 1987) 687-717. Comstock provides an important classification and examination of two major methodological approaches to contemporary narrative theology: Yale vs. Chicago or the "pure" vs. the "impure" narrative hermeneutic. Also, for an excellent study of the Yale hermeneutic in dialogue with Chicago concerns see Mark I. Wallace, *The Second Naivete: Barth, Ricœur, and the New Yale Theology* (Macon, GA: Mercer University Press, 1990). It must be noted, however, that several in the so-called New Haven circle nervously reject Comstock's Yale vs. Chicago typology, suggesting that it applies primarily to older Yale scholars such as George Lindbeck, Hans Frei, and Paul Holmer. Indeed, several younger theologians associated with Yale (as faculty or Ph.D. graduates) have made some interesting although modest moves beyond their mentors' Barthian, pure narrative confessionalism. I am thinking especially of Placher, Tanner, Thiemann, and Werpehowski. Nevertheless, Comstock's typology remains a useful indicator of two moods in contemporary theology if it is remembered that both "schools" are in process. In fact, Kathryn Tanner is now on the faculty at Chicago.

GEERTZ AND LINDBECK

George Lindbeck's influential work, *The Nature of Doctrine: Religion and Theology in a Postliberal Age*, serves as the centerpiece of the Yale hermeneutic.[3] Lindbeck appropriates his reading of sociologists and anthropologists for what he terms a cultural-linguistic model for understanding religion and theology. For Lindbeck and the Yale school, theologians writing in the postmodern or postliberal age must write like sensitive anthropologists and careful linguists as they concern themselves with description rather than explanation of religious narratives.

Anthropologist Clifford Geertz has been influential in the development of Lindbeck's thought.[4] Geertz's theories of how religion functions as a cultural system have been well reviewed in interdisciplinary studies of religion and culture. Geertz's work chronicles the shift in modern anthropological discussions of religion from an earlier concern with religious thought as an interior psychological or mental state to the current understanding of religion as an external, historically constructed symbol system shaping the psychological and social lives of religious devotees. In Geertz's anthropological theory of religion, the focus of study is not on subjective life or even on outward behavior but on the socially available "systems of significance" — beliefs, rites, meaningful objects — in terms of which subjective life is ordered and outward behavior

---

[3] George Lindbeck, *The Nature of Doctrine: Religion and Theology in a Postliberal Age* (Philadelphia, PA: Westminster Press, 1984). For a fine collection of essays evaluating Lindbeck's program see Bruce D. Marshall, *Theology and Dialogue: Essays in Conversation with George Lindbeck* (Notre Dame, IN: University of Notre Dame Press, 1990). An entire issue of *Modern Theology* 4 (January 1988) was devoted to a critical consideration of Lindbeck's thought.

[4] See Clifford Geertz, "Religion as a Cultural System," in his *Interpretation of Cultures* (New York: Basic Books, 1973) 87-125.

guided."[5] Geertz explains that this approach "is neither introspectionist nor behaviorist; it is semantic."[6]

George Lindbeck is quite attracted to Geertz's semantic approach to religion and culture. Following Geertz, Lindbeck understands religions as cultural systems governed by their own rules of grammar and therefore analogous to linguistic systems.[7] He writes:

> In the account that I shall give, religions are seen as comprehensive interpretive schemes, usually embodied in myths or narratives and heavily ritualized, which structure human experience and understanding of self and world.... Stated more technically, a religion can be viewed as a kind of cultural and/or linguistic framework or medium that shapes the entirety of life and thought.[8]

Lindbeck explains that most theories of religion take either a propositionalist form or an experiential-expressivist form. The propositionalist theory "emphasizes the cognitive aspects of religion and stresses ways in which church doctrines function as informative propositions or truth claims about objective realities."[9] The experiential-expressivist theory "interprets doctrines as noninformative and nondiscursive symbols of inner feelings, attitudes or existential

---

[5] Clifford Geertz, *Islam Observed* (New Haven, CT: Yale University Press, 1968). An important selection from this text, "From *Sine Qua Non* to Cultural System," is included in Walter H. Capps, *Ways of Understanding Religion* (New York: Macmillan, 1972) 183-186. My citation is taken from Capps, 183-184.

[6] *Ibid.*, 184.

[7] Although he uses the theories of Geertz to support and verify his cultural-linguistic model of understanding religion and theology, Lindbeck has also been greatly influenced by the linguistic philosophies of Peter Winch and Ludwig Wittgenstein. The most explicit use of Wittgenstein by a member of the Yale school can be seen in the work of Lindbeck's colleague, Paul Holmer, in "The Grammar of Faith," *The Grammar of the Heart; New Essays in Moral Philosophy*, ed. Richard H. Bell (New York: Harper and Row, 1988) 3-20. For the purposes of this consideration, however, I have limited my analysis of influences on Lindbeck's thought primarily to Geertz's idea of religion as a cultural system.

[8] Lindbeck, *The Nature of Doctrine*, 32-33

[9] *Ibid.*, 16.

orientations."[10] The propositionalist is concerned with the correspondence between religious doctrines or narratives and "truth." The experiential-expressivist judges religious doctrines and narratives in terms of how well they "articulate or represent and communicate that inner experience of the divine... which is held to be common to all."[11]

Rejecting both propositionalist and experiential-expressivist models for understanding religion, Lindbeck proposes his cultural-linguistic paradigm. In this model narratives refer not to the truthfulness of objective realities nor to an existential or mystical experience of the divine; instead, they function "as communally authoritative rules of discourse, attitude, and action."[12] Lindbeck clarifies his proposal as follows: "The proper way to determine what 'God' signifies, for example, is by examining how the word operates in a religion and thereby shapes reality and experience rather than first establishing its prepositional or experiential meaning and reinterpreting or reformulating its uses accordingly."[13] Like Geertz, Lindbeck insists that a narrative text or a religious practice must be interpreted in terms of the "grammatical rules" which govern its use and place in a particular culture or religion. A religion, like a language, has its own rules for judging intelligibility and appropriateness. As such, it cannot be either legitimated or criticized by appeal to criteria beyond its texts, traditions, and practices. The theologian is thus concerned with intrasystematic coherence rather than connection to truth claims or experiences beyond the defined borders of her cultural-linguistic community.[14]

---

[10] *Ibid.*

[11] Lindbeck, *The Nature of Doctrine*, 47.

[12] *Ibid.*, 18.

[13] *Ibid.*, 114.

[14] For a very helpful discussion of Lindbeck's self-referential, intratextual theological model see William C. Placher, *Unapologetic Theology: A Christian Voice*

For the purposes of this study, George Lindbeck's postliberal
program for theology can be summarized under three of his guiding concerns: theology and narrative, theology and language, and
finally, theology and intratextuality.[15]

THEOLOGY AND NARRATIVE

Like others associated with the Yale style of theological reflection,
as a Christian theologian Lindbeck understands the church as a
"story-shaped church."[16] His program emphasizes the primacy of

in a Pluralistic Conversation (Louisville, KY: Westminster/John Knox Press,
1989) 155-170. Placher brings Lindbeck's model into conversation with revisionist
and correlational theologies like David Tracy's to illustrate that in the Yale
hermeneutic any apologetics must be considered only ad hoc. Placher is a product of Yale and his fine work moves beyond the older Lindbeck-Frei-Holmer
model and charts a theological method somewhere between New Haven and
Chicago.

[15] Two readers sympathetic to the Yale style of theology who saw an earlier
draft of this paper commented that I offer a rather "hard" reading of Lindbeck,
presenting him as a kind of radical Barthian merely hiding behind the theories of
Geertz and others as a cover for his neo-orthodox ideology of the "Word-Event."
They suggest "softer" readings are also possible. Perhaps, however, this so-called
"hard reading" is also reflected in other recent critical studies of Lindbeck. See
Terrence Tilley, "Incommensurability, Intratextuality, and Fideism," Modern The-
ology 5 (January 1989); John E. Thiel, Imagination and Authority: Theological
Authorship in the Modern Tradition (Minneapolis, MN: Fortress Press, 1991);
Werner Jeanrond, "Theology in the Context of Pluralism and Postmodernity:
David Tracy's Theological Method," Postmodernism, Literature and the Future
of Theology, ed. David Jasper (New York: Saint Martin's Press, 1993). Also,
David Tracy charges that Lindbeck and others in the Yale circle produce a
"methodologically sophisticated version of Barthian confessionalism." He
observes, "The hands may be the hands of Wittgenstein and Geertz but the voice
is the voice of Karl Barth," The Thomist 49 (1985) 465.

[16] George Lindbeck, "The Story-Shaped Church: Critical Exegesis and Theological Interpretation," Scriptural Authority and Narrative Interpretation, ed.
Garrett Green (Philadelphia, PA: Fortress Press, 1987) 161-178. Also, George

narrative as an interpretive category for understanding the Bible and the Christian faith. He believes the church is first and fundamentally characterized by its story. The story is logically prior to the specific meaning of its images, concepts, theories, and doctrines. For Lindbeck the focus on the primacy of narrative is meant to refer to the historical realities of empirical churches — to particular, concrete groups of people — and not to something trans-empirical or universal. We have no access to a common or generic human story beyond the particular narratives in which we find ourselves and others. In a carefully nuanced way this suggests that for the Christian, the story of the church is prior to the "human story."[17]

The Yale school prides itself on being "antifoundationalist," grounded in a realistic reading of the biblical narrative. This means the theologian must be attentive to the language of the Bible's own literary genre rather than the language of some general, generic, or so-called universal human experience. Lindbeck's late Yale colleague, Hans Frei, through his work in hermeneutics, attempted to demonstrate that the central narrative of the New Testament addresses the particularity of the life, death, and resurrection of Jesus Christ. As such it is not a philosophical account or explanation of a universal, foundational, or even an authentically "religious" or

Lindbeck, "Scripture, Consensus, and Community," *This World: A Journal of Religion and Public Life* 23 (Fall 1988) 5-24.

[17] Lindbeck's antifoundationalist methodology reminds us that all religious thought and practice is historically situated — grounded in a particular language and culture. The theologian does not have a direct or unmediated access through raw experience or religious vision to a universal human or divine story. She sees the world living in her skin and looking out through a given cultural-linguistic lens. No revisionist theologian would quarrel with this. However, the problem with Lindbeck's program, as this chapter will argue, is that he limits theological vision to one's own community's theological reading and its rather tight communal construing of knowledge.

ethical mode of being in the world.[18] It is instead an account of the radical particularity of the incarnation and an unapologetic invitation to salvation by entering its story-shaped community called the church. Frei's agenda for theology insists that the theologian must engage in a realistic reading of the gospels and must resist the temptation to demythologize or simply collapse the language of the Bible into modern categories of ultimate concern, being itself, or authentic existence. Biblical narratives must be allowed to catch the reader up into the sacred world of the text. Indeed, the Bible must be permitted to absorb the world into its unique world. The language of the biblical narrative must shape the world of human experience as members of the church community become disciples of a language larger than their individual utterances and subjective experiences.

In Lindbeck's model of narrative theology, a religion with its central stories functions as a language and its doctrines serve as a grammar. As such, doctrines do not claim to present first-order propositional truths or correspond to some extratextual objective reality. Instead, they perform the second-order task of defining the intrasystematic rules or truths that contribute to the coherence of the story.

---

[18] Even as Lindbeck looks to Geertz for his anthropology and to Wittgenstein for his linguistic philosophy, he looks to Frei for his biblical hermeneutics. Frei's intra-textual reading for the "plain sense" of the text is greatly indebted to the literary theory of Erich Auerbach and bears family resemblances to the now old New Criticism and formalist theories. For an examination of Frei's method within the context of formalist theories see Lynn M. Poland, *Literary Criticism and Biblical Hermeneutics: A Critique of Formalist Approaches* (Chico, CA: Scholars Press, 1985) 107-156. For Frei's clearest writing on the distance between the Yale and the Chicago approaches to textual interpretation see Hans Frei, "The Literal Reading of the Biblical Narrative in the Christian Tradition: Does It Stretch or Will It Break?," *The Bible and the Narrative Tradition*, ed. Frank McConnell (New York: Oxford University Press, 1986) 37-77. Also, Hans Frei, *Types of Christian Theology* (New Haven, CT: Yale University Press, 1992).

THEOLOGY AND LANGUAGE

Lindbeck's theological reading of anthropologists and linguists leads him to conclude that "just as an individual becomes human by learning a language, so he or she begins to become a new creature through hearing and interiorizing the language that speaks of ✓ Christ."[19] The idea of a Christian preconceptual and preverbal experience of salvation is viewed as unreal and mythological by those who understand religious experience in strict cultural-linguistic terms. For one to become religious one must become skilled in the language, the symbol system of the given religious community. Lindbeck explains: "To become a Christian involves learning the story of Israel and of Jesus well enough to interpret and experience oneself and one's world in its terms. A religion is above all an external word, a *verbum externum*, that molds and shapes the self and its world, rather than an expression or thematization of a ʳ preexisting self or of preconceptual experience."[20] The ancient formula *extra ecclesiam nulla salus* (no salvation outside the church) is articulated and affirmed in the new Yale theology with a postmodern, postliberal sophistication.

The relationship of language to experience is a central concern in Lindbeck's program. He is convinced that language creates the possibility of religious experience. God spoke the world into being. Likewise, language creates worlds to inhabit. Lindbeck, a Lutheran, illustrates this point from the life of Martin Luther. He argues that Luther did not invent his doctrine of justification by faith because he had a tower experience; but instead, the famous tower experience was made possible because Luther first discovered the doctrine in the world of the text, in the Bible. Then, and only then, did

[19] Lindbeck, *The Nature of Doctrine*, 62.
[20] *Ibid.*, 34.

he have a religious experience as he stood under the life-shaping Word of the text.

Lindbeck is clear that different religious discourses are not pointing to some common religious feeling prior to their diverse linguistic expressions. Different religions are not merely different expressions or manifestations of a common religious or human experience. Lindbeck, who has devoted many productive years to ecumenical conversations and concerns, sees enormous ecumenical possibility in his thesis. In the Lindbeckian method of interpreting religion and theology one is freed from the impossible task of trying to translate diverse texts and traditions into some general philosophy of "the religious" in the name of ecumenical understanding, co-operation, and mutuality. In Lindbeck's program religions in dialogue "are not forced into the dilemma of thinking of themselves as representing a superior (or an inferior) articulation of a common experience... They can regard themselves as simply different and can proceed to explore their agreements and disagreements without necessarily engaging in the invidious comparisons that the assumption of a common experiential core make [sic] so tempting."[21]

THEOLOGY AND INTRATEXTUALITY

As we have seen, the vocation of the theologian in Lindbeck's cultural-linguistic model is primarily that of keeping the stories of her own faith community straight as she guards her religion's texts from being absorbed into the world. Theology in this model is

[21] *Ibid.*, 55. For a sympathetic and fair discussion of the ecumenical possibilities of Lindbeck's program see William C. Placher, "Revisionist and Postliberal Theologies and the Public Character of Theology," *The Thomist* 49 (1985) 392-416.

"intrasemiotic or intratextual." According to Lindbeck, "Intratextual theology redescribes reality within a scriptural framework rather than translating Scripture into extrascriptural categories."[22] Theological reflection and discourse must inhabit its own semiotic world. This model of doing theology challenges the liberal theological tradition and its correlational methodology in which the theologian brings her religious texts and traditions into a mutually critical conversation with contemporary culture, not merely as a witness, but as an authentic quest for meaning and truth in a graced but fallen world.

George Lindbeck constantly reminds his readers that his understanding of intratextuality is postliberal or postcritical. His strategy for reading the Bible intratextually for its "plain sense" is not to be confused with a precritical biblicism. Viewing the Bible as a realistic narrative for the faith and practice of the church, one can freely affirm that the biblical stories are "history-like" even when they are not "likely-history."[23] The rendering of God's character in scriptural texts is not dependent upon the historical or scientific factuality of the story. Yet the story must remain normative and regulative for the identity, faith, and practice of church community.

Lindbeck's *The Nature of Doctrine* is an important attempt to rethink theological method in light of the challenges and insights of postmodernism. But he too easily dismisses public and revisionist theological projects like University of Chicago professor David Tracy's as "experiential-expressivist." Again, in the Lindbeckian typology, this means religious language is simply noninformative and nondiscursive symbols of inner feelings, attitudes, or existential orientations reflecting some universal religious core. Tracy considers this a serious misreading of his work and the work

---

[22] Lindbeck, *The Nature of Doctrine*, 118.
[23] *Ibid.*, 122.

of his "Chicago" colleagues. Let us turn to a consideration of
Tracy's thought in light of the phenomenological hermeneutics of
his friend and conversation partner, Mircea Eliade.

ELIADE AND TRACY

Tracy finds it strange that Lindbeck reads his work as articulating
a unilateral understanding of the relationship between experience
and language or expressing the belief that inner experiences are
prior to expression or communication. Following Hans-Georg
Gadamer and Paul Ricœur, Tracy's theological agenda has been to
rethink the dialectical relationship between language and experience. His program moves beyond the Schleiermacher —Tillich —
Rahner — Lonergan experiential paradigm to an explicitly
hermeneutical one.[24]

While hermeneutically-informed theologians like Tracy see great
value in cultural-linguistic "thick descriptions" of religions and
their semiotic codes, they also believe mere grammatical analysis
is not enough. Tracy contends that theologians need to move on to
rhetorical analysis. This is of course the classical discipline which
is the correlate of modern hermeneutics. Because there is an
unavoidable political agenda encoded in all religious narratives,

[24] David Tracy, "Lindbeck's New Program for Theology: A Reflection," *The
Thomist* 49 (1985) 460-472. Tracy finds it "bizarre" that Lindbeck would label
Paul Ricœur an experiential-expressivist. Ricœur's philosophy has carefully decon-
structed "the dream of total mediation of the self to itself as an absolute subject."
His work seeks to demonstrate that there is no self-understanding that is not medi-
ated through signs, symbols, and texts. See Ricœur's *Oneself as Another* (Chicago,
IL: University of Chicago Press, 1992). It has been suggested accurately that
David Tracy's theology is a careful theological performance of Ricœur's philosophical hermeneutics. See Kevin J. Vanhoozer, *Biblical Narrative in the Philosophy of Paul Ricœur* (New York: Cambridge University Press, 1990) 156.

grammar and rhetoric interact in all concrete interpretations. Both code and use are important hermeneutically.[25] Rhetorical-hermeneutical analysis of religious stories moves from semiotics to a greater cultural-historical-political awareness and thus can move theology from the service of the ethos of a particular cultural-linguistic community to involvement with the public concerns of the interdependence and interconnection of all life.

David Tracy's hermeneutics encourages theologians to move beyond dialogue with anthropologists like Geertz and into conversation with historians of religion or phenomenologists of religion like Mircea Eliade. While members of the Yale school are drawn to Geertz's cultural-linguistic interpretation of truth and meaning to validate their intratextual narrative claims, Tracy finds the work of Eliade congenial to his understanding of the manifestation of sacred presence and mystery in a plurality of texts, traditions, and experiences. The creative hermeneutics of Eliade does not limit the task of interpretation to scriptural or communal texts but explores the manifestations of the sacred in symbol, image, icon, ritual, logos, and cosmological theologies. "In the final analysis," Eliade wrote, "the world reveals itself as language."[26] Tracy's theology displays his appreciation for Eliade's work, which Tracy says, "profoundly broadened my sense of religious pluralism." Commenting on the

---

[25] Tracy acknowledges the value of reading for "thick descriptions" in Lindbeck's program in his "On Reading the Scriptures Theologically," *Theology and Dialogue: Essays in Conversation with George Lindbeck*, ed. Bruce D. Marshall (Notre Dame, IN: University of Notre Dame Press, 1990) 35-68. However, he argues theologians must move beyond Lindbeck's kind of grammatical analysis to rhetorical analysis, in his "Lindbeck's New Program for Theology: A Reflection," *The Thomist* 49 (1985) 469. For a fine study of rhetoric and theology by a specialist in the field of theology and literature see David Jasper, *Rhetoric, Power and Community* (Louisville, KY: Westminster/ John Knox Press, 1993).

[26] Mircea Eliade, *Myth and Reality* (New York: HarperTorch Books, 1963) 141.

legacy of his late Chicago colleague, Tracy concludes, "No single Western thinker seems as able as Eliade is at disclosing this radical sense of belonging to, even saturated by, the rhythms of the / cosmos, the whole, as sacred power."[27]

Eliade was one of the finest 20th-century interpreters of religion. His creative work opened the borders between history, myth, fiction, and imagination in religious studies.[28] He was concerned not only with the historical origins of the great religions but also with the primordial manifestations of the cosmos at the origins of all religions. Although intrigued by a phenomenology of the sacred in the cosmos, Eliade did not believe the historian of religions could simply isolate some pure or primal religious core or essence. His understanding of cosmic religiosity was always attentive to ethnological distinctions and religious differences in the human need to bring some symbolic order to life. Yet he did believe that despite the vast cultural and religious differences within the human community, religious symbols come from a universal human need to find a narrative or mythological world that gives ultimate meaning to life beyond the burdens and terrors of history.

Mircea Eliade's personal pilgrimage and professional vocation led him beyond the sanctuary of his Orthodox Christian tradition to an adventure of tracking the movements of gods, hearts, minds, and bodies as he looked for traces of the sacred in the cosmos. A striking passage from his journal describing this quest merits quotation at length:

---

[27] David Tracy, "The Challenge of the Archaic Other: The Hermeneutics of Mircea Eliade," in Tracy's *Dialogue with the Other: The Inter-Religions Dialogue* (Louvain/Grand Rapids, MI: Peeters Press/Eerdmans, 1990) 67.

[28] Norman J. Girardot and Mac Linscott Ricketts, eds.; *Imagination and Meaning: The Scholarly and Literary Worlds of Mircea Eliade* (New York: Seabury Press, 1982).

I have spent thirty years and more now among the exotic, barbaric, indomitable gods and goddesses, nourished on myths, obsessed by symbols, held in the spell of so many images swimming back up to me from worlds long submerged beneath time past. Those thirty years now appear to me as so many stages in a long initiation. Each of those divine forms, those myths or symbols, represents a danger confronted and overcome. How many times I have just escaped "losing" myself — losing my way in that labyrinth where I was in danger of being killed, sterilized, "emasculated" (by one of those terrible mother goddesses, for example). An infinite series of intellectual adventures — and I use that word "adventure" in its primary sense as an existential risk. They were not, all those things, mere items of "knowledge," acquired piecemeal and at leisure from books; they were so many encounters, confrontations, and temptations. I am perfectly aware, now, of all the perils I skirted during that long "quest": first and foremost, the danger of forgetting that I had a goal, that I was directing my footsteps toward something, that I was trying to reach a "center."[29]

As this journal entry illustrates, Eliade was not a nine-to-five phenomenologist of religions. His spiritual and intellectual curiosity threw him existentially into the terror, joy, mystery, and ambiguity of encountering otherness in trying to reach a "center" — [in trying to interpret and understand the human situation *from within* the deeper, indeed archaic, meanings of its mythological creations and myths.]

Eliade's uninhibited use of terms like "center," "sacred," "hierophany," and "cosmic rhythms," along with his revisionary use of the language of Romantic hermeneutics, have led some to misread his work as just another expression of the Romantic tradition. But a close reading of Eliade reveals a post-Romantic creative

[29] Eliade discusses this journal entry and the existential risks and terrors of encountering the radically other, in Mircea Eliade, *Ordeal by Labyrinth: Conversations with Claude-Henri Rocquet*, trans. Derek Coltman (Chicago, IL: University of Chicago Press, 1982) 119-126.

hermeneutics of the "other."[30] [Eliade does not imply that consciousness is immediate or solitary.] The human person does not have a pure, Romantic, or unmediated access to a core self, sacred presence, or the divine. We always see through the contingencies of languages, historical communities, and wounded, emerging egos. [Yet, unlike the strict cultural-linguistic model of interpreting religious experience within the context of tight communal boundaries, Eliade's method suggests that a deepened self-consciousness, God-consciousness, or cosmic-consciousness comes through a hermeneutics of genuine conversation with the other — through encountering communities, persons, places, things, and stories of difference.]

Eliade's fascination with religious and human diversity, and his search for connections, patterns, structures and essential or primordial meanings in and between religions, did not, as some suggest, lead him to elevate a sacred essence as something separate in existence or in thought from the particular or accidental. For Eliade, essence "exists only in and through the particular and can be known only by opening our eyes and hearts to the sensuous living world."[31]

---

[30] Lindbeck places Eliade in the Romantic tradition. Tracy reveals Eliade's distance from that tradition through considering his hermeneutics of the other. Tracy, *Dialogue with the Other*, 51. Ricœur's reading of Eliade confirms Tracy's interpretation. He writes that in Eliade's theory, the "great myths of origins come to light as bearers of irreducible difference." As such they carry an inexhaustible capacity for reinterpretation and resist being easily absorbed into the morphology of the sacred. See Ricœur's review of Eliade's *History of Religious Ideas*, in *Religious Studies Review* 1 (1976) 3.

[31] Girardot and Ricketts, eds., *Imagination and Meaning*, 1-16, provide a clear introduction to Eliade's notion of the inseparability of accident and essence. The ideal *becomes* real and is known only accidentally in the "sensuous living world" (p. 3). The question of the existence of a Platonic *eidos*, or the speculative questions about the existence of an extrahistorical or extracosmic presence or reality separate in existence or thought from the accidental or particular are not the most interesting questions for those who take Eliade's hermeneutics seriously. A far more interesting question is whether imagination and history can ever be separated.

This creative hermeneutics calls the reader to lift her eyes from her faith community's revelatory texts to gaze into the eyes of the other as she moves through the sensuous living world, which is itself the labyrinth of meaning and understanding.

Eliade was convinced that it is only through encountering the other that we can understand ourselves. Indeed, Tracy sees Eliade's work as addressing contemporary hermeneutics at the point where it most needs a rigorous challenge, namely, around the question and concept of the "other." Eliade's work not only engages the other in the so-called "great" world religions; it is concerned with the "projected other" — the "pagan," "the archaic," and those "others" who have been interpreted and even invented by the projected fears and desires of the Western hermeneutical tradition. Tracy values Eliade's program because, like Gadamer, Eliade understands hermeneutics as conversation with the other, yet unlike Gadamer, he risks authentic encounter and dialogue with the *radically other.*[32]

Creative links between Eliade's work and concerns and David Tracy's theological hermeneutics can be seen by a brief consideration of three themes central to Tracy's developing project: the analogical imagination, the mystical prophetic paradigm, and dialogue with the other.

The Analogical Imagination

David Tracy's hermeneutical theology begins with the recognition that the contemporary theologian lives, works, and writes in a world of profound pluralism and ambiguity. Like William James, Tracy is interested in the "buzzing, blooming confusion of experience,"

---

[32] Tracy, *Dialogue with the Other*, 48-51.

and like James, he resists taming or controlling this pluralism by
bringing it under the discipline of a monotheory.[33] Tracy asserts
that since reality itself appears diverse or plural, any second-order
account of reality must also be pluralistic. Further, Tracy argues
that pluralism is an important hermeneutical option since it
demands that we listen to the voices of others as we attempt to
understand ourselves and our communities in an increasingly global
village alive with unfamiliar and indeed different understandings of
selves, communities, and that which is ultimate.

The reality of pluralism should teach the theologian that there are
many possible modes of being-in-the-world. It is through conversation with others, Tracy suggests, that we begin to see many possible disclosures to enrich our culture and ourselves. He believes
conversation is the pluralist strategy par excellence for reading our
world and our lives. While this reading acknowledges radical difference and diversity, it also is attentive to connections, to the possibility of similarity-in-difference. Tracy calls this strategy the
"analogical imagination."

Unlike strategies that stress the incommensurable between religions or cultures, or those that search for some lowest common
denominator and then call it a "universalism," the analogical imagination attempts to take both "otherness" and "similarity" quite
seriously.[34] Concerning the analogical imagination Tracy writes:

---

[33] Tracy, *Dialogue with the Other*, 28.

[34] Jean-Francois Lyotard's postmodern reading of "little narratives" after the
collapse of the grand metanarratives of the West stresses the incommensurable.
See his *The Postmodern Condition: A Report on Knowledge*, trans. Geoff Bennington and Brian Massumi (Minneapolis, MN: University of Minnesota, 1989).
In contrast, the work of a scholar like Huston Smith seeks to absorb difference too
easily into a universalism, or in his words, "the human unanimity." See his *Forgotten Truth: The Common Vision of the World's Religions* (San Francisco, CA:
Harper and Row, 1992).

That imagination bluntly claims, first, that we understand one another through some analogies to our own experience or not at all. To understand the other *as* other, the different *as* different is at the same time to recognize it as possible; to understand the other *as* possible is to recognize some similarity, analogy to our actuality. Second, and just as important, an analogical imagination also insists that analogies are not simple similarities but similarities-in-difference. The difference of the other (and thereby the otherness of the other) must be maintained for any proper analogy. In fact, that difference provokes the disclosure of possibility.[35]

Possibility becomes the primary category of an active analogical imagination. This possibility does not suggest that one can or should take on the identity of the other. This interpreted possibility instead renders the Other as a different yet possible way of being-in-the-world. This disclosure of possibility recognizes and respects difference while affirming the possibility of similarity-in-difference.[36] It is to acknowledge the other world of meaning as in some sense an authentic possibility which can not only inform but also transform one's understanding of self, community, culture, and the movements of the gods.

The analogical imagination insists that there must be a mutually critical correlation between the texts of one's religious community and common human language and experience. Anticorrelational or intra-textual theologies like Lindbeck's Geertz-like approach to theology as communal, descriptive anthropology fail, it seems, to understand the phenomenon of intertextuality and thus neglect the voice of the other as a genuine possibility of disclosure inviting transformation.

---

[35] David Tracy, "Christianity in the Wider Context — Demands and Transformations," *Religion and the Intellectual Life* 4 (Summer 1987) 16. Also, David Tracy, *The Analogical Imagination: Christian Theology and the Culture of Pluralism* (New York: Crossroad, 1981).

[36] *Ibid.*, 13.

[Tracy's rigorous hermeneutical readings of both the classics of
the Christian canon and other people's stories demonstrate there
are no autonomous texts. His work reveals the inevitable intertextuality of all seemingly stable, autonomous texts. Tracy's colleague
Paul Ricœur defines intertextuality as "the work of meaning
through which one text, in referring to another text both displaces
this other text and receives from it an extension of meaning."[37]
Tracy closely follows Ricœur's theoretical work in textuality and
intertextuality which appropriates and extends various understandings of intertextuality in current post-structuralist criticism. The
theory of intertextuality assumes there are no pure texts or stories.
Every text is an intertext as pieces and traces of other texts find
their way into the production of new texts with their influences,
sources, metaphors, allusions, archetypes, and expressions of both
a cultural consciousness and a cultural unconsciousness.[38] A critical and analogical reading of texts will disclose numerous points
of intersection with other texts.

Even as there are no pure or stable texts, there are no passive
or objective readers.[39] Readers hear the voice of the text within
the world of their "buzzing, blooming confusion of experience."
There is then always a conversation or interaction between reader
and text in the process of interpretation and understanding. It
could be said that the intertextuality of all texts reflects the great

[37] Paul Ricœur, "The Bible and the Imagination," *The Bible as a Document
of the University*, ed. Hans Dieter Betz (Chico, CA: Scholars Press, 1981) 53.

[38] Jay Clayton and Erie Rothstein (eds.), *Intertextuality and Influence in Lit-
erary History* (Madison, WI: University of Wisconsin Press, 1991). Also, Vincent
B. Leitch, *Deconstructive Criticism: An Advanced Introduction* (New York:
Columbia University Press, 1983) 123-163.

[39] Edgar V. McKnight, *Post-Modern Use of the Bible: The Emergence of
Reader-Oriented Criticism* (Nashville, TN: Abingdon Press, 1988). Also, see
Tracy on reader-response, *Plurality and Ambiguity: Hermeneutics, Religion, Hope*
(San Francisco, CA: Harper and Row, 1987) 17-21.

intertextuality of the human story. The theologian who values the analogical imagination will be careful therefore to recognize points of connection as well as expressions of radical difference in the search for human understanding, not merely as an exercise of intellectual curiosity, but as a theological, indeed, a spiritual commitment.

THE MYSTICAL-PROPHETIC PARADIGM

David Tracy's earlier work treated the traditional Christian dialectic of sacrament and word within the more primordial religious dialectic of manifestation and proclamation. His more recent work, greatly influenced by the inter-religious dialogue, attempts to rethink manifestation and proclamation theologically as mystical-prophetic.[40]

Like Eliade and Ricœur, Tracy is intrigued by the hermeneutical notion of truth as manifestation or disclosure. Tracy suggests that "the truth of religion, like the truth of its nearest analogue, art, is primordially a truth of manifestation."[41] Tracy's work seeks to demonstrate how this disclosure is operative in both "classics" and in the extraordinary power of ordinary experience. He is most interested, however, in what happens when we experience a classic or paradigmatic work of any culture.[42]

---

[40] David Tracy, "God, Dialogue and Solidarity: A Theologian's Refrain," *The Christian Century* (October 10, 1990) 900-904. Also, Tracy, *Dialogue with the Other*.

[41] David Tracy, "The Uneasy Alliance Reconceived: Catholic Theological Method, Modernity and Postmodernity," *Theological Studies* 50 (1989) 548-570.

[42] For a discussion of Tracy's understanding of the classic within the wider context of his thought see Werner G. Jeanrond, *Text and Interpretation as Categories of Theological Thinking* (New York: Crossroad, 1988) 129-153.

According to Tracy, a classic work of any culture — a work of art or literature, music, thinking, religion, or action — calls forth a response of "recognition" of the disclosure of something extraordinary. Whether one calls this recognition an "aha experience!" or a "yes, yes, that's it experience," this experience of classic disclosure and recognition is familiar to all who open themselves to the sounds, sights, and sensations of life. Although these "classics" are highly specific in their origins and modes of expression, they bear an "excess and a permanence of meaning," always calling for further interpretation and reflection and always pointing to something beyond themselves.[43]

The hermeneutical language of manifestation or disclosure is in some sense analogous to the spiritual and poetic language of classical religious mystics who see the diverse expressions of an internally related, sacramental cosmos as revelatory texts to be read as scripture. The mystical religious impulse celebrates the connections between word and image, self and other, similar and different, God and world, spirit and flesh, in a language affirming the structural relationships of God-world-soul-body. The mystical imagination uncovers the "religious dimension" of worldly human language and experience.

Mircea Eliade asked, "Do modern Christians and Jews any longer *feel* the world as God's creation?"[44] Eliade's work, grounded in a hermeneutics of manifestation, challenges theologians living in a religion of the book not to neglect their traditions' own archaic roots in the rhythms of the cosmos. Archaic religions remind us that by entering the spiritual and sensual otherness of the ritual, the dream, the symbol, the festival, the dance, the myth,

---

[43] Tracy, "The Uneasy Alliance Reconceived," 560-564. Also, Tracy, *Plurality and Ambiguity*, 28-46. In addition, see Tracy's chapter, "The Classic," in *The Analogical Imagination*, 99-153.

[44] Cited by Tracy in *The Analogical Imagination*, 381.

or the story we can participate in a reality beyond the ordinary and enter the sacred time and place of the origins of the cosmos through the disclosure of the extraordinary power and presence of the whole.[45]

Tracy suggests that Eliade's method reveals the importance and the possibility of a creative and mystical retrieval of the archaic and pagan roots of Christianity.[46] The prophetic attacks on Canaanite nature religion and the destruction of the archaic and indigenous traditions of the Americas by Christian colonizers of minds, bodies, and lands serve as haunting reminders that in this era of increasing nationalism, tribalism, and sectarian violence, we must never again allow the pagan or archaic other to become the mere projected other, the invented embodiment of our worst fears and most egocentric, ethnocentric, or nationalistic desires:

The mystical imagination with its relentless call for a radical participation in the whole, sacred cosmos reflects a creative hermeneutics of connection. Yet there exists within the mystical vision a temptation simply to collapse the otherness of the other into a generic humanism, a naive universalism, a cosmic metanarrative, or an uncritical pluralism. David Tracy recognizes the truth in Simone de Beauvoir's cynical charge that "pluralism is the perfect

---

[45] For an analysis of Eliade's theory of escaping the "nightmare" of history and the "terror" of ordinary rime through the otherness of sacred myth, ritual, or symbol to assert that "only the paradigmatic is the real," see Tracy, *The Analogical Imagination*, 202-218. Also, Tracy's *Dialogue with the Other*, 48-67. For another helpful study here, see Guilford Dudly III, *Religion on Trial: Mircea Eliade and his Critics* (Philadelphia, PA: Temple University Press, 1977).

[46] Tracy, "The Uneasy Alliance Reconceived," 565. Also, Mircea Eliade, *The Myth of the Eternal Return* (New York: Harper and Row, 1959). In recent years a number of feminist theologians have been experimenting with retrievals of the pagan roots of Christianity as a way to affirm a spiritual ecology of both body and earth. See especially, Carol P. Christ, *Laughter of Aphrodite* (San Francisco, CA: Harper and Row, 1987).

ideology for the bourgeois mind."[47] He therefore understands the need for mystical claims of manifestation to enter the dialectic of prophetic correction and critique through the hermeneutics of suspicion. This prophetic reading will carefully examine and evaluate the ethical, ideological, and political implications of these claims. A prophetic hermeneutics will not simply celebrate a romantic notion of the interconnection of all life; it will strive to assure that connection through a language of resistance and a political struggle for justice on behalf of those who are indeed marginalized or excluded from the dominant narrative or cosmic text by privileged readers.

David Tracy's thinking concerning the prophetic has been informed by his interdisciplinary appropriation of the hermeneutics of suspicion: the Hebrew prophets, Freud, Lacan, Marx, Nietzsche, and Derrida.[48] The prophetic word shatters any comfortable and secure understanding of genuine participation in the cosmos:

> This prophetic word comes also as stark proclamation, as kerygma, to disconfirm any complacency in participation, to shatter any illusions that this culture, this priesthood, this land, this ritual is enough, to defamiliarize us with ourselves and with nature, to decode our encoded myths, to inflict its passionate negations upon all our pretensions, to

[47] Tracy, "Christianity in the Wider Context: Demands and Transformations," 12.

[48] David Tracy uses these masters of suspicion and their "deconstructive" analyses not to forever ground a theological position but as linguistic therapy to expose the illusions of our familiar accounts of knowledge, reality, and language. See Tracy, *Plurality and Ambiguity*, 47-65. Unlike many theologians who simply dismiss thinkers like Derrida as nihilists, Tracy writes, "Like a Zen master, Derrida has exposed an illusion, the illusion that we language-sated beings can ever be fully present to ourselves or that any other reality can be fully present to us either," *Ibid.*, 59. Indeed, Derrida has insisted, "I totally refuse the label of nihilism which has been ascribed to me and my American colleagues. Deconstruction is not an enclosure in nothingness, but an openness towards the other" (Kearny, *Dialogues with Contemporary Continental Thinkers*, 123-124).

suspect even our nostalgic longings for the sacred cosmos, to expose
all idols of the self as projections of ourselves and our mad ambitions,
to expose all culture as contingent, even arbitrary, all philosophic
wisdom as foolishness, to demand disillusionment as the precondi-
tion of insight; to make us recognize that Judaism and Christianity
disclose a radical world-affirmation only because they have first
undergone a radical, decentering experience of world negation in the
kerygmatic, proclamatory word of address of prophetic religion.[49]

Tracy recognizes that this strong word of prophetic address can
make the mystical claims regarding manifestation and radical participation in the cosmos seem extravagant and even idolatrous. But
he insists that the mystical and the prophetic must be held together
in critical, self-correcting tension. His theological program advocates both mystical and prophetic readings of religious, personal,
and social narratives. Yet he remains most interested in the hyphen
of the mystical-prophetic paradigm, for it is in this rich space that
the vision of the mystic and the word of the prophet embrace and
salute one another.

DIALOGUE WITH THE OTHER

Tracy's method of doing theology demands conversation with the
other. He often quotes one of his most influential theology teachers, Bernard Lonergan, on the rules of this dialogical approach to
theology: ["Be attentive, be intelligent, be responsible, be loving,
and, if necessary, change."[50] The possibility of change or transformation is central to Tracy's understanding of authentic conversation. Although some theologians have recently argued that in the

---

[49] Tracy, *The Analogical Imagination*, 211.

[50] David Tracy, *Blessed Rage for Order: The New Pluralism in Theology* (New
York: Seabury Press, 1975) 12.

inter-religious dialogue we must move beyond dialogue to mutual
transformation, in Tracy's theory of conversation, as we have seen,
the serious dialogical encounter with the other which leads to a
recognition of similarity-in-difference is itself an experiment in
mutual transformation or mutual conversion as one begins to understand "oneself as another."

Tracy's hermeneutics places "the other," not "the self," as the
dominant focus of theological interpretation. He believes if one is
to encounter the "other" not as a projected but as a genuine other,
one must be willing to put everything at risk, even one's sacred
truths.[51] He argues that only when the subject-matter and not the
subject's consciousness is allowed to be heard can true conversation occur.[52] The Christian theologian of course enters the conversation as a Christian. She must have enough self-respect to take
seriously her discourse and experience.[53] She must acknowledge
and even value her intellectual and social location within the frame
of her primary cultural-linguistic community or communities, for
she will always hear the story of the other from her position of difference. She will always hear differently or not at all. However,
she must also risk the possibility of transformation as she engages
the other — the religious other, the cultural other, the sexual other,
the stranger of the covenant, and perhaps even as Levinas reminds
us, "the terrifyingly other."[54]

---

[51] Tracy, *Dialogue with the Other*, 95. Such a proposal may in fact require the
theologian to move beyond conventional and classical understandings of theism.
In fact, Tracy's current work in progress is exploring "The End of Theism and
the Renaming of God."

[52] *Ibid.*

[53] Tracy's criteria for entering the conversation can be found in his "Christianity in the Wider Context: Demands and Transformations," 17-20.

[54] Simon Critchley, *The Ethics of Deconstruction: Derrida and Levinas* (London: Blackwell Publishers, 1992).

This hermeneutical strategy of conversation must not be construed as a mere ethical or cultural relativism with a goal of some vague and spiritless inclusiveness in philosophical, theological, and civic discourse. Tracy contends that genuine dialogue must be accompanied by real solidarity in social practices. The hope for mutual transformation through dialogue is to identify and construct more just and humane modes of being in the world with others. It seeks to include those who have been silenced or marginalized, whether by violent oppression, authoritarian ideologies, totalist narratives, or polite party politics. It therefore asserts that certain expressions of otherness and difference must be excluded from the conversation, not included in it.[55] Racism, sexism, classism, and religionism are forms of difference that must be met with the prophetic language of resistance, for they betray the vision of including all justly in social practices jealously guarding the interconnection and interdependence of life.

David Tracy s hermeneutical model of dialogue takes seriously the postmodern critique of the possessive and consumerist modern self that represents the other, if at all, as a projection of its own conflicted desires. This critique correctly signals a shift from the centrality of the modern self to the priority of the postmodern other in critical reflection and theory. As a Christian theologian he also takes quite seriously the classical theological language of sin and grace that once spoke of a decentered self as powerfully as the most controversial French post-modernists.[56] Indeed, the classical Christian texts remind us that in order to find ourselves we must first lose ourselves. Tracy's model suggests that to find ourselves and the fullness of grace in our fragmented world we must risk entering

---

[55] David Tracy, in a "Review Symposium" of his *Plurality and Ambiguity*, in *Theology Today* 44 (January 1988) 514.

[56] Tracy, *Dialogue with the Other*, 2.

into dialogue and solidarity with the other, and through the conversation and praxis discern new ways of "naming ourselves and
rendering God's name in history."

HOW DO STORIES SAVE US?

George Lindbeck and the Yale school's intratextual style of doing
theology suggests that the theologian's vocation is primarily that of
guardian and interpreter of her community's canon. The church, not
the world, is affirmed as the privileged and proper theological reality. The world becomes an *object* of theological description and
prophetic critique, rarely a rich and mystical *source* for imaginative and revisionary theological thought and writing. Indeed, the
sacred world of the church's story, if entered faithfully by the
believer, promises to "absorb the world" into its unique world or
new creation with little human or cosmic surplus left to interpret or
exegete. Salvation, like theology, appears rather well managed and
clean; it is intratextual and communal: *extra ecclesiam nulla salus.*

While Yale theologians seem most interested in keeping their
community's story straight, those drawn to the work of David Tracy
and the Chicago school are much more interested in doing theology while listening to other people's stories.[57] For them theology
is viewed as a pluralistic, interdisciplinary, intertextual, and revisionary project in which the theologian brings the texts, traditions,

[57] I am not suggesting that those influenced by the New Haven theological
mood are uninterested in other stories or other canons. Nor am I suggesting that
they are uninterested in dialogue. Certainly, the Christian tradition can be *a particular* dialogue partner too. It seems, however, that in the intratextual style of theology, dialogue with the other can become an occasion for *understanding* but not
transformation since the anticorrelational theologian cannot risk his or her "center" in conversation; he or she cannot be "converted" by the other without becoming internally conflicted and incoherent.

and practices of her community into conversation with others, especially communities of difference, in the search for greater insight, understanding, humane presence and connection with the divine. There is the hope that narrative slices of life, both our own stories and the stories of others, will open us to meaning, truth, and the sacred. It is therefore not enough for the theologian to master the stories of her religion's canon; she must be attentive to the plots and narrative turns in the other's story even as she attempts to write her community's evolving story.

Lindbeck's postliberal theological method correctly attempts to guard communities of cultural and religious difference from the imperialism of those who would impose a metanarrative or a story of God upon them in the name of civility, truth, or the Holy.[58] There is ecumenical and political wisdom in this antifoundationalist approach to truth and theological method. However, it seems this strategy can in the end do more to protect privileged, white, male, middle-class theologians from the risk of transformation or conversion to something other than it does to insure the dignity and well being of the other.[59] In effect, since it is assumed that the

---

[58] A strong and articulate case for this approach can be found in Kathryn Tanner, "Respect for Other Religions: A Christian Antidote to Colonialist Discourse," *Modern Theology* 9 (January 1993) 1-18.

[59] My point here is that an intratextual, anticorrelarional theology can easily become sectarian or insular and thus protect the self-interests of its privileged readers and interpreters from the voices of oppositional others. However, conversations with my "Yaley" friends convince me that it doesn't *have* to function this way. For example, it could be argued that undivided attention and faithfulness to the church's story demands that one practice justice, love mercy, and walk humbly before God in the presence of the "other." The Christian is under a scriptural and communal obligation *(Ordnung)* to attend to the cries of the poor, oppressed, and marginalized if he or she takes the Jesus story seriously. Lindbeck's productive work in ecumenical concerns testifies to this truth. I am also quite struck by the work of Yale theologian Kathryn Tanner. Applying an intratextual methodology, or in her words, an "internal critique" of the Christian

stories of the other cannot or should not be included in the canonical readings of autonomous theological traditions advocated by Lindbeck, if they are heard at all, are not these other voices denied their revelatory and salvific power?

Gordon Kaufman has observed that it is unfortunate Lindbeck has put such a clear and needed exposition of the cultural and linguistic grounding of all religious thought and practice into the service of such a theologically conservative agenda.[60] Theologians consciously writing in the shadow of postmodernism will not quarrel with Lindbeck's understanding that all God-talk is historically situated.[61] We do indeed see God and the world through the lenses of languages, historical communities, and wounded, decentered egos. But does this mean, as Lindbeck's model implies, that the theologian should live and work and think in singular churchly communities of interpretation? Should the theologian limit her faith and theological vision to the narratives and practices of one cultural linguistic community?[62]

beliefs, she presents a prophetic reading of Christianity which strongly challenges the ecclesiastical and political status quo. See her *The Politics of God* (Minneapolis, MN: Fortress Press, 1992). For another example of this approach see Ronald F. Thiemann, *Constructing a Public Theology: The Church in a Pluralistic Culture* (Louisville, KY: Westminster/John Knox Press, 1991).

[60] Gordon Kaufman, review of *The Nature of Doctrine*, in *Theology Today* 42 (1985) 241.

[61] For an excellent collection of essays, several of which bring Lindbeck's communal construing of theology into conversation with the more public model of Gordon Kaufman, see Sheila Greeve Davaney (ed.), *Theology at the End of Modernity* (Philadelphia, PA: Trinity Press International, 1991).

[62] For three challenging and imaginative calls to expand one's hermeneutical horizon through encounters with interpretive communities of difference, see: Henry Louis Gates, Jr., *Loose Canon: Notes on the Culture Wars* (New York: Oxford University Press, 1992); Philomena Mariani (ed.), *Critical Fictions: The Politics of Imaginative Writing* (Seattle: Bay Press, 1991); Rick Simonson and Scott Walker (eds.), *The Greywolf Annual Five: Multi-Cultural Literacy* (Saint Paul, MN: Greywolf Press, 1988).

Such a strategy can indeed shield the confessional theologian from the difficult demands of multicultural and multilingual literacy and from the invitation to public solidarity in praxis if she can in fact imagine herself as living only in her tradition, her text, and her privileged reading. One could almost excuse a fundamentalist for advocating such a sectarian imagination in defense of her tribal gods and goods. But for a post-critical Christian theorist who values close readings and thick descriptions to retreat from the public square into the world of the text, pretending she has found a separate, autonomous world, is not only bad faith, it is bad fiction.[63]

David Tracy's important work teaches us that there are no innocent texts, including scripture; there are no innocent readings, including confessional readings, and there are no innocent traditions. One can never hide from the buzzing, blooming world of confusion by rushing into the safety of a cloistered text — for there are no pure texts or narratives.[64] Even if a text were to fall out of the sky like a stone from heaven, one could only enter the text by reading it, and it would thus be defiled by the impurity of the reader's horizon of expectations emerging from her psychological, social, and political location in life.[65]

---

[63] I am using "bad faith" not in the conventional theological sense, but in the existentialist sense of a failure of nerve; a failure to risk conversion through encounter with the other.

[64] For Tracy's most explicit treatment of intertextuality, see *Plurality and Ambiguity*, 78. Tracy writes, "Postmodernity demands multiple discourses for interpretation itself. As postmodern writers and thinkers remind us, we live within intertextuality."

[65] In addition to Tracy's work, reader-response criticism is instructive here. See Wolfgang Iser, *The Act of Reading: A Theory of Aesthetic Response* (Baltimore, MD: Johns Hopkins University Press, 1978). Also, Hans Robert Jauss, "Literary History as a Challenge to Literary Theory," in *Toward an Aesthetic of Reception*, trans. Timothy Bahti (Minneapolis, MN: University of Minnesota Press, 1982) 3-45.

A close theological reading of the Bible and other religious texts reveals a rich intertextuality. The Bible itself is a complex intertext. The theory of the Russian critic Mikhael Bakhtin's dialogical principle is instructive here.[66] Bakhtin discovered the world of the text to be an intersection of textual surfaces rather than a fixed point of static meaning. For Bakhtin, every text represents a kind of dialogue among and between several writings. Each text is an intersection of texts where writings other than the plain sense of the text can be identified and read. He writes, "Each word tastes of the contexts in which it has lived its socially charged life."[67] Bakhtin argued that all existence is dialogical in this sense and always in danger of being "monologized" by authoritarian political, moral, or religious discourses and interpretations.

As we have seen, Paul Ricœur's work in biblical hermeneutics confirms Bakhtin's theory of intertextuality as it relates to the world of the biblical text. Ricœur shows us that there is nothing pure or stable about the Bible; in fact, a variety of worlds exist in the biblical material.[68] There are traditions and counter-traditions in the

[66] Mikhael Bakhtin's dialogical principle, or "dialogism," argues that the capacity to have consciousness is based on *otherness*. See Michael Holquist, *Dialogism: Bakhtin and his World* (New York: Routledge, 1990). Bakhtin developed his theories of dialogue and intertextuality in his, *The Problems of Dostoyevsky's Poetics*, ed. and trans. Caryl Emerson (Minneapolis, MN: University of Minnesota Press, 1984). Also see *The Dialogic Imagination: Four Essays by M. M. Bakhtin*, ed. Michael Holquist, trans. Caryl Emerson and Michael Holquist (Austin, TX: University of Texas Press, 1981). Julia Kristeva has done much to extend Bakhtin's theory of intertextuality. See Kristeva, *Desire in Language: A Semiotic Approach to Literature and Art*, ed. Leon S. Roudiez, trans. Thomas Gora, Alice Jardine and Leon S. Roudiez (New York: Columbia University Press, 1980), 66, 69, 86-87.

[67] Aileen Kelly citing Bakhtin in a review article, "Revealing Bakhtin," *The NewYork Review of Books* (September 24, 1992) 44.

[68] For the most complete study of Ricœur's biblical hermeneutics, see Vanhoozer, *Biblical Narrative in the Philosophy of Paul Ricœur*. Also, Ricœur, *The Bible and the Imagination*. Finally, Paul Ricœur, *Essays on Biblical Interpretation*, ed. Lewis S. Mudge (Philadelphia, PA: Fortress Press, 1980).

biblical text. For example, there are scriptural accounts of women who found identities in prophetic words and deeds contrary to the representational control of reality by the patriarchy, yet their voices and memories were later eclipsed by the discourses and social practices of patriarchy. Recent dialogical and oppositional readings of the text by feminist theologians are retrieving those subversive memories repressed by the monologized tradition of patriarchy.[69] This recovery of a repressed counter-tradition has been made possible only by. the marginalized but empowered social praxis of women entering into critical and demanding conversation with the text and its often resistant communities of interpreters.

David Tracy's revisionary and constructive theology reminds us that life, the world in front of the text, like the textual world, is terribly and wonderfully polysemic, intertextual, and dialogical. In the spirit of many great storytellers, Tracy's work demonstrates that *we tell a story to find yet another story.* Following Tracy, the Christian theologian with an active analogical imagination knows that if she is to find salvation in history she must learn to read the rich intertextuality of the human and cosmic story as carefully and as seriously as she approaches the privileged texts of her primary community, always attentive to points of connection and always suspicious of claims that too easily tame plurality or absorb ambiguity. She knows she must leave the comfort and security of home to journey through many strange and unfamiliar worlds. There she must learn new and difficult languages if she hopes to meet the mystic, embrace the prophet, and do theology in dialogue with the radically other.[70]

---

[69] Elizabeth Schussler Fiorenza, *In Memory of Her: A Feminist Theological Reconstruction of Christian Origins* (New York: Crossroad, 1984). Also, E. Schussler Fioreaza, *Bread Not Stone: The Challenge of Feminist Biblical Interpretation* (Boston, MD: Beacon Press, 1984).

[70] The thought of Julia Kristeva concerning otherness and the stranger is insightful. In her exploration of the stranger, the foreigner, and the outsider, she also considers the idea of "strangeness" within the self. Her illuminating work

She also knows the existential risks of this adventure into the story-shaped worlds of the other: the risks of becoming lost in the labyrinth of exotic gods and goddesses, enchanting myths, spell-binding images, intoxicating scents, swimming symbols, and dangerous dances with strangers. Yet she has counted the cost. She is convinced that a deepened self-consciousness, God-consciousness, and cosmic-consciousness comes only through a creative hermeneutics of genuine conversation with the other: through encountering communities of difference — through reading oppositional narratives — through hearing the cries of the poor and the oppressed — through listening to the articulate silence of night dreams and the languages hidden in her body and in the face of the other — through traveling to unknown regions far beyond the churchyard gate. Less-demanding proposals for telling the stories of God, in the end, will seem like bad fictions.

David Tracy's many productive conversations around the topic of narrative theology and hermeneutics led him to think more broadly about "theology as writing." He suggests that the new theories of writing are helping to develop Jewish and Christian hermeneutical understandings. Now more theologians are viewing the central role of Scripture and other classic texts not merely as testimony to past presence but "as writing." Theology is indeed a kind of writing. But what kind of writing is it? We turn now to a consideration of that question.

suggests that we can only learn to live in peace with the strangers around us if we acknowledge and tolerate the strange-ness or otherness in ourselves, for we are indeed "strangers to ourselves." Kristeva, *Strangers to Ourselves*, trans. Leon S. Roudiez (New York: Columbia University Press, 1991).

THEOLOGY IS A KIND OF WRITING:
NARRATIVE AND THEOPOETICS*

> *Hence the new theories of writing help
> Jewish and Christian (and, even more,
> Islamic) understandings of the central
> role of Scripture as not merely testimony
> to past presence but as **writing**
> David Tracy*

INTRODUCTION

Many still remember when that terrible twister ripped through the Kansas flatlands. As Frank Baum remembers it, the sky turned grayer than peasant life on the prairie. From the north came the low wail of the wind and suddenly Uncle Henry stood up. "There's a cyclone coming, Em!" he called to his wife. Toto jumped out of Dorothy's arms. The house whirled around two or three times and rose slowly through the air. Dorothy felt as if she were going up in a balloon.

Most know Baum's account of Dorothy's story.[1] A tornado sweeps Dorothy away from Kansas to the land of Oz. Even under the magical spell of Oz she is convinced: "There's no place like home, there's no place like home." The lion, the scarecrow and

---

* A somewhat parallel — yet different — version of this chapter was first read at a conference celebrating Gordon Kaufman's retirement from Harvard, then at a meeting of the American Society for Aesthetics in New York, and finally published in *Cross Currents* 47 (1997) 317-331.

[1] Frank Baum. *The Wonderful Wizard of Oz*, originally published in 1900 (New York: Knopf, 1992).

the tin man travel with her down the yellow brick road, which she hopes will take her to the Wizard and then home, for there's no place like home.

After a terrifying yet exciting adventure in the labyrinth of Oz, her wish is granted and she leaves the colorful world of Oz and re-enters the drab, black and white tones of her Kansas farm. Auntie Em, Uncle Henry and the hired help gather around her bed and assure her that she is all right, that she has returned to *reality*. Oz was only a bad dream from a bump on the head. Against their patronizing dismissals Dorothy cries, "It wasn't a dream, it was a place, a real, truly live place! Doesn't anyone believe me?" They didn't.

Many people, however, did believe her. They wanted to believe her. They needed to believe her. So Frank Baum wrote another Oz book, after the *Wizard*, in which Dorothy takes Uncle Henry and Auntie Em with her to Oz, where she becomes a princess, far from the Kansas flatlands. Salman Rushdie, who knows much about home and perhaps too much about exile, provides this commentary on the stories of Oz:

> So Oz finally *became* home; the imagined world became the actual world as it does for us all, for the truth is that once we have left our childhood places and started out to make up our own lives, armed only with what we have and what we are, we understand that the real secret of the ruby slippers is not that "there's no place like home," but rather that there is no longer any such place as home: except, of course, for the home we make, or the homes that are made for us, in Oz; which is anywhere, and everywhere, except the place from which we began.[2]

Many good storytellers through the ages have joined the creative writers of Genesis in reminding us that we can never really go

---

[2] Salman Rushdie, *The Wizard of Oz* (London: British Film Institute, 1992) 57. For a further discussion of home and exile in light of the Oz stories see my "So Many Good Voices in My Head," *Soundings* 79 (1996) 19-31.

home. We all now live east of Eden. With the loss of the Garden many have attempted to build mighty towers that reach all the way to the heavens. Those towers become dungeons in the air and fall to the earth with the noise of the crash of Babel. Their collapse, like the first fall, is a fall into consciousness: the awareness that Infinity resists and limits all historical totalities and that logos can never finally tame and tutor the wild mystery of theos. It is the awareness that the story of redemption began in a garden but will end in a city–not in a literal Zion but in the imaginary homeland of a New Jerusalem, which, like Oz, is anywhere, and everywhere, except the place from which we began. We live only what we imagine.[3]

One of the happiest turns in postmodern thought for persons of imagination and faith is the turn from a reified metaphysics to a poetics. Theology as invention and imaginative construction joins the disciplines of literary theory, cultural studies and philosophy in viewing itself as composition, construction and for some even "a fictive enterprise with emancipatory intentions."[4] We now live east of Eden and its pure and perfect foundations. The safely detached "observation towers" where men once sat to colonize reason, homogenize language, unify ethics and thus domesticate the Divine have forever fallen. With this fall comes the consciousness that theology is *rhetoric* in its most robust sense, written and spoken by

[3] For clear treatments of postmodern philosophical antifoundationalism and its implications for theology see John E. Thiel, *Nonfoundationalism* (Minneapolis, MN: Fortress Press, 1994) and Stanley Hauerwas, Nancey Murphy and Mark Nation (eds.), *Theology Without Foundations: Religious Practice and the Future of Theological Truth* (Nashville, TN: Abingdon Press, 1994). *Theology Without Foundations*, a Festschrift for narrative theologian James McClendon, includes several essays written from Anabaptist perspectives, including John Howard Yoder's "Walk and Word: The Alternatives to Methodologism." Church of the Brethren theologian Nancey Murphy's study seeks to overcome the liberal/fundamentalist impasse through nonfoundationalism: *Beyond Liberalism and Fundamentalism: How Modern and Postmodern Philosophy Set the Theological Agenda* (Valley Forge, PA: Trinity Press International, 1996).

authors, not by mere auditors of a self-validating revelation. Commenting on the rhetorical vocation of the theologian, Mark Wallace reminds us that:

> [theology] is increasingly recognizing itself to be an exercise in persuasion and pragmatics, a conversation partner in many persons' collective search for meaning and understanding, not a royal road to reality immediately and incorrigibly self-present to the subject.[5]

Indeed, the recent work of David Tracy explicitly states that the theologian must be more attentive to the fact that *theology is writing.* Tracy contends that this reminder about writing and attention to current theories of writing can help Jewish and Christian (and Islamic) understandings of the central role of scripture "as not merely testimony to past presence but *as writing.*"[6] Tracy believes that when scripture is viewed as writing beyond naïve notions of logocentrism, it can in fact "expose all pretensions to full self-presence and correct the fatal repressions and hierarchizations that have plagued much of Western thought and existence."[7] Tracy's attention to material culture, and to "the materiality of writing" in particular, challenges many modern assumptions that language is rooted in ideation not physicality. It applies a hermeneutics of suspicion to any easy notion that the human agent's rational intent comes before form or that idea comes prior to embodiment and creative activity or performance.

---

[4] Theologian Mark Wallace joins other poststructuralists in making the case that theology, like postmodern philosophy, is "fictive" in the most profound sense — Wallace, *Fragments of the Spirit* (New York: Continuum, 1996): "Theology, Rhetoric, and Postmodernism," 15-34. Following Derrida, Richard Rorty first explicitly made the case to an American audience that philosophy must be viewed "as writing." See "Philosophy as a Kind of Writing: An Essay on Derrida," *New Literary History* 10 (Autumn 1978) 141-60.

[5] Wallace, *Fragments*, 19.

[6] David Tracy, "Writing," *Critical Terms for Religious Study*, ed. Mark C. Taylor (Chicago, IL: University of Chicago Press, 1998) 391.

[7] *Ibid.*

THEOLOGY AS WRITING

Theology is a kind of writing. But what kind of writing is it? Following current, creative research in hermeneutics and literary theory, I suggest that theology in our postmodern condition can best be understood first as a poetics, not a dogmatics or systematics. I am of course not suggesting that all postmodern theology must be written in poetic verse, although that would be lovely indeed. I am, however, arguing that whether theology is inscribed in the genre of poetry, in the form of narrative, or in a thicker; theoretical style of prose, it remains a *poiesis:* an inventive, imaginative act of composition performed by authors.

Literary theorist Paul de Mann's work on rhetoric addresses the imaginative character of all humanistic disciplines, including philosophy and theology. He makes a distinction between figural and metafigural writing.[8] Figural works are poems, parables, plays and novels that rely on various artistic styles of speech, while metafigural works consist of self-reflective, theoretical writing about which figures are most adequate to the subject matter at hand. Yet both are funded by a poetics or an artisanship. In making this distinction de Mann seeks to preserve the imaginative character of all writing, while noting the very different rhetorical styles and strategies operative in the process of composition. In this model of the writing life, the creative theorist may indeed be recognized as "a strong poet."

The grand preacher, poet, and philosopher Ralph Waldo Emerson was making much the same point when he suggested that we must work by art, not metaphysics. Unhappy with both moral philosophers and philosophical theologians, Emerson declared that

---

[8] Paul de Mann, *Allegories of Reading: Figural Language in Rousseau, Nietzsche, Rilke, and Proust* (New Haven, CT: Yale University Press, 1979) 14-25. Also see Mark Wallace's discussion of figural and metafigural writing. *Fragments*, 19-20.

philosophy would one day be taught by poets.[9] From Plato to Heidegger to Gadamer and Levinas, poetry has often been understood as a branch of philosophy, and hence as a potential expression of truth and knowledge. Yet as we shall see below, in the end poets in Plato's Republic could not pass his strict truth test and they were banished.

Aristotle is more helpful than Plato in his treatment of poetry and poetics. He understands poetry not merely as a branch of philosophy but also as one of the arts. In a wonderful passage from his *Poetics*, he writes, "The difference between a historian and a poet is not that one writes prose and the other in verse ... The real difference is this, that one tells what happened and the other what might happen." Aristotle goes on to contend that the poet must be a "maker" [*poietes*] not merely of verses but of stories, that he is a poet in virtue of his "re-presentation." What does he represent? He represents the world of action.[10]

The hermeneutics of Paul Ricœur and David Tracy are indeed congenial to this understanding of poetry and poetics. Unlike the so called anticorrelational or "pure narrative" theologians who insist on the "plain sense," realistic reading or *sensus literalis* of the text, because the hermeneutical methods of Tracy and Ricœur see an extravagance or a surplus of meaning within texts, even

---

[9] Emerson is quoted here by John Dewey in his University of Chicago lecture, "Emerson, the Philosopher of Democracy." — John Dewey, *Characters and Events* (New York: Holt, Rinehart and Winston, 1929) 70. Emerson, of course, influenced Nietzsche. See George J. Stacy, *Nietzsche and Emerson: An Elective Affinity* (Athens, OH: Ohio University Press, 1992). With art over metaphysics in view, Nietzsche demonstrated a writing genre of "philosophy as literature" or philosophy as a kind of writing. See Bemd Magnus, Stanley Stewart, and Jean-Pierre Mileur, *Nietzsche's Case: Philosophy As/And Literature* (New York: Routledge, 1993).

[10] Aristotle, *Poetics*, translated by W. Hamilton Fyfe (Cambridge, MA: Harvard University Press, 1960) 36-37.

within biblical narratives (or perhaps especially in biblical narratives!), they favor a model of theology as metaphoric, poetic discourse over theology as simply descriptive discourse. Following, yet extending, Aristotle's theory of mimesis presented in the *Poetics*, Ricœur (and Tracy following him) insists that his understanding of representation or reference does not imply a mirror relation to reality. This is why he does not translate mimesis by use of the term "imitation." Mimesis designates not a mere imitation, but also involves a dynamic, imaginative composition and production of reality.

Thus, Ricœur acknowledges that narrative and poetic renderings of life are in fact "semantic innovations."[11] As such, through narrative plots and poetic tropes, something new — not yet said — arises in language. Language refers to a world in front of the text, but its referential movement is not direct. All reference is in fact reference by redescription and re-presentation. This process of composition allows us to see the world in a new way. Our mimetic language does not duplicate reality but recreates it. As Mario Valdes correctly observes, Ricœur's theory of narrative and metaphorical language reaches for a connection to, rather than a congruence with, the world as signified.[12] In Ricœur's philosophical hermeneutics as well as in David Tracy's theological hermeneutics, naming ourselves and rendering God's name in history is always a process of imaginative composition and construction as the textual world meets the sensuous living world of the philosopher or theologian. This is in part what Tracy understands as "the materiality of writing."

---

[11] Paul Ricœur, *Time and Narrative*, Vol. 1., trans. Kathleen Mclaughlin and David Pellauer (Chicago, IL: University of Chicago Press, 1985) ix.

[12] Mario J. Valdes (ed.), *A Ricœur Reader: Reflection and Imagination* (Toronto, Ont.: University of Toronto Press, 1991) 25.

THE FLESH BECOMES WORD: A POETICS OF THE HEART'S DESIRE

In her thought-provoking book, *Poetic Justice: The Literary Imagination and Public Life*, moral philosopher Martha Nussbaum likewise resists the unproductive, modern division of labor between poets and philosophers.[13] Nussbaum has given the greater part of her career to the recovery and rehabilitation of poetry for philosophical inquiry. As a classicist, Professor Nussbaum takes us behind modernity to interrogate this unfortunate division of labor. She writes:

> For the Greeks of the fifth and fourth centuries B.C., there were not two separate sets of questions in the area of human choice and action, aesthetic questions and moral-philosophical questions to be studied and written about by mutually detached colleagues in different departments. Instead, dramatic poetry and what we now call philosophical inquiry in ethics were both typically... seen as ways of pursuing a single and general question: namely, how human beings should live.[14]

---

[13] Martha C. Nussbaum, *Poetic Justice: The Literary Imagination and the Public Life* (Boston, MA: Beacon Press, 1995).

[14] *Ibid.*, xii-ix. Martha C. Nussbaum, *Love's Knowledge: Essays on Philosophy and Literature* (New York: Oxford University Press, 1990), 3-53. Nussbaum's pre-modem or classical program is Aristotelian in its ethical stance, which enables her to accept a Kantianism modified so as to "give the emotions a carefully demarcated cognitive role." This is an important corrective to Cartesian dualism. However, since Aristotle goes to some length to separate *poiesis* (artisanship) from *phronesis* (practical wisdom or moral action which draws from general rules) and since, I shall argue, Kant's imagination is too bounded by a metaphysics of morals, the postmodern theopoetic project advocated in this chapter seeks to move to a more explicit claim that aesthetics precedes ethics. See Aristotle, *Nicomachean Ethics*, in *The Basic Works of Aristotle*, ed. Richard McKeon (New York: Random House, 1941) 1140a, 1-24. Addressing this Aristotelian divide, a significant work by ethicist Richard Miller advocates a "poetics of practical reasoning" in which a poetic ethical method (inductive, interpretive, particular) is contrasted with a theoretical rationality which applies general rules and essentialist

Nussbaum concludes that pre-modem philosophy and literature were rhetorics with different styles of addressing the same existential end: *eudaimonia*, a word often translated as "happiness" but rendered by Nussbaum and other linguists as "human flourishing."

Nussbaum makes her impassioned, theoretical agenda clear: she wants to return us to the richness of our emotional lives, lives that freely acknowledge the cognitive power of the emotions. Deep, embodied feeling, she contends, is part of thought. Only the rationalist presuppositions of modem philosophy and its handmaidens could have convinced us otherwise. Thus, she writes books like *Love's Knowledge*, in which she argues that some kinds of knowledge are accessible only when we experience the emotion of love. She continues to develop this satisfying insight in her study, *The Therapy of Desire*, where she explores the wisdom of the senses in doing moral philosophy. Her methodological move privileges intuitive perceptions and improvisational responses over rule-based systems of ethics.

After centuries of unproductive dualisms in Western thought which pried apart reason and emotion, body and soul, ethics and aesthetics, poetry and prose, Desire has again returned poetry to the republic of philosophy and its theological territories.[15] With the

principles deductively. See *Casuistry and Modem Ethics: A Poetics of Practical Reasoning* (Chicago, IL: The University of Chicago Press, 1996).

[15] Postmodernism tends to be split along a fault line of the "ludic" and "anti-ludic" (the ecstatics and the ethicists) relative to the problems and possibilities of desire. My theory follows "ludic feminism." See Teresa Ebert, *Ludic Feminism and After: Postmodernism, Desire, and Labor in Late Capitalism* (Ann Arbor, MI: University of Michigan, 1996). Ludic feminists have been influenced by postmodern philosopher Gilles Deleuze and his psychoanalyst collaborator Felix Guattari. They see desire as a mode of production which constitutes the underpinning of culture and history. Desire is treated not as lack but as positive energy. See Ronald Bogue, *Deleuze and Guattari* (New York: Routledge, 1989). Note especially Daniel Smith's "Deleuze's Theory of Sensation: Overcoming Kantian Duality," *Deleuze: A Critical Reader*, ed. Paul Patton (Cambridge: Blackwell, 1996) 29-56.

return of Desire comes the postmodern return of God, and how could it be otherwise? For Emmanuel Levinas reminds us that the relation to the Infinite is not a knowledge but a Desire.[16] The relationship to the Infinite is not gnosis but an eros toward God and an eros toward the world.

What a frightening assertion this can be to those who live and move and have their being in a realm of pure or even practical reason, detached from the heart's desire. It may in fact be here, in the realm of Desire, that the Pietistic education of Immanuel Kant strangely failed him.[17] Some of the most interesting characters in the history of Pietism, like Gottfried Arnold, for example, became heretical preachers and provocative poets, not moral philosophers. The Pietistic educations of the great poets Goethe and Novalis made them keenly aware of the sensual, spiritual and metaphorical nature of all thinking. This led Novalis to conclude: "The seat of the soul is where the inner world and the outer world meet. Where they overlap, it is in every point of the overlap."[18] In face of epistemology's many gaps and fissures, Goethe yielded to the mystery

[16] Emmanuel Levinas, *Totality and Infinity*, trans. Alphonso Lingis (Pittsburgh, PA: Duquesne University Press, 1969). Those who understand the program of Levinas to be centered in "ethics as first philosophy" might find this citation odd. However, there is an artisanship in the creative ethics of Levinas, for it is "the face of the Other," not morality or metaphysics, "from which all meaning appears" (299). For further discussion see Edith Wyschogrod, "The Art in Ethics: Aesthetics, Objectivity, and Alterity in the Philosophy of Emmanuel Levinas," *Ethics as First Philosophy*, ed. Adriaan T. Peperzak (New York: Routledge, 1995) 137-148.

[17] As a young man, Kant was so oppressed by the moral perfectionism of some expressions of German Pietism that he also turned from the movement's more passionate and poetic possibilities. Note the intellectual biography by Ernst Cassirer, *Kant's Life and Thought*, trans. James Haden (New Haven, CT: Yale University Press, 1985).

[18] Cited in Phil Cousineau, ed., *Soul: An Archaeology: Readings from Socrates to Ray Charles* (San Francisco, CA: Harper, 1994) 31.

of grace as he confessed: "It is the nature of grace always to fill spaces that have been empty."[19]

Kant of course understood all of this. That is why he struggled so profoundly with the dance of the noumenal and the phenomenal. Yet in the end, perhaps because the shadow of Plato's cave was so safely seductive, he went with the philosopher and turned away from the poet of his Pietist roots. Let me explain.

As a librarian and lecturer in the city of Konigsberg, Kant began his intellectual career writing about the sublime, the aesthetic, natural philosophy and science, and the poetic. So impressive was his corpus of critical writings that finally, at the age of 42, he was invited to the University of Berlin to take up a full professorship in poetics. He refused and stayed in Konigsberg to give himself to his evolving interests in formal, critical philosophy. Not until four long years after the Berlin invitation was he appointed to the chair of logic and metaphysics at the University of Konigsberg in 1770.

He published nothing for the next ten years. He was at work, however, on a problem he had written by hand in his own published copy of the book that helped make him famous: *Observations on the Feeling of the Beautiful and the Sublime*. In the front of that book Kant wrote:

> Everything goes by like a river and the changing taste and various shapes of men make the whole game uncertain and delusive. Where do I find fixed points in nature, which cannot be moved by man, and where can I indicate the markers by the shore to which he ought to adhere?[20]

Where indeed? Kant's longing for fixed points, for a metaphysics of morals over a poetics of obligation, was finally satisfied in his

---

[19] Robert Bly (ed.), News *of the Universe: Poems of Twofold Consciousness* (San Francisco, CA: Sierra Club Books, 1995) 30-77.

[20] Immanuel Kant, *Observations on the Feeling of the Beautiful and Sublime*, trans. John T. Goldthwait (Berkeley, CA: University of California Press, 1960) 8.

trilogy, *The Critique of Pure Reason, The Critique of Practical Reason* and *The Critique of Judgment*. This was philosophy so discursive and dense it bewildered even Kant's smartest friends and colleagues. The unruly passions of the poet were eclipsed by the more fixed propositions of the critical philosopher. Philosopher Richard Rorty concludes that Kant the philosopher turned inward like a poet, yet pushed thought beyond the concrete, idiosyncratic contingencies of the poetic imagination to discover a "common moral consciousness." Therefore, in Kant's program even the strongest poet must become a dutiful fulfiller of universal obligations.[21]

The Kantian imaginary enters into communion with Platonic reason at this point, for both thinkers contend that we must bring particular sensations, desires and actions under general principles if we are to be moral. Although Kant returned to his early love of aesthetics in his third critique, he produced a rather disembodied doctrine of "aesthetic disinterestedness" wherein ethics precedes aesthetics.[22] The transgressive body of the strong poet must now submit to that which underwrites the categorical imperative, the philosopher's reason. This of course was also Plato's problem.

Plato banished many poets from his Republic, his perfect society. He was convinced that poets (especially the dramatic poets) were politically and morally dangerous. He was certainly right. Poet John Hollander, in a brilliant essay, suggests that Plato was

---

[21] This critical reading of Kant follows the work of Richard Rorty, *Contingency, Irony, and Solidarity* (New York: Cambridge University Press, 1989); Terry Eagleton, *The Ideology of the Aesthetic* (Cambridge: Blackwell, 1990); and Mary Bittner Wiseman, "Beautiful Exiles," *Aesthetics in Feminist Perspective*, ed. Hilde Hein and Carolyn Korsmeyer (Bloomington, IN: Indiana University Press, 1993) 169-178.

[22] A comparison of Kant's theory of "aesthetic disinterestedness" with Freud and the enigma of pleasure in view is found in Hubert Damisch, *The Judgment of Paris* (Chicago, IL: University of Chicago, 1996).

most afraid of the poet within himself.[23] Plato the philosopher, like the early Kant, was in many ways wonderfully poetic but he finally repressed and renounced the poet within. Why? Because poetry is not as clean as philosophy, or theology for that matter. Poetry is connected to the concrete, contingent, complicated realm of embodied passion and as such threatens the rule of reason.

Mark Edmundson, in an important piece of literary criticism entitled *Literature Against Philosophy, Plato to Derrida*, explains:

> Literary criticism in the West begins with the wish that poetry disappear. Plato's chief objection to Homer is that he exists. To Plato poetry is a deception: it proffers imitations of imitations when life's purpose is to seek eternal absolute truth. Poetry stirs up dangerous emotions, challenging reason's rule.[24]

Plato argues that poetry's appeal to the passions is also an appeal to more passionate, reckless, dangerous citizens. Consider Plato's warning from his *Republic:*

> So we shall be justified in not admitting [the poet] into a well-ordered commonwealth, because he stimulates and strengthens an element which threatens to undermine reason... The dramatic poet sets up a vicious form of government in the individual soul: he gratifies that senseless part which cannot distinguish great and small, but regards the same thing as now one, now the other.[25]

Plato likes the philosopher because he is a member of the elite, while the poet is a democrat, a man of the crowd. Plato is especially distressed by the way in which poets lean into common feelings.

---

[23] John Hollander, "The Philosopher's Cat: Examples and Fictions," in *Melodious Guile: Fictive Patterns in Poetic Language* (New Haven, CT: Yale University Press, 1988) 207-232.

[24] Mark Edmundson, *Literature Aganst Philosophy, Plato to Derrida: A Defence of Poetry* (New York: Cambridge University Press, 1995).

[25] Plato, *The Republic*, trans. Francis McDonald Cornford (London: Oxford University Press, 1941) 337.

He charges that it makes them childish and feminine and even womanish; it makes reasonable men write like women and children! Furthermore, poets tell lies — fictions — in the name of making meaning. They manipulate language and care little about accuracy. Philosophers make the eternal Logos, Word or Reason inhabit political structures and moral forms, but poets, dangerous poets, make the flesh become word.

Poetic language, as Plato feared, is a sensuous style of reasoning. The literate voice emerges from the deepest realms of Desire. The award winning film *Il Postino (The Postman)* explores this beautifully.[26] In fact, it could be said that *The Postman* explores through the art of film what Paul Ricœur explores through the "art of theory" in his celebrated *The Rule of Metaphor.*[27]

The story of *The Postman* concerns the democratic friendship of a local postman with the famous poet Pablo Neruda, who is exiled from his native Chile and living on an island off the coast of Italy. When Neruda recites a poem to Mario the postman, Mario says, "Strange." Neruda thinks the postman is a rather harsh critic but Mario explains. He didn't mean that the poem was strange but that he *felt* strange when he heard Neruda's poem.

Some of the best scenes in the film involve Mario's awkward courtship of the local beauty. She completely ignores Mario until he begins to speak to her through Neruda's sensual poetry. She listens to the postman's lovely words and returns home love-struck. Her mother asks, "What did he say to you?" The young woman replies dreamily, "Metaphors!"

[26] *Il Postino [The Postman]*, directed by Michael Radford, Miramax Films, 1996. Based on Antonio Skarmeta, *The Postman*, trans. Katherine Silver (New York: Hyperion Miramax Books, 1995).

[27] Paul Ricœur, *The Rule of Metaphor: Multi-disciplinary Studies of the Creation of Meaning in Language*, trans. Robert Czerny (Toronto, Ont.: University of Toronto Press, 1977).

The mother almost faints. "Not metaphors!" she moans. The mother remembers the passions of her own youth and trembles. "What harm can words do?" the daughter asks. "Words are the worst things in the world," the mother answers.

What did the poet say that made the postman feel so strange? He said, "Love is so short, forgetting is so long." He also said:

> And it was at that age... poetry arrived
> in search of me. I don't know, I didn't know where
> it came from, from winter or a river.
> I don't know how or when,
> no, they were not voices, they were not
> words, nor silence,
> but from a street I was summoned,
> from the branches of night,
> abruptly from the others,
> among violent fires
> or returning alone.
> there I was without a face
> and it touched me.
> I did not know what to say, my mouth
> had no way
> with names, my eyes were blind,
> and something started in my soul,
> fever or forgotten wings,
> and I made my own way, deciphering
> that fire,
> and I wrote the first faint line,
> faint, without substance, pure
> nonsense, pure wisdom
> of someone who knows nothing,
> and suddenly I saw
> the heavens
> unfastened
> and open,
> planets,
> palpitating plantations,

shadow perforated,
riddled
with arrows, fire, and flowers,
the winding night, the universe.
And I, infinitesimal being,
drunk with the great starry
void,
likeness, image of
mystery,
felt myself a pure part
of the abyss,
I wheeled with the stars,
my heart broke loose on the wind.[28]

The *Postman* is quite romantic, yet in the movie the postman and the poet remind us that the same id of Desire that calls forth the language and experience of romance and sex also invokes the prophetic words and work of political action and social transformation. The romantic Neruda was also a passionate Marxist. The poetic impulse that causes sensual satisfaction and personal pleasure also gets people killed on behalf of social justice. In the end, Mario is killed as a result of his connection with oppositional communist politics and the communist poet. Desire gives rise to both poetry and politics and refuses to separate the personal from the political.[29]

---

[28] Pablo Neruda, "La Poesia," *Love: Ten Poems by Pablo Neruda from the Movie The Postman*, comp. Francesca Gonshaw, trans. Alastair Reid (New York: Hyperion Miramax Books, 1996) 6-9.

[29] Pablo Neruda, *Song of Protest*, trans. Miguel Algarin (New York: Murrow, 1976). Note also Martin Espada (ed.), *Poetry Like Bread: Poets of the Political Imagination* (Willimanic, CT: Curbstone Press, 1994) and Carolyn Forche (ed.), *Against Forgetting: Twentieth Century Poetry of Witness* (New York: W.W. Norton, 1993).

ART AS RELIGION'S NEAREST ANALOGUE

Because Desire and God have returned together in our postmodern condition, in the interest of constructive theology, following David Tracy's claim that art is religion's nearest analogue, I am prepared to argue that aesthetics precedes ethics. We work by art, not by an inherited ethics. Aesthetics precedes ethics because the grand story of creation precedes the story of church and society.[30] Contrary to the claims of at least some metaphysicians and natural lawyers, Genesis is not the beginning of religion and morality; Genesis is the beginning of Desire.

To turn to aesthetics is of course to turn to the carnal body.[31] Aesthetics is more than mere art. As the Greek term *aisthesis* implies, aesthetics takes us into the whole embodied realm of human perception and sensation, beyond the reasonable and responsible domain of conceptual thought. Aesthetics signals the body's long symbolic rebellion against the tyranny of a reified metaphysics, theology and ethics.

[30] I am most grateful for engaging conversations with poet Julia Kasdorf which have both challenged and critically confirmed my work in progress on theology and the arts, ethics and aesthetics. For a very helpful collection of essays on ethics and aesthetics see "Art and Ethics: A Symposium," *Salmagundi* 111 (Summer, 1996) 24-145.

[31] Within our diverse Anabaptist traditions, our poets and literary critics have much to teach our theologians about the turn to the body. See especially Di Brandt's *Dancing Naked* (Stratford, Ont.: The Mercury Press, 1996) and Julia Kasdorf's new collection of poems, *Eve's Striptease* (Pittsburgh, PA: Pittsburgh University Press, 1998). Also, for an insightful article on Janet Kauffman's "Bodyfictions" see Amy Hollywood, "On the Materiality of Air: Janet Kauffman's 'Bodyfictions'," New *Literary History* 27 (1996) 529-543. Robert Detweiler's work of literary criticism turns explicitly to a "body poetics and politics." See *Uncivil Rites* (Champaign, IL: University of Illinois Press, 1996). For a theological criticism of Anabaptist body metaphors see my "Communal Hermeneutics as Body Politics or Disembodied Politics?" *Brethren Life and Thought* (Spring 1995) 94-110.

Postmodern theory's strong linguistic turn eventually evolved into a narrative turn with a plot which has now taken our theoretical attention to the body.[32] David Tracy reminds the contemporary theologian to be attentive to the voices of those who have been marginalized or exiled or even silenced by dominant systems, voices that may emerge as strangely and startlingly other. I turn now to two rather recent books authored by feminist theologians from my own tradition. They have helped me better reflect upon the strange and satisfying carnalities of contemporary theology as well as trace the interesting dance of what Tracy has called the analogical and dialectical movements of the religious imagination. Both works enter into some conversation with Gordon Kaufman's modern project of theology as imaginative construction, yet move beyond Kaufman's neo-Kantian ethics to a theology more fully inspired and informed by the aesthetic: Melanie May's *A Body Knows: A Theopoetics of Death and Resurrection* and Diane Prosser MacDonald's *Transgressive Corporeality: The Body, Poststructuralism, and the Theological Imagination.*[33] Both theologians turn to the body as the site for imaginative theological construction.

Melanie May, in addition to being a theologian, is an ordained minister in the Church of the Brethren. She writes that her study with Gordon Kaufman remains formative in reminding her that all her words about God are in fact *her* words: always incomplete,

---

[32] Postmodernism has reminded us that we come to consciousness in language. Thought is cultural-linguistic. The linguistic turn of postmodern thought in the past decade has moved through narrative texts to what is now an intense attention to the body. Almost weekly a new book or article is published with "body" in the title. There is even a scholarly journal devoted exclusively to body theory: *Body and Society*, published in London by Sage Publications since March 1995.

[33] Melanie May, *A Body Knows: A Theopoetics of Death and Resurrection* (New York: Continuum, 1995); Diane L. Prosser MacDonald, *Transgressive Corporeality: The Body, Poststructuralism, and the Theological Imagination* (Albany, NY: SUNY, 1995).

inadequate, and always inviting self-conscious responsibility. Her imaginative book is a marvelous blending of personal narrative, poetry, doxology and theory in the service of theological composition. Resisting the style of the systematic theologian, May honors *poesis* as the process "of making and remaking without ceasing." With intelligence and intuition, she moves God-talk from theology to theopoetics.

May's incarnational theopoetics is articulated with a Hebrew rather than a Greek accent. This is apparent as she cites Naomi Goldenberg: "As women speak more and more in public settings, hermeneutics might then discover the original text, that is, the human body. In the beginning was definitely not the Word... It is flesh that makes the words."[34]

May takes us to the original, bio-historical text of our flesh. Yet unlike some who now celebrate the flesh so much in their theory that the unnuanced turn to the body appears to be little more than a new and improved essentialism — simply replacing word with flesh, Being with body–May's body poetics understands the difficult dialectics of word and flesh, of eros and thanatos, of calamity and bliss, of abjection and celebration. She understands well what Judith Butler terms "the body as a discursive territory."[35] Bodies are inscribed with various vocabularies even as language itself is embodied and material. As she quotes her grandmother's wise words, "A body knows," the surface of May's own body shows her readers the sobering scars of a cancer survivor as well as the satisfying yet difficult mysteries of human and divine love. In the voice of a preacher and poet May declares: "[The] body is made of mud and the wild holiness of wind."[36]

---

[34] May, *A Body Knows*, 23.

[35] Judith Butler, *Bodies That Matter: On the Discursive Limits of Sex* (New York: Routledge, 1993). Also note Elizabeth Grosz, *Space, Time, and Perversion: Essays on the Politics of Bodies* (New York: Routledge, 1995).

[36] May, *A Body Knows*, 20.

This is important for both good art and good theology, for *the Creator God of Genesis is both poet and potter.* God created with both word and hand.

Without this awareness, the return to the body in critical theory risks falling into a new essentialism in which it is almost implied that there is a "natural" state of embodiment outside of cultural-linguistic scripts and symbols.[37] This biological and geographical determinism almost forgets that "nature" is not our only home; language and culture, art and religion are also our homes. Many have been saved from the tyranny of tribal gods and oppressive ancestral landscapes by art and religion. This has much to do with "transcendence" — not the disembodied transcendence of a transcendental signified, but a complicated recognition of the body's limits and boundaries and an imaginative openness to that which exceeds our dreams and bones: God as well as the otherness of the Other.

On the other hand, seeking to avoid any trace of essentialism, some poststructuralists write as if the body is merely a passive site for linguistic inscription, cultural control and social discipline. Even Foucault, who constantly argued that we are inscribed by the technologies of power, also insisted that we are not reducible to those technologies, nor to consciousness, nor to the structures of language, for we are "bound to the back of a tiger."[38]

This leads us into the fine work of Diane Prosser MacDonald. MacDonald, a former Mennonite pastor, teaches us to transgress. The goal of her project is not a new way of systematizing the movement of the sacred in human history but rather a bold transgression of those orders of thought and salvation that in fact resist the call of the sacred. Creative transgression is central to MacDonald's theology. Much like writer Jeanette Winterson, her thought celebrates

---

[37] *Ibid.*, 111-112, n. 13.
[38] MacDonald, *Transgresive Corporeality*, 55-85.

"ecstacy and effrontery" as prior to epistemology and ethics. Much like poet bell hooks, she embraces an erotic pedagogy wherein transgression itself exposes and undermines the politics of domination and domestication.[39]

In a delightful move of friendship evangelism, MacDonald invites Friedrich Nietzsche and Michel Foucault to church to help her do a theology which will enter the "blessed madness" of the limits. She is most interested in the sublime, sensuous "remainders" on the margins of thought–that which cannot be easily managed by morality or metaphysics.

MacDonald's study reminds us that, long before Jacques Derrida announced that metaphysics is violence, Nietzsche taught us that the will-to-truth is rooted in an anti-aesthetic, a hatred of the body; that is, the wish to make everything "comprehensible, practical, useful and exploitable." From Foucault she has learned that our bodies may indeed be the sites of the interplay of power/knowledges but that they will not and cannot be tamed by those discourses because, as embodied beings, we are also "bound to the back of a tiger." Foucault also taught her that the soul is the prison of the body, not the other way around, as a Christendom informed by neo-Platonism implies. The socially constructed soul, with its high walls and watchful wardens, has placed the body in an iron cage of rationalities and moralities. MacDonald suggests that through a "somatology of wild love," the power of the body, in all its fright and beauty, must be unleashed against the soul: transgressive corporeality.

What does this mean? MacDonald acknowledges her indebtedness to Gordon Kaufman and the entire modern project of theology

---

[39] Jeanette Winterson, *Art Objects: Essays on Ecstacy and Effrontery* (New York: Knopf, 1996). bell hooks, *Teaching to Transgress: Education as the Practice of Freedom* (New York: Routledge, 1994).

as imaginative construction.[40] Yet she dissents from that project in at least two ways: First, she questions the interweaving of epistemology and ethics wherein any deconstruction of epistemology appears valid only if it is in the interests of a public or common ethical consciousness. In this model she argues, true knowledge is always linked to *true moral consciousness*. MacDonald joins postmodern theologian Mark Taylor in his critique of hegemonic truths underwritten by utilitarian relations by stressing instead the primacy of the limits, the margins, the remainders, as the neglected sites of theological construction. Here, we must return again to the image of Bloch and Metz standing outside the cathedral. Here, we must ask, with David Tracy, again and again, "Do we meet God in the center or on the margins of history?" This is a question no Anabaptist or Catholic can easily ignore.

Second, MacDonald worries that contemporary constructive or revisionist theologians are simply not sensual enough. Like Kant, they are not sure what to do with the "sensual remainders" that spill over the top of the imaginary given to social ethics and personal morality. Here both ethics and epistemology need a more carnal education, which is a transgressive education, an artistic education.

So MacDonald teaches us to transgress. When we do, we of course find ourselves in the good company of many saints, mystics, ecstatics, prophets, poets, pietists, heretics and anabaptists who said no to their assigned places in the plot of the inherited master narrative. They knew that God no longer came to them in the given order of sin, repentance and redemption. A God beyond epistemology and ethics instead came as transgression, excess and gift.[41]

---

[40] Gordon Kaufman, *The Theological Imagination: Constructing the Concept of God* (Philadelphia, PA: Westminster Press, 1981).

[41] The current work of David Tracy is very instructive here. See *On Naming the Present: God, Hermeneutics, and Church* (Maryknoll, NY: Orbis Books,

With their hearts they believed unto righteousness and with their bodies they confessed unto salvation.

David Tracy's recent work welcomes the radical irruption of voices such as May's and MacDonald's. In an astonishing essay in *Concilium* entitled, "The Return of God in Contempory Theology," Tracy argues that the two classic analogical clues for understanding God's reality — love and intelligence — must now return in new, postmodern dialectical forms and sometimes formlessness.[42] He insists that "God is Love" now becomes an occasion not to show the reasonableness and relationality of the Divine Reality to the "modern mind." Instead, he contends that in the great tradition of Dionysius the Areopagite — the tradition of God beyond Being — love now returns, not as a predictable relationality, but rather, and I am quoting Tracy here, "first as transgression, then as excess, and finally the transgressive excess of sheer gift."[43] Like love, intelligence returns in our postmodern condition with a new face. The modern *logos* can no longer control *theos*. The reasonableness of modern theo-logy must yield to yet another transgression. Here, according to Tracy, the profoundly apophatic tradition of Meister Eckhart's God beyond God returns to remind theologians, philosophers and poets of a God beyond even the most lovely *logos*.[44]

For David Tracy, the greatest puzzles and complexities in the claim that theology is a kind of writing lie not in the old debates between "scripture alone" versus "scripture and tradition." Rather, they lie in the newer hermeneutical challenges of confronting the

1994) 36-46. Also see Edith Wyschogrod, *Saints and Postmodernism: Revisioning Moral Philosophy* (Chicago, IL: University of Chicago Press, 1990).

[42] David Tracy, "The Return of God in Contemporary Theology," *Concilium* (1994) 6, *Why Theology?*, edited by Werner Jeanround and Claude Geffre. This piece is reprinted in David Tracy, *On Naming the Present: God Hermeneutics and Church* (Maryknoll, NY: Orbis Press, 1994) 44.

[43] *Ibid.*

[44] *Ibid.*

presence-oriented category of "Word." However, poetic and
metaphorical language (for in the rule of metaphor "it is and is
not" both and at the same time) help express the reality of the Word
(and words) as both self-presencing Logos *and* self-distancing
Kerygma.[45] Here postmodern concerns around language, presence
and absence intersect with the beauty of classical Christian categories and images such as analogy/dialectic, sacrament/word,
proclamation/manifestation, mystic/prophetic incarnation/cross,
nature/grace, creation/redemption, cosmos/history, the comprehensible and the incomprehensible as well as the hidden God and the
revealed God.

The Return of God

Even we constructive and revisionist theologians who have become
skilled in redeeming the pleasures of Babel with an analogical
imagination in the task of public theology need to be reminded not
to neglect the dialectical edge of the voices from the margins. The
spiritually sensuous ones are becoming easier for most of us to
hear, but the suffering ones still speak. Even now, the blood of
tigers and martyrs mingles as the voices of drowned anabaptists
cry out from the rivers of Europe and from high church baptismal
fonts. Their broken bodies still lie on the altars of orthodoxy and
their blood still drips from the eucharist cups of Christendom,
reminding us that this too is transgression, this too is excess, this
too is gift!

   Good theology is a kind of transgression, a kind of excess, a
kind of gift. It is not a smooth systematics, a dogmatics, or a reified metaphysics; as a theopoetics it is a kind of writing. It is a

---

[45] David Tracy, *Writing*, 389.

kind of writing that invites more writing. Its narratives lead to other narratives, its metaphors encourage new metaphors, its confessions invoke more confessions and its conversations invite more conversations.

David Tracy boldly declares, "Desire, body, love, gift have all returned to allow God-as-God to be named anew."[46] Indeed, Melanie May and Diane Prosser MacDonald remind us that theological writing is not driven by mere duty or discipleship but is itself a light in the head and a fire in the belly. It is passion. With the return of Desire to theology there is less austerity, humility, morality and self-rejection and more play, poetry, story, irony, mystery, grace, carnal vitality and creative power in the blessed work of theological composition. With the return of Desire we may again know *jouissance*, the pleasure of the text, for with the return of Desire, God has returned, and with the return of God, you see, we have the return of the strong author.

---

[46] David Tracy, "The Return of God," *On Naming the Present*, 45.

EVEN THE POSTMODERN STORY HAS A BODY
NARRATIVE, POETRY & RITUAL*

The tongue is both an organ of language and taste
Maurice Merleau-Ponty

INTRODUCTION

We have seen how David Tracy understands theology within the theoretical context of "the materiality of writing." Resisting a pure narrative theology and situating his hermeneutics within a theology of material culture in the world in front of the text, he understands how the metaphorical and poetic languages of scripture and faith refer not only to a sensuous, living world in front of the text but also to articulate flesh, to the human body. Indeed, if the surpluses and excesses of meaning in the metaphorical language of faith stories lead us not merely to more texts but also to the world as text and to the body as text, then it seems that a true narrative theology must move from a hermeneutics of the text to a hermeneutics of the gesture. This chapter in the genre of a theopoetic exploration and reflection begins to bring narrative, poetry and ritual together within the theoretical and theological context of the possibilities of sacramental presence in a postmodern world come of age.[1]

---

* The text of this chapter has been published in *The Presence of Transcendence*, ed. Lieven Boeve and John C. Ries (Leuven: Peeters, 2001) 239-253.

[1] I have published several theological articles that enter into some conversation with postmodernism, some on narrative, some on poetry, and some on ritual. However, this chapter, indeed this dissertation, seeks to bring these themes together. In the long process of my research and writing it became evident to me that even as the text returns us to an embodied world, so a hermeneutical,

Paul Ricœur's former student Jacques Derrida, writing on the visual arts, has confessed, "It is true that only words interest me."[2] Indeed, in most postmodern theory, it is the linguistic text and not the author or his or her material culture which becomes the body of theory. It is well known that in the postmodern imagination the author was killed in Paris, embalmed at Yale, and pronounced dead again and again in English departments and divinity schools from Paris to New Haven to Durham.

The body of the text has also dominated contemporary conversations in theology. While the hermeneutics of Paul Ricœur is more attentive to the world in front of the text, that is, the intertextuality of the narrative text, author, authorial context and audience than his deconstructive students, his radical Huguenot Protestantism — where the Word-Event is central — whispers through all his theory. It has been correctly observed that the work of the Catholic theologian David Tracy is a "theological performance of the hermeneutics of Paul Ricœur." As we have seen, while Tracy does turn to Eliade to explicate and exegete a phenomenology of the sacred, nevertheless, his hermeneutic remains deeply indebted to his former Chicago colleague Ricœur. In most contemporary hermeneutic or narrative theologies, whether pure or impure, anti-correlational or correlational, there is the assumption that one can move from text to ethical action, from story to morality, without much conscious attention to ritual, liturgy, sacrament or spirituality.

narrative theology carries us to a ritual, sacramental theology. See Scott Holland, "How Do Stories Save Us?," *Louvain Studies* 22 (1997) 328-351, and Scott Holland, "Signifying Presence: The Ecumenical Sacramental Theology of George Worgul," *Louvain Studies* 18 (1993) 38-55.

[2] Jacques Derrida, "The Spacial Arts: An Interview with Jacques Derrida," *Deconstruction and the Visual Arts*, ed. Peter Brunette and David Wells (London: Cambridge University Press, 1994) 19.

Interestingly, David Tracy has been stuck, by his own admission, on how to move on to book three of his projected trilogy: the work on practical theology. Likewise, Paul Ricœur has failed to fully produce his promised "poetics of the will." In his insistence that one must move from text to ethical action Ricœur senses that something else must be addressed. A poetics of the will?

In the rich history of both Catholicism and Protestantism, "orthodoxy" has never been understood as mere cognitive correctness in either theology or ethics; it has been concerned with right worship. This is no small matter, for it implies that there may in fact be a ritual, liturgical, sacramental, indeed aesthetic, "consummation of theology,"[3] which spills over into productive public life, not simply from the surplus of meaning in the text, but from the poetics *and* performance of the prayer, the liturgy, the hymn, the homily, the Eucharist — *the performance of doxology*. Theology in the Hebrew and Christian traditions, in the end, yields to a doxology against all idolatry and ideology, even the idols of dogma and ethics.

Recently, the fields of narrative theology and hermeneutical theology have been vigorously challenged by the innovative discipline of ritual criticism.[4] Ritual critics remind us that every story, every text, happens some*where* and in some*body* as well as some*time*.

Drawing from ritual critics such as Ronald Grimes and sacramental theologians such as George Worgul, my evolving work suggests that the self is performatively constituted as well as narratively

---

[3] In this context I have been fascinated by Catherine Pickstock's *After Writing: On the Liturgical Consummation of Philosophy* (Oxford: Blackwell, 1998). However, I find her and her "radical orthodox" colleagues [see *Radical Orthodoxy* (London: Routledge, 1999)] too bound by the theology, sacramentology and philosophy of the late Middle Ages. I am more attracted to the understanding of liturgical and ritual innovation outlined in Nathan D. Mitchell's study, *Liturgy and the Social Sciences* (Collegeville, MN: The Liturgical Press, 1999).

[4] See Ronald L. Grimes, *Ritual Criticism: Case Studies in Its Practice, Essays on Its Theory* (Columbia, SC: University of South Carolina Press, 1990).

constituted. I claim that "ritual knowing" is not epistemologically inferior to "narrative knowing" on the way to naming ourselves and rendering God's name in history, for even the stories of God are told and enacted some*time*, some*where* by some-*body*.

THE EMBODIED MIND

Those who read postmodern thought know that the earlier postmodern "linguistic turn" in critical theory gradually evolved into a "narrative turn" which is now clearly becoming an intense *turn to the body*. Phenomenologically, this is because, as Merleau-Ponty always knew, "The tongue is both an organ of language and taste."[5] Theologically, this is because the Creator God of Genesis is both *poet* and *potter*.

Ricœur and Tracy, in their rich conversations with postmodernism, have demonstrated that the quest for philosophical understanding and theological meaning demands hermeneutical detours, for the only path of the self to itself is through the other. Consciousness must pass through the unconscious (the semantics of desire); intuition must pass through critical interpretation (the hermeneutics of suspicion); reason must pass through language (linguistics and rhetoric); and reflection must pass through imagination (poetics).

Following yet extending their fine work, I am contending through this theopoetic reflection what every good poet, priest and preacher already knows: all narratives must pass through the body — *the hermeneutics of gesture* — for "Even the Postmodern Story

---

[5] Maurice Merleau-Ponty, "La Conscience et l'acquisition du langage," *Bulletin de psychologie* 18 (1964) 226-259. Also see Monila M. Langer, *Merleau-Ponty's Phenomenology of Perception: A Guide and Commentary* (Tallahassee, FL: Florida State University Press, 1989).

Has A Body." My evolving work and its attention to the body pries open space for the postmodern return of the strong author (poet, priest, prophet, mystic — for William James taught us that "religious thought is carried on in terms of personality") and this embodied space likewise provides both mystical and carnal possibilities for the postmodern return of God, even, at least in moments of grace, through a consummation of the signified and signifier on the tongue.

I suppose I am prepared to argue that "since we are not Greeks," metaphorically speaking, the body knows as much as the soul.[6] Let me explain. George Lakoff and Mark Johnson have recently published their capstone work collecting important and even astonishing empirical research on the history and nature of human perception, consciousness and cognition. Their study will be received with great satisfaction by ritual critics, sacramental theologians, poets and preachers. It is a huge and happy book and it is entitled, *Philosophy in the Flesh: The Embodied Mind and Its Challenge to Western Thought.*[7]

Lakoff and Johnson's findings can be summarized under the three central theses of the book: First, most thought is unconscious. Second, abstract concepts are largely metaphorical. The richness of life is found in the rule of metaphor. Third, the mind is inherently embodied. Thought requires a body — not in the trivial sense that you need a physical brain with which to think, but in the profound sense that the very structure of our thoughts comes from the nature of the body. The mind is inherently embodied. This

[6] In the statement, "since we are not Greeks," I am speaking in the language of poetic excess linking this line with the poetic assertions of Yeats and Cairns later in this chapter. Thus, this is not philosophical history but metaphorical exaggeration.

[7] George Lakoff and Mark Johnson, *Philosophy in the Flesh: The Embodied Mind and Its Challenge to Western Thought* (New York: Basic Books, 1999).

conclusion of cognitive science is so important for sacramental theology that I must say a bit more about it before I extend my claim that a theopoetics and a hermeneutics of gesture finally meet on the tongue of language and taste. Consider this summation of Lakoff and Johnson on the embodied nature of thought:[8]

- Reason is not disembodied, as the tradition has largely held, but arises from the nature of our brains, bodies, and bodily experience. This is not just the innocuous and obvious claim that we need a body to reason; rather, it is the striking claim that the very structure of reason itself comes from the details of our embodiment. The same neural and cognitive mechanisms that allow us to perceive and move around also inform our conceptual systems and modes of reason. Thus, to understand reason we must understand the details of our visual system, our motor system, and the general mechanisms of neural binding. In summary, reason is not in any way a transcendent feature of the universe or of disembodied mind. Instead, it is shaped crucially by the peculiarities of our human bodies, by the remarkable details of the neural structure of our brains, and by the specifics of our everyday functioning in the world.
- Reason is evolutionary, in that abstract reason builds on and makes use of forms of perceptual and motor inference present in "lower" animals. The result is a Darwinism of reason, a rational Darwinism: Reason, even in its most abstract form, makes use of, rather than transcends, our animal nature. The discovery that reason is evolutionary utterly changes our relation to other animals and changes our conception of human beings as uniquely rational. Reason is thus not an essence that separated us from other animals; rather, it places us on a continuum with them.
- Reason is not "universal" in the transcendent sense; that is, it is not part of the structure of the universe. It is universal, however, in that it is a capacity shared universally by all human beings. What allows it to be shared are the commonalties that exist in the way our minds are embodied.

[8] *Ibid.*, 4.

- Reason is not completely conscious, but mostly unconscious.
- Reason is not purely literal, but largely metaphorical and imaginative.
- Reason is not dispassionate, but emotionally engaged.

These empirical findings from cognitive science confirm what every priest and poet knows: the body is cognitive, not stupid; and likewise, the mind is embodied. Further, these findings link language to the body, especially the movement of metaphor and the dance of poetry. They also suggest much about the human movement from narrative to lyric to drama.[9]

THE PRIMAL ORIGINS OF ART AND RELIGION

My own work has emphasized the emergence of theopoetics beyond a reified metaphysics, systematics and dogmatics, joining theologians like David Tracy in announcing the return of God in our postmodern condition.[10] Yet this call to theopoetics is not novel. Consider the dated yet timely words of that preacher-poet Samuel Taylor Coleridge: "We need not wonder that it pleased Providence that the divine thoughts of religion should have been revealed to us in the form of poetry: and that at all times, poets, not the slaves of any particular sectarian opinions, should have joined to support

[9] For a very satisfying study tracing the creative movement of "narrative, lyric and drama" in the religious construction of the self, see Frederick J. Ruf's *Entangled Voices: Genre and the Religious Construction of the Self* (New York: Oxford University Press, 1997). Another important treatment of the self as formed not merely in discourse but through performance is Calvin O. Schrag's Gilbert Ryle Lectures, *The Self After Postmodernity* (New Haven, CT: Yale University Press, 1997).

[10] Scott Holland, "Theology is a Kind of Writing: The Emergence of Theopoetics," *Cross Currents* 47 (1997) 317-331.

those delicate sentiments of the heart ... which may be called the feeding streams of religion."[11]

Poets have been teaching me much recently about the tongue as an organ of both language and taste. Like most modern and post-modern thinkers, I am tempted by the primacy of the text and by the pleasures of imaginative textual production. "Imaginative construction!" This can almost falsely imply that language precedes both the world and the body. Indeed, in my earlier work on theology as imagination, I constructed too much on an epigraph by Robert Ganzo: "Invent, there is no lost feast at the bottom of memory!"[12]

A poet, who is also a smart theorist, challenged me on this point by asking, "Are you quite sure?" She helped me see again what I already knew. Although all knowledge and memory is composed, there is a feast at the bottom of memory: a carnal knowledge, a bodily intelligence, a primal pulse, an animal faith, an eros toward God and the world; indeed there is a Eucharistic hunger under all our loves and longings and losses. Herein are the origins of art and religion. This claim is confirmed in the work of Ellen Dissanayake as she explores the origins and meaning of art.[13] Dissanayake contends that art was central to human evolutionary adaptation and that the aesthetic faculty is a psychological component of every human being. She argues that art is closely linked to the origins of religion and to the rituals of birth, death, transition and transcendence.

The astonishing work of anthropologist Roy Rappaport, which he completed on his deathbed, confirms and extends the findings

---

[11] S. T. Coleridge in *Biographia Literaria*, cited in Kathleen Norris, *Amazing Grace: A Vocabulary of Faith* (New York: Riverhead Books, 1998) 380.

[12] "Theology is a Kind of Writing," 317.

[13] Ellen Dissanayake, *Homo Aestheticus: Where Art Comes From and Why* (Seattle: University of Washington Press, 1992).

of Dissanayake on the bio-historical origins and evolutionary inter-connections of art, ritual and religion.[14] Some critics have suggested that Rappaport's final work is the most important and original social scientific study of the foundations of religion and culture since Durkheim. Combining cognitive and adaptive approaches to the study of human behavior, he examines the centrality of ritual and religion in evolution and argues that they are co-extensive with the invention of language and thus with culture. Indeed, Rappaport establishes the centrality of ritual for what it means to be human. Importantly, his work is "real anthropology" in contrast to the highly philosophical, disembodied anthropology that informs much postmodern theory and theology. His project demonstrates that ritual is not merely an alternative way to express certain things; on the contrary, he shows that certain things can be expressed *only* in ritual.

Like Dissanayake, Rappaport is attentive to the evolutionary links between art, ritual and religion, or what he calls "art and grace." As an anthropologist he is interested in the neurological union of opposites in human biology, history and culture. This includes the union of the discursive and non-discursive and the sacred and the profane. He writes that the union of opposites, the vision of some harmony with the universe in the midst of conflicts and contradictions, is what R. Otto called approaching "the holy" but what he, following William James and Gregory Bateson, calls "grace." In this anthropological understanding, grace is related to integration, especially what is to be integrated in the diverse parts of the mind, the multiple levels of experience that at one level is termed consciousness and at another level is called the unconscious. Here Rappaport quotes Bateson, "For the attainment of grace, the

---

[14] Roy A. Rappaport, *Ritual and Religion in the Making of Humanity* (Cambridge: Cambridge University Press, 1999).

reasons of the heart must be integrated with the reasons of reason."[15] Concluding a brilliant career as an anthropologist, Roy Rappaport suggests that reason, ritual, religion and art cannot be pried apart in any epistemology that takes seriously the complexity, contradictions and wonder of human behavior and the making of meaning, which is to say the artful making of culture.

A poet and theological thinker, Catherine Madsen, insists that knowledge is more than something merely constructed. She writes, "Knowledge at its best is not transmitted in increments, but comes whole into the mind, and then must be filled in, thickened in density, to achieve its potential: it is not like a wall built of separate stones but like a child's body, feeding. Knowledge is carnal. It is metabolized, not acquired; perhaps at that level it is not even 'constructed'."[16] As Jorge Luis Borges insists, "Thinking, analyzing, inventing are not anomalous acts; they are normal respiration of the intelligence." "Let all that has breath praise the Lord." "Taste and see that the Lord is good."

The good work of theology is the embodied work of narrative, lyric and drama. Narrative language desires dramatic performance; Poetic language hungers.[17] Rather than take my readers through more theory and theology proper, which preceded this chapter and which will indeed follow this chapter, I want to invite the reader into the pleasure of the text, some poetic texts, as we consider this claim that language is hungry because it is "indeed of the body." This hunger, as we shall see, is both Eucharistic and erotic. Let us consider some poetic "fragments."

---

[15] *Ibid.*, 383.

[16] Catherine Madsen, "Intellectual Light," *Cross Currents* 49 (1999) 299-302.

[17] See the collected essays, *Liturgy and the Body*, edited by Louis-Marie Chauvet and Francois Kabasele Lumbala, *Concilium* (Maryknoll, NY: Orbis, 1995). Also see Jonathan Bishop, *Some Bodies: The Eucharist and Its Implications* (Macon, GA: Mercer University Press, 1992).

THEOPOETIC FRAGMENTS

David Tracy has recently written that "fragments" rather than systems or totalities are indeed the marks of the spiritual situation of our times.[18] He observes that there are at least three kinds of contemporary thinkers for whom the category of "fragments" is important: first, the radical conservatives who view fragments with regret and nostalgia as markers of all that remains of what was once a unified culture; second, the postmodernists in their love of extremes tend to see fragments as a welcome emancipation from the reigning totality systems of rationality and onto-theology; the third group of thinkers interests Tracy most for they see fragments "theologically as saturated and auratic bearers of an infinity and sacred hope, fragmentary of genuine hope in some redemption."[19] He sees Walter Benjamin and Simone Weil as suggestive representatives of this third group.

In her *Spiritual Autobiography*, Simone Weil, the French philosopher and scholar of classics, records two personal epiphanies of sacred presence in her fascinating yet tormented spiritual journey. One occurred at Assisi while praying where Francis once prayed in the chapel of Santa Maria degli Angeli. The other epiphany came through a poem she memorized which, in her words, "took on the virtue of a prayer." Weil had been drawn to the so-called metaphysical English poet-priests. During her recitation of a poem by George Herbert she had an experience much like her epiphany at Assisi through which she declared, "Christ came down and took possession of me." She calls the encounter "a real

---

[18] David Tracy, "Fragments: The Spiritual Situation of Our Times," *God, The Gift, and Postmodernism*, ed. John D. Caputo and Michael J. Scanlon (Bloomington, IN: Indiana University Press, 1999) 170-184.

[19] *Ibid.*, 173.

contact, person to person, here below, between a human being and God." She confesses feeling "the presence of Love."[20]

The poem by Herbert is entitled "Love," which is his theopoetic synonym for "God" or "Lord" or "Christ," or "Sacred Presence." Consider the words of the poet-priest:[21]

"LOVE" BY GEORGE HERBERT

Love bade me welcome; yet my soul drew back,
Guiltie of dust and sinne.
But quick-ey'd Love, observing me grow slack
From my first entrance in,
Drew nearer to me, sweetly questioning,
If I lack'd any thing.
A guest, I answer'd, worthy to be here:
Love said, You shall be he.
I the unkinde, ungratefull? Ah my deare,
I cannot look on thee.
Love took my hand, and smiling did reply,
Who made the eyes but I?
Truth Lord, but I have marr'd them: let my shame
Go where it doth deserve.
And know you not, sayes Love, who bore the blame?
My deare, then I will serve.
"You must sit down, sayes Love, and taste my meat"
So I did sit and eat.

---

[20] Cited by Doris Grumbach in her *The Presence of Absence: On Prayer and an Epiphany* (Boston, MA: Beacon Press, 1999) 52.

[21] I am using here the modern translation of Herbert's text from the collection, *George Herbert: The Country Parson, The Temple*, edited with an introduction by John N. Wall, Jr., with a preface by A. M. Allchin, *Classics of Western Spirituality* (New York: Paulist Press, 1981) 45.

George Herbert's "Love" concludes his collection of poems, *The Temple*, with an expression of almost reckless grace, which I shall suggest, integrates the beauty of holiness on the tongue of taste and language. Herbert was perhaps the greatest poet-priest writing in the school of the great master John Donne. T. S. Eliot has noted that in the preaching and poetry of Donne, thought seems in control of feeling. However, in Herbert, he suggests, feeling seems in control of language.[22] This produces a more "intimate" tone of speech, Eliot argues. It also produces a graceful image of "talking and tasting."

In a lovely, engaging lecture at The University of Chicago at a conference entitled, "Mystics: A Conference on Presence and Aporia,"[23] Regina Schwartz accented Herbert's "Love" poem. Her lecture was called, "From Ritual to Poetry: A Mystic Eucharist." Schwartz discussed a movement from "from ritual to poetry" in the work of Herbert and other metaphysical poets. She noted the emergence of the "Eucharistic" significance of poetic language itself, especially in Herbert, beyond rites and rituals. There is a "Eucharistic" dimension in the linguistic expression itself. Thus, she argued, we see an aesthetic movement from ritual to poetry as a locus of sacred presence.

I agree. The metaphysical poets were fine preachers because of their theopoetic understanding of the sacramental possibilities of artful language, of the Word-Event. Poetic language is able to do more with the dance of the signified and signifier than is possible in propositional or purely descriptive language. A number of recent books are making this claim about the sacramental possibilities of language. I am thinking especially of Philip Ballinger's *The Poem*

---

[22] T. S. Eliot, *George Herbert* (London: The British Council and the National Book League by Longmans, Green & Co., 1962) 17.

[23] "Mystics: A Conference on Presence and Aporia," Kent Hall, The University of Chicago, 13-14 May 1999.

as Sacrament and Theresa DiPasquale's *Literature and Sacrament: The Sacred and the Secular in John Donne.*[24] This work really echoes the earlier theory of David Tracy's former Chicago colleague, Nathan Scott. Scott, a religion and literature specialist and an Episcopal priest, wrote widely on "visions of presence in poetry" and on "the poetics of belief." In poetic or metaphorical language, the signified and signifer at times seem to embrace and kiss in moments of artful manifestation.

Yet in the end is not the manifestation of sacred presence experienced in both the sacrament of Word *and* ritual? Consider the embodied, phenomenological movement of Herbert's poem. It is saturated with grace. As the poet encounters Divine Love, he does not merely rest in the assurance communicated in the language of love nor does his meditation end in the artful liturgy of love. Love's invitation is far more carnal and corporeal. Love "takes his hand" and says, "taste my meat." He did indeed sit and *EAT!* In the liturgy of life the tongue is an organ of both language and taste.

Spiritually-awake poet William Butler Yeats seemed to understand how talk and taste meet on the tongue, how in artistic moments, indeed, in graceful movements, we cannot know the dancer from the dance, because "we are not Greeks." Consider this famous fragment from his "Among School Children":[25]

---

[24] Philip A. Ballinger, *The Poem as Sacrament: The Theological Aesthetics of Gerard Manley Hopkins* (Leuven/Grand Rapids, MI: Peeters Press/Eerdmans, 2000). Theresa M. DiPasquale, *Literature and Sacrament: The Sacred and the Secular in John Donne* (Pittsburgh, PA: Duquesne University Press, 1999). Nathan A. Scott, Jr., *The Poetics of Belief* (Chapel Hill, NC: University of North Carolina Press, 1985). Also see the following: L. William Countryman, *The Poetic Imagination: An Anglican Spiritual Tradition* (Maryknoll, NY: Orbis Press, 1999) and Douglas F. Ottati, *Hopeful Realism: Reclaiming the Poetry of Theology* (Cleveland, OH: The Pilgrim Press, 1999). Also, Andrew M. Greeley makes similar arguments about poetic language in *Religion as Poetry* (New Brunswick: Transaction Publishers, 1995).

[25] William Butler Yeats, *Selected Poems and Four Plays*, edited with an introduction by M. L. Rosenthal (New York: Scribner Paperback Poetry, 1996) 121.

Plato thought nature but a spume that plays
Upon a ghostly paradigm of things;
Solider Aristotle played the taws
Upon the bottom of a king of kings;
World-famous golden-thighed Pythagoras
Fingered upon a fiddle-stick or strings
What a star and careless Muses heard:
Old Clothes upon old sticks to scare a bird...

Labour is blossoming or dancing where
The body is not bruised to pleasure soul,
Nor beauty born out of its own despair,
Nor bleared-eyed wisdom out of midnight oil.
O chestnut tree, great rooted blossomer,
Are you the leaf, the blossom or the bole?
O body swayed to music, O brightening glance,
How can we know the dancer from the dance?

How indeed? The distinguished American poet Scott Cairns, like
Yeats, is interested in a spirituality where the body is not bruised
to pleasure the soul nor is the dancer removed from the dance. His
recent collection of work is entitled *Recovered Body*. His poem,
"Loves," is subtitled, "Magdalen's Epistle," and in it he explores
incarnational love through Mary's voice. Here is a fragment of that
lengthy poem:[26]

...I have received some little bit

about the glib divisions which
so lately have occurred to you
as right, as necessary, fit —
That the body is something less
than honorable, say, in its
...appetites? That the spirit is

something pure, and — if all goes well —

---

[26] Scott Cairns, *Recovered Body* (New York: George Braziller Publisher, 1998)
66- 67.

potentially unencumbered
by the body's bawdy tastes.

This disposition, then, has led
to a banal and pious lack
of charity, and, worse, has led

more than a few to attempt some
soul-preserving severance — harsh
mortifications, manglings, all

manner of ritual excision
lately undertaken to prevent
the body's claim on the *heart*

or *mind*, or (blasphemy!) *spirit* —
whatever name you fix upon
the supposed *bodiless*.

I fear that you presume — dissecting
the person into something less
complex. I think you forget

you are not Greek. I think that you
forget the very issue which
induced the Christ to take on flesh.

All loves are bodily, require
That the lips part, and press their trace
of secrecy upon the one

beloved...

Because we are not Greeks, Cairns contends, all loves are bodily
and require that the lips part and press their trace of secrecy upon
the one beloved. Some saints and mystics through the centuries
have in fact believed that the lips are the holiest of all the body's
members because through them pass not merely the language and
kisses of love, but the Eucharist. The body knows as much as the
soul. Cairns is currently at work on some essays tracing his own

spiritual journey into what he is calling a "sacramental poetics."[27] He claims that his own work as a poet led him to reflect beyond literature into the experience of sacramental presence. Interestingly, his spiritual autobiography validates the claim I am making about the "hunger" of poetic language. Raised in the Baptist Church, Scott Cairns now worships in communion with the Russian Orthodox Church because the rich, poetic language of the liturgy consummates on the tongue where talk and taste meet, and signified and signifier together dwell in the beauty of holy mystery.

I turn now to a beautiful poem by the Mennonite-Brethren poet Jean Janzen. True to her Anabaptist heritage, Janzen sees that sacred presence and Eucharistic satisfaction of our holy and fleshly hungers are found outside of temples made with human hands in a sacramental universe. Churchly sacraments open one who eats and drinks to another hunger, a holy desire, indeed, to a eucharistic eros toward the world. Those who love God must also love the world, filled as it is with such pain and such indescribable beauty. You can not merely theorize it or even describe it; *you have to eat it.*[28]

WILD GRAPES BY JEAN JANZEN

Grandfather, dying in November,
asked for wild grapes from
a distant creek. He remembered them,
sweet under the leaves, sent Peter,
his eldest, on horseback.

---

[27] I have been in correspondence with Scott Cairns about this and I am grateful for his insights on sacramental poetics.

[28] Jean Janzen, *Snake in the Parsonage* (Intercourse, PA: Good Books, 1995) 57. Used with permission.

Through the window the light,
golden as broth, filled his bedside cups,
and the dusty air shimmered.

I have known others, who, at the end,
crushed the flesh of nectarine against
the dry palate, or swallowed bits
of cake, eyes brimming.

What to drink in remembrance
of each morning that offered itself
with open arms? What food
for the moments we whispered
into its brightness?

Grandfather, the last pain-filled days,
dreamed cures. He who loved God,
who would go to him, but who also
loved this world, filled as it is
with such indescribable beauty,
you have to eat it.

As I finish this theopoetic reflection, a new book has arrived on my desk, Antonio Damasio's *The Feeling of What Happens*.[29] Damasio is a professor of neurology and the author of the award-winning book, *Descartes's Error*, which has been translated into seventeen languages. This new work explores the centrality of body and emotion, beyond and perhaps even before language and reason, in the making of human consciousness. It parallels the findings of Lakoff and Johnson. The distinguished neurologist begins his book with a poetic epigraph which sets the tone for the following four hundred pages of scientific and humanistic investigation into the nature of consciousness. I will conclude where Damasio begins:

[29] Antonio Damasio, *The Feeling of What Happens: Body and Emotion in the Making of Consciousness* (New York: Harcourt Brace & Company, 1999).

Or the waterfall, or music heard so deeply
That it is not heard at all, but you are the music
While the music lasts. These are only hints and guesses,
Hints followed by guesses; and the rest
Is prayer, observance, discipline, thought and action.
The hint half guessed, the gift half understood, is Incarnation.
                         – T. S. Eliot, "Dry Salvages" from *Four Quartets*

Because of the mystery of the Incarnation, because the God of creation is both Poet and Potter, the human person is both narratively and performatively constituted. We will now turn to an exploration of this claim.

PART THREE

SIGNIFYING PRESENCE
THE NARRATIVE AND PERFORMATIVE CONSTITU-
TION OF THE SELF

There is nothing deep down inside us except what we have put there
ourselves, no criterion that we have not created in the course of
creating a practice, no standard of rationality that is not an appeal to
such a criterion, no rigorous argumentation that is not obedience to
our own conventions.
Richard Rorty, Consequences of Pragmatism

The specific experience I'm talking about has given me one certainty:
consciousness precedes being, and not the other way around, as the
Marxists claim. For this reason the salvation of the human world lies
nowhere else than in the human heart, the human power to reflect, in
human meekness and responsibility
Vaclav Havel, Time, March 5, 1990

INTRODUCTION*

Richard Rorty, the neopragmatist philosopher of postmodernity,
speaks for many in the contemporary academic community when
he contends that there is nothing deep down inside us except what
we have put there ourselves. Rorty, in the company of postmodern thinkers, identifies the collapse of all metanarratives, master-
stories, first principles or general standards of rationality, and
thus, the collapse of any hope for a metaphysics of presence. With
the postmodern deconstruction of both classical and modern
understandings of 'presence' follows the deconstruction of the

---

* An earlier version of this study appeared in *Louvain Studies* 18 (1993) 38-
55.

possibility of identifying a core self, an authentic self, or a unify-
ing mystical core within the human person. There is nothing deep
down inside us except what we have put there ourselves.[1]

In contrast, Vaclav Havel, the playwright president of Czechoslovakia, reflecting on years of struggle, suffering, imprisonment
and persecution for his political and moral convictions concludes:
consciousness precedes being. The artist-politician Havel believes
that one can speak meaningfully of that which lies in the human
heart and the human power to reflect out of a consciousness that
precedes being.[2]

A few years ago when I had begun my research on the question
of "How Do Stories Save Us?," I visited David Tracy in his Swift
Hall office at the University of Chicago. I had scheduled an interview to discuss narrative theology in light of his evolving theological project. In preparation for my visit he had pulled from
unruly shelves sagging under the weight of thousands of books and
journals a copy of George Worgul's *From Magic to Metaphor.* He
expressed appreciation for the book and noted how it presented a
phenomenological validation of the sacraments by attending well
to the linguistic category of metaphor and to the behavioral sciences. However, he suggested he found it curious that my dissertation was being directed by a "sacramental specialist" rather than
one who specialized more in hermeneutical theology since the
debate and dialogue around narrative theology was largely cast in
hermeneutical terms.

---

[1] Richard Rorty, *Contingency, Irony, and Solidarity* (Cambridge: Cambridge
University Press, 1989).

[2] An intelligent treatment of conscience and the problem of human consciousness in light of an interdisciplinary approach to moral theology may be
found in Sidney Callahan's *In Good Conscience: Reason and Emotion in Moral
Decision Making* (San Francisco, CA: Harper, 1991). She cites Havel on consciousness, p. 1.

I told Professor Tracy that I indeed understood the highly textualized tone of the conversations around narrative — "To what do the texts *refer* and how?" — but that I had an intuitive and intellectual sense, in progress, that the narrative question needed to move on to a consideration of performance: to a creative movement from the hermeneutics of the text to a hermeneutics of the gesture. After all, I wondered aloud, if like Tracy and Ricœur and unlike Frei and Lindbeck the text took me to the world in front of itself rather than to some pure intratextual reality, was not this a necessary theoretical and theological move? Tracy indicated that he thought this kind of question and exploration "had promise." At the time I didn't realize how the question would take me on such a long exploration from narrative to ritual and from hermeneutical theology to sacramental theology.

Now, a few years later, David Tracy is highlighting an important claim in the work of historian of religions Lawrence Sullivan in his "Putting an End to the Primacy of the Text."[3] Joining other historians of religions, anthropologists and behavioral as well as cognitive scientists, Sullivan has argued that the primary attention to written texts (from scripture to classics to contemporary scholarly analysis) has led to the unfortunate disregard for the fact that material realities other than writing play central roles in religious imagination, experience and practice. Sullivan and a growing number of scholars are reminding us that although the use of print media and the activity of writing have been the primary material focus for conceptualization during the past three hundred years in Western culture, we now must acknowledge that *religious and cultural understandings are negotiated and communicated through a variety of material forms.*

[3] Lawrence E. Sullivan, "Putting an End to the Text as Primary," *Beyond the Classics? Essays in Religious Studies and Religious Education*, ed. Frank E. Reynolds and Sheryl L. Burkhalter (Atlanta, GA: Scholars Press, 1990) 41-59.

To attend to this claim and its importance for theological understanding, this chapter will explore the ecumenical significance of
George Worgul's sacramental theology of presence in an age characterized by postmodern suspicion and despair. The central issue
of narrative and performance or behavior will be kept in constant
view. Professor Worgul, S.T.D., is an alumnus of the Faculty of
Theology at the K.U. Leuven, where he wrote his dissertation under
the direction of Piet Fransen. He is currently Professor of [Sacra-
mental] Theology and Associate Director of the Institute for the
Study of the Family at Duquesne University. Worgul's important
study, *From Magic to Metaphor*, will serve as the centerpiece of
this critical consideration.[4]

Professor Worgul's symbolic-realist hermeneutic is rich with the
language of 'pre-conscious convictions', 'unconscious first principles', 'the a priori constitution of the imagination', and the 'root
metaphor'.[5] His creative method seems congenial to the convictions of President Havel, indeed; consciousness precedes being.
However, Worgul's careful scholarship is also attentive to the questions, concerns and critiques of religious presence that emerge
where traditional, modern, and postmodern world-views intersect.

---

[4] George S. Worgul, *From Magic to Metaphor: A Validation of the Christian
Sacraments* (New York: Paulist Press, 1980) or the reprint from University Press
of America, 1985. Other works by Worgul discussed and cited in this essay
include: "Ritual, Power, Authority and Riddles: The Anthropology of Rome's
Declaration on the Ordination of Women," *Louvain Studies* 14 (1989) 38-69;
"Ritual as the Interpreter of Tradition," *Louvain Studies* 10 (1984) 141-150;
"Imagination, Ritual and Eucharistic Real Presence," *Louvain Studies* 9 (1982)
198-210.

[5] The phrase, "symbolic-realist hermeneutic," is used by sociologist of religion
Robert Bellah to describe any method of interpretation, including his own, that
would assert that as humans we can only think in symbols and thus interpret any
experience in symbols. For Bellah, the symbol is not a decoration, but our only
way of apprehending the real. Indeed, 'reality' is symbolically constructed and
constituted. See his *Beyond Belief* (New York: Harper and Row, 1970) 237-257.

His informed methodology is not grounded in a Romantic or naive notion of unmediated consciousness or presence. Neither does his method present a static, physicalistic interpretation of nature, reason, essence, being, or the human person. His program affirms a foundational 'presence' in both the cosmos and the human heart, yet that presence or reality is always mediated through the contingency of language (thus his focus on how language and other symbol systems function), the contingency of self (thus his careful attention to the behavioral sciences), and the contingency of historical communities (thus his interest in the components and operational features of culture).[6]

While Richard Rorty, like most eliminative postmodern philosophers, would argue that there is 'nothing beyond the text' (read nothing beyond the human text) or nothing but the endless play of signifier upon other signifiers, nothing, no presence outside of the social register, Worgul, like Havel, wagers on the possibility of presence.[7] George Worgul's theory of symbolization not only suggests that theological symbols do in fact point to a "Transcendental Signified," but that they *really* make present the reality they signify.

I will organize this examination of Worgul's thought around four of his favorite themes: root metaphors, ritual, imagination and real presence. The chapter will conclude with some reflections on the importance of his theological proposals for the Christian community at the end of the twentieth century with the issues of narrative and performance in view. However, first a brief summary of his method is in order to provide a context for this thematic consideration.

---

[6] The contingency of language, self, and community is a Rortyan concern (see Rorty, *Contingency, Irony, and Solidarity*, 3-44), yet I am suggesting that the theologian's constructions of reality are informed by presence rather than by a postmodern fall into absence.

[7] The 'nothing beyond the text' assertion of course belongs to Jacques Derrida, yet this idea is expressed in other forms through the work of Roty, Jean Francois

ON METHOD: THE THEOLOGICAL REALITY IS GROUNDED IN THE
HUMAN REALITY

As a specialist in sacramental theology, Professor Worgul's
method, following the phenomenological insights of G. Van der
Leeuw and others, defends the claim that sacraments must be
understood and interpreted within the context of the human phenomenon "which gives rise to and remains present in the sacramental action."[8] Worgul suggests that every sacrament is connected
to a particular human experience, be it a meal, an initiation, or an
act of service. Greatly influenced by the phenomenological-exis-
tential methods of Husserl, M. Blondel, and David Tracy, Worgul's
work explores the anthropological dimensions of the sacraments
and then successfully integrates that anthropological analysis and
phenomenological description of human ritual and symbol into a
theological interpretation of the Christian sacraments. Thus, the
theological reality is grounded in the human reality.

George Worgul's understanding of both contemporary theology
and the behavioral sciences contributes to a well-developed theory
of human ritual and symbolic activity. As he brings the traditional
rituals and symbols of the Christian church into conversation with
the recent theories of Kohlberg, Erikson, Turner, Bellah, and others, he succeeds where many sacramentologists fall short in inte-
grating the sacraments into all of human experience. It is the
humanity of Jesus that in Worgul's thought becomes the core of

Lyotard and others. 'Eliminative postmodernism' is taken from the helpful typological study of postmodernism of David Ray Griffin with William A. Beardslee
and Joe Holland, *The Varieties of Postmodern Theology* (Albany, NY: SUNY
Press, 1989). This work contends that a number of postmodern paradigms are
operating in the contemporary theological academy from the most radical eliminative or deconstructive genre (the theological use of Derrida and company) to
more conservative or post-liberal expressions.

[8] *From Magic to Metaphor*, 34.

sacramental theology since "it binds together the human phenomenon of symbolic activity with the offer and attainment of divine life."[9] The church, as a community of persons and therefore a sociological entity, expresses and reflects the life of the risen Lord in history. Worgul's careful grounding of theology within the rich and complex web of human experience clearly moves the religious understanding of sacraments from magic to metaphor.

ROOT METAPHORS: ANALOGICAL, PRIMORDIAL, AND OPERATIONAL

The literary critic John Middleton Murry wrote: "Metaphor is as ultimate as speech itself, and speech as ultimate as thought. Metaphor appears as the instinctive and necessary act of exploring reality and ordering experience."[10] Recent studies in epistemology confirm that metaphorical thinking is indigenous to all human constructions of reality. Theorists in the humanities, the social sciences, and the physical sciences are affirming the primacy of the metaphor for all human learning and knowing.[11] The interdisciplinary theological proposals of George Worgul share this understanding that metaphors are not mere linguistic ornaments or decorations; rather, they are our only way of apprehending the real. Worgul's work demonstrates what the American philosopher Charles Peirce suggested about the 'vague' power of myths, symbols and metaphors to guide personal and social human development. Metaphors are

[9] *Ibid.*, 34.

[10] Murry is cited by Sallie McFague in her very fine book, *Metaphorical Theology: Models of God in Religious Language* (Philadelphia, PA: Fortress Press, 1982) 32.

[11] See especially George Lakoff and Mark Johnson, *Metaphors We Live By* (Chicago, IL: University of Chicago Press, 1980) and George Lakoff and Mark Turner, *More Than Cool Reason: A Field Guide to Poetic Metaphor* (Chicago, IL: University of Chicago Press, 1989).

appropriately vague; *they are conceptually imprecise but symbolically precise* and thus call into question conventional presumptions and expectations of the real by offering new visions and possibilities of reality.[12]

The theological program of Professor Worgul is attentive to a particular type of metaphor: the root metaphor. He credits Stephen Pepper for coining the term in his *World Hypothesis* where he wrote:

> A man desiring to understand the world looks around for some clue to its comprehension. He pitches upon some area of common sense fact and tries to see if he cannot understand other areas in terms of this one. The original area then becomes his basic analogy or root metaphor.[13]

Citing Pepper's 'common sense fact', Max Black's 'conceptual archetype', David Tracy's 'analogical clue', Newman's 'first principles', and Ortega y Gasset's '*creencias*', Worgul's work describes root metaphors as operative in the human endeavor for grasping a wholeness in the midst of life's complexities. As an organizing principle, he defines a culture's root metaphor as "the corporate ground and basis for a common interpretation of experience and from this — corporate life and action."[14] The fact that cultures find it necessary to employ root metaphors to make common slices of life comprehensible and connected to some stable pole of reality, suggests, Worgul argues, that reality is "not immediately revelatory of an inner consistency, connectedness, or integral meaning."[15]

[12] Bellah discusses Peirce in *Beyond Belief*, 201-203. Also see: James Hoopes (ed.), *Peirce on Signs: Writings on Semiotic by Charles Sanders Peirce* (Chapel Hill, NC: University of North Carolina Press, 1991).

[13] Stephen Pepper, *World Hypothesis* (Berkeley, CA: University of California Press, 1942) 38-39. Cited by George Worgul in his "Ritual as the Interpreter of Tradition," *Louvain Studies* 10 (1984) 143.

[14] George Worgul, "Imagination, Ritual and Eucharistic Real Presence," *Louvain Studies* 9 (1982) 199.

[15] *Ibid.*, 200.

Meaning is not self-evident. Perceived reality is complex, ambiguous, paradoxical and pluralistic. The paradoxes and binary oppositions of life, brilliant light and haunting darkness, unspeakable joy and deep sorrow, life and death, are given meaning, order, coherence, and a sense of integration in and through root metaphors. When the sting of death often seems so relentless and unmerciful, Christian pastors have witnessed the uncanny power of central metaphors to lead mourners through the rocky terrain and uncharted geography of the valley of the shadow of death as symbolically precise yet conceptually imprecise words are articulated, "The Lord is my shepherd... yea though I walk through the valley... I will fear no evil..." When the burden of loss seems too heavy for anyone's solitude to bear, a mystical presence may come to help carry the unbearable weight of absence and sorrow as the community gathers and embraces the mourner in the name and spirit of the one who said: "I am the resurrection and the life, those who believe in me, although they were dead yet shall they live."

Worgul explains that a root metaphor may emerge through a person, an idea, or a significant event such as the passion of Christ. He believes these metaphors are operative on two levels of culture: first, in the perception of reality held by social groups expressed in and through language, patterns of behavior, and social institutions; and second, in the unconscious first principles and beliefs which ground and sustain what is expressed more consciously in language, behavior and social structure.

Drawing from the important field studies of anthropologist Victor Turner and the hermeneutical theory of Paul Ricœur, Worgul's emerging system identifies the subversive potential of root metaphors to challenge and transform the institutions, norms, practices, and ideologies of a given social structure. Root metaphors do indeed provide meaning, stability, order and coherence for a culture, yet because they also relentlessly call for fidelity to their expressed presence and meaning system, they are reformatory and at times even revolutionary.

Victor Turner's work is significant because his theory, unlike earlier theories of Weber, Durkheim, and others, focuses not on the social conservatism of metaphors, symbols and rituals, but on their function in originating culture.[16] He contends that root metaphors arise within a social drama between social structure, that which is a given in the historical moment, and antistructure, that which might alternatively be a new and fresh possibility of expression and meaning. Thus, root metaphors exercise a social correction. The ritual expression of a culture's root metaphor challenges the ritual community to evaluate how closely the community's institutions and behavioral patterns connect with the spirit and meaning of the metaphor. This ritual enactment serves to remind the community of the need for constant revision and correction in any system as it enters the dialectical dance with what is and what might be, for in every metaphor there exists a creative tension between the 'is' and the 'is not'.[17]

In like manner Paul Ricœur's hermeneutics of metaphorical discourse suggests that through metaphor we experience a metamorphosis of language and reality. He argues that by interrupting conventional understandings through a shattering of language, metaphors neither act "to improve communication nor to insure a univocity in argumentation," but rather act to "shatter and increase our sense of reality by shattering and increasing our language."[18]

---

[16] For a good treatment of Turner's theories on ritual and cultural formation and transformation, see Ronald L. Grimes, *Beginnings in Ritual Studies* (Lanham, MD: University Press of America, 1982) 133-159.

[17] McFague comments on this creative tension in her *Metaphorical Theology* (cited above). Because there is an excess of meaning in metaphors they stretch the imaginative construction of reality beyond static or conventional limits as they whisper 'it is but it is not' (pp. 13-14).

The Biblical witness to this profound shattering of normal language is well known: 'the first shall be last', 'to save your life you must lose it', 'unless you eat the flesh of the Son of Man and drink his blood, you have no life in you'. "Symbols give rise to thought" Ricœur reminds us, and in the metaphor there exists "a surplus of meaning." Thus, our most conceptually precise philosophical and theological thought experiments and proposals must be open to constant revision as the symbolically precise yet conceptually imprecise rule of the metaphor meets us anew in each historical moment.[19]

George Worgul's appropriation of the work of Turner and Ricœur reminds us that the ritual enactment by a community of its root metaphor must be a creative and originating performance, putting the community in touch with the life, the human phenomenon, and indeed, with the primordial presence that must form, inform, and transform all social structures. Worgul's focus on ritual performance for formation and transformation is central to his program. While a culture's root metaphors are functioning in several layers of social life, Worgul insists that the root metaphor "finds its keenest expression in a culture's ritual behavior."[20]

---

[18] Paul Ricœur, "Creativity of Language," *Philosophy Today* 17 (1973) 97-112. Also see Ricœur's *The Rule of Metaphor* (Toronto, Ont.: University of Toronto Press, 1977) 65-100. For an example of Worgul's use of Ricœur see his "Ritual, Power, Authority and Riddles," 39-41.

[19] Paul Ricœur, *Interpretation Theory: Discourse and the Surplus of Meaning* (Fort Worth, TX: Texas Christian University Press, 1976). For the most recent collections of Ricœur's work on metaphor, hermeneutics and criticism see Mario J. Valdes (ed.), *A Ricœur Reader: Reflection and Imagination* (Toronto, Ont.: University of Toronto Press, 1991) and Ricœur, *From Text to Action: Essays in Hermeneutics* (Evanston, IL: Northwestern University Press, 1991).

[20] Worgul, "Imagination, Ritual and Eucharistic Real Presence," 200.

RITUAL: THE SYMBOLIC TRANSFORMATION OF EXPERIENCE AND THE
PERFORMATIVE CONSTITUTION OF THE SELF

Informed by some of the best scholarship in the disciplines of cultural anthropology and ritual studies, Worgul agrees with philosopher Susan Langer that: "Ritual is a symbolic transformation of experience that no other medium can adequately express." He points to anthropological studies which verify that all cultures ritualize their particular root metaphors. So convinced is Worgul of the importance of ritual performance that he speculates that a successful repressive action against a particular culture might do well to first focus on a termination of ritual performance and only secondarily on a battle of ideas or philosophy.[21]

"Consciousness precedes being and not the other way around," says Havel. Perhaps it is of greater human significance than political analysts care to admit that the revolution in Czechoslovakia first found its voice and empowerment not in the tomes of academic philosophy nor in the clever arguments of the lawyers, nor even in the diplomatic rhetoric of the politicians, but through the playwrights and dramatists of the theater and through the imaginative work of poets and novelists! With the sensitivity to the profound reality of the unconscious, the human heart, and the power of the imagination, is not the artist and the theologian in touch with the same presence? The creative theology of George Worgul is indeed congenial to this possibility.

Ritual is central to human existence. Ritual enactment is necessary for both the constitution of the self and the community. It is the home of the root metaphor. Worgul writes, "Ritual is the domicile, par excellence, of root metaphors."[22] He continues:

---

[21] *Ibid.*

[22] Worgul, "Ritual, Power, Authority and Riddles," 41.

Ritual comes into being when an event, person, or idea emerges as the cultural root metaphor. Its interpersonal, repetitive, and adaptive characteristics equip it well to be the custodian of root metaphors. Ritual gathers the metaphor's audience, drawing them from their individuality into a social community. It calls them from their unique experience of life into a common horizon of interpretation. Ritual's repetition sustains and reinforces the root metaphor. This return, over and over again, to the metaphor is a testimony to the metaphor's vital ability to address new experiences and maintain its potency for meaning.

Ritual's adaptive value exhorts the community to faithfully apply the metaphor to life and live out its exigencies and demands.[23] Worgul's program testifies to the power of ritual. Utilizing the disciplines of sociology and anthropology his work demonstrates the importance of ritual for an integrated world-view. He shows us that these disciplines indicate that there are three primary factors that make up the world-view of any person or social group: language, behavior patterns, and social structure. Ritual is indigenous to each of these factors.[24]

Language discloses meaning. Language does not merely describe reality, but language, by its ability to disclose meaning, can in fact discover, construct, or shape reality. Words are of course part of a symbol system and linguists tell us that the development of language is closely linked to ritual.

Worgul is careful in his system to show how language and ritual must be integrated in the process of thinking, knowing and being. "Ritual language interprets ritual behavior," he essays, and thus it is the "narrative or myth which guides and directs the interpretation of ritual behavior."[25]

---

[23] Worgul, *From Magic to Metaphor*, 70-110.
[24] Worgul, "Ritual, Power, Authority and Riddles," 40.
[25] *Ibid.*

Ritual, of course, is itself a pattern of behavior. While ritual reflects or expresses humanness, it also does much more. Worgul explains that it is in fact an articulation in that it shapes or constructs human behavior. Ritual can articulate humanness as ritualized behavioral patterns function to call forth and shape human persons and communities.

Worgul is convinced that without such ritual performance there could be no social structure or community. Without the ritual enactment of common symbols and root metaphors, community is impossible. Ritual reaffirms common symbols and thus provides a foundation for meaningful social relationships. As such ritual is a source of social stability. Yet as we have seen concerning the subversive possibilities of metaphors, when ritual is linked with a group's root metaphor it has the power to challenge the status quo and thus call forth a new order or paradigm. Rooted in the drama of human experience, ritual may evoke new symbols or root metaphors as the social praxis demands them. These symbols may first appear as 'anti-symbols' or 'antistructural elements' (Turner) as they challenge the old order and affirm a new language, a new pattern of behavior, and a new social structure.

It is Worgul's attention to the integration of language and ritual that makes his method quite relevant to contemporary theological conversations and debates concerning the centrality of narrative or story for theological reflection and construction. His program reminds us that *the human person is not only narratively constituted; the human person is also performatively or ritually constituted.*

Even as some in the Roman Catholic tradition have mistakenly viewed the sacraments in a magical rather than a metaphorical way, many Protestants have focused on the priority of the 'Word-Event' to the extent that it became an almost magical act for them.[26] The

---

[26] It was the theology of Karl Barth that in this century elevated what he called the Word-Event or the priority of the preached and proclaimed Word of God.

elevation of the homiletical, doctrinal or narrative word and the devaluation of ritual and liturgy in the theology and worship of many Protestant traditions has not only contributed to an aesthetic and sensual sterility in worship; it has led to an impoverished theology that while skilled in a hermeneutics of linguistic texts, has little to contribute to a hermeneutics of living, breathing, dancing, singing, performing texts.

The current emphasis in theological circles on the central role of narrative in human experience has been well reviewed. Stephen Crites helped set the tone for this discussion in his celebrated essay, "The Narrative Quality of Experience," in which he argues that "the formal quality of experience through time is inherently narrative."[27] Many 'pure narrative' or 'story only' theologians from Yale to Notre Dame to Berkeley are suggesting that story-shaped methods of interpretation are not only in harmony with the best of the Biblical tradition, but also with universal human experience.[28] However, Ronald Grimes, a leader in ritual studies, strongly challenges this thesis.

In a seminal article Grimes seeks to add balance to the current overemphasis on the Word-Event in the theological academy by presenting his claim that the self is performatively as well as narratively constituted.[29] Most narrative theologians base their argument for the primacy of story on their understanding that the Bible is itself a collection of stories, and narrative must, therefore, be the foundation for theological and ethical reflection and method.

[27] Stephen Crites, "The Narrative Quality of Experience," *Journal of the American Academy of Religion* 39 (1971) 291.

[28] For a review and critique of pure narrative hermeneutics see Scott Holland, "A Critique of the Hauerwas Reading of the Jesus Story," *Conrad Grebel Review* 10 (Spring 1992) 157-168.

[29] Ronald Grimes, "Of Words the Speaker, of Deeds the Doer," *The Journal of Religion* 66 (1986) 1-17.

Further, they would claim that everyone tells stories, that story-telling is pan-human. Grimes rejects both assertions by reminding the reader that the Bible contains the genres of poetry, dream accounts, aphorisms, legislation, and other non-narrative forms. He then raises serious questions about the ethnocentrism that lies behind the claim that narrative is pan-human. He points to the anthropological research on the Ilongots by R. Rosaldo who reports that they have no biographies or autobiographies, to argue that in some cultures selfhood is constituted more through ritual than narrative. He makes his case for a performatively-grounded hermeneutic by insisting that it has wider applicability because "it does not imply that storytelling, or worse, literacy, is a condition for human selfhood."[30]

In his ritual theory Grimes seeks to illustrate that 'ritual knowing' is not epistemologically inferior to 'narrative knowing' on the way to religious and ethical practice. He also expresses his concern that in the study of religion time should have no more privileged status than space. Grimes examines a case study of neurologist Oliver Sacks, whose work was popularized by Robin Williams' portrayal of the interesting doctor in the film, *Awakenings*, to support his claims concerning space and time. One of Sacks' patients, Jimmy R., has no memory for the period from 1945 to the present. Since Sacks believes that memory, temporality, and narrative constitute selfhood, he asks some nuns in the hospital if they think Jimmy has a soul. The sisters advise, "Watch him in chapel and judge for yourself." The striking and beautiful passage from Dr. Sacks' work deserves to be quoted at length:

> … I was moved, profoundly moved and impressed, because I saw here an intensity and steadiness of attention and concentration that I

[30] *Ibid.*, 6.

had never seen before in him or conceived him capable of. I watched him kneel and take the Sacrament on his tongue, and could not doubt the fullness and totality of Communion, the perfect alignment of his spirit with the spirit of the Mass. Fully, intensely, quietly, in the quietude of absolute concentration and attention, he entered and partook of the Holy communion. He was wholly held, absorbed, by a feeling. There was no forgetting, no Korsakov's then, nor did it seem possible or imaginable that there should be; for he was no longer at the mercy of a faulty and fallible mechanism — that of meaninglessness sequences and memory traces — but was absorbed in an act, an act of his whole being, which carried feeling and meaning in an organic continuity and unity, a continuity and unity so seamless it could not permit any break. The sisters were right — he did find his soul here... I have known Jim now for nine years — and neuro-psychologically, he has not changed in the least. He still has the severest, most devastating Korsakov's cannot remember isolated incidents for more than a few seconds, and has dense amnesia going back to 1945. But humanly, spiritually, he is at times a different man altogether... rich in all the Kierkegaardian categories — the aesthetic, the moral, the religious, the dramatic.[31]

Despite the absence of narrative and a sense of time in Jimmy's life, Sacks identifies the presence of a soul or a core self as he is held in the mass by a ritualistic intentionality and intimacy. The work of both Ron Grimes and George Worgul must serve as a reminder to narrative theologians and narratologists that there may indeed be a presence to touch and a story to see, smell, taste and hear beyond the linguistic narrative text.[32]

[31] *Ibid.*, 13. Also see Oliver Sacks, "The Lost Mariner," *New York Review of Books* 31 (1984) 14-19.

[32] In addition to the works of Grimes already cited in this essay, see his excellent *Ritual Criticism: Case Studies in Its Practice, Essays on Its Theory* (Columbia, SC: University of South Carolina Press, 1990). Despite the unfortunate use

IMAGINATION AND PRESENCE

Two wise and beautifully written books have appeared during a
decade of intense debate about the "deconstruction of presence,"
both of which posit that there can be no major literary, artistic or
musical creations in the absence of a presence which is at its core
theological. Both George Steiner's *Real Presences* and Ralph
Harper's *On Presence* call for a recovery of a metaphysics of presence in an age of deconstruction. Literary critic Steiner's work in
aesthetics lead him to conclude: "The ascription of beauty to truth
and meaning is either rhetorical flourish, or it is a piece of theology."[33] Pastor and humanities professor Harper believes that an
intimacy of Being underwrites all earnest grasps for the meaning
of meaning and connection. He writes: "The metaphysician uses
the same language, out of desperation as the mystic; and the mystic uses the same language as the man or woman in love."[34]

Joining the late philosophy of Heidegger with ecumenical theological reflections, Steiner and Harper present an intriguing and
satisfying aesthetics of presence. On the difficult journey to a metaphysics, George Worgul's program adds depth, texture and validation to the humanistic studies of Harper and Steiner as he brings his
nuanced work in ritual studies and the structured imagination to

---

of 'magic' in its title, a very good theological study of ritual has just been published by Protestant theologian Tom F. Driver, *The Magic of Ritual: Our Need
for Liberating Rites That Transform Our Communities* (San Francisco, CA: Harper
San Francisco, 1991). Specialists in narrative theory can be instructed by Mieke
Bal who creatively addresses the problematic word-image dualism in *Reading
Rembrandt: Beyond the Word-Image Opposition* (New York: Cambridge University Press, 1991).

[33] George Steiner, *Real Presences* (Chicago, IL: University of Chicago Press,
1989) 216. Also see Nathan Scott's review essay, "Steiner on Interpretation,"
Religion and Literature 22 (1990) 9-20.

[34] Ralph Harper, *On Presence: Variations and Reflections* (Philadelphia, PA:
Trinity Press International, 1991) 126.

the questions, problems and possibilities of real presence. Worgul writes: "When a culture's ritual clearly expresses its root metaphor, a presence with the community's charter-event materializes among the ritual participants. Ritual succeeds in this effort through a unique utilization of language and specific structuring of behavior patterns."[35] 'Worgul further essays that, through this structuring of behavior, ritual effects intimacy, social direction, interiorization and presence. Through ritual enactment, members of the ritual community are connected with their origins and with one another. This activity is both personal and corporate and thus intimate, as the community is called and challenged to interiorize the meaning of the root metaphor.

In Worgul's model, intimacy, social direction and interiorization come together to attain the final goal of ritual: presence, indeed, a real presence. The question his model boldly asks is: How is this presence realized? His answer is that it is through the human imagination which empowers these features of ritual to attain presence.

For Worgul, imagination is not the fancy or fantasy of a Walt Disney screenwriter. The German term for imagination, *Einbildungskraft*, begins to provide a picture of the human person's structured imagination. Literally it means, 'the power to form into one'. As Worgul understands the imagination, it is the integrative, constructive, creative human interplay with the world of symbols. *Following David Tracy, Worgul contends that above all else, imagination defines the human.* It is irreducible to cognitive or even intuitive thought. Worgul asserts, "It is not identical to concept imaging but it is an *a priori* condition for its possibility."[36]

It must be noted that in Worgul's understanding of the imagination, it is both a priori and a posteriori in its functional constitution. Citing the work of Gilbert Durland, Worgul explains: "In

[35] Worgul, "Imagination, Ritual and Eucharistic Real Presence," 203.
[36] *Ibid.*, 206.

the interaction of innate image formation and imaging praxis in concrete cultural history, the individual structured imagination emerges."[37]

Let me unpack this distinction, drawing from Worgul's writing on the imagination. He views the pre-conscious and unthematized constitution of the a priori side of the imagination as an incorporating and empowering power above all powers. He sees it actively seeking communion, connection, intimacy and integration with the whole of being. In this context he writes almost confessionally when he declares: "Every practical presence of a reality or a person is at the same time analogically a presence of the whole."[38] A postmodern critic like Richard Rorty would reject this definition of imagination as being hopelessly ontotheological and Romantic. This view of imagination does resonate with the credo of John Keats, "I believe in nothing but the holiness of the heart's affections and the truth of the imagination."

Yet Worgul also defines imagination as a posteriori to the human faculties as its successful operation depends on cognition, memory, feeling, action, will, etc. He explains that these faculties judge and evaluate the imagination's presentations of the 'real' and the 'truthful' by bringing imagination into critical conversation with the complexity of social life and public discourse. It is thus in this creative and critical dialogue between innate image formation and imaging praxis that the structured imagination finds its voice.

It is the structured imagination in Worgul's theory that opens the individual to presence and Being as it calls persons to transcend and journey beyond their individualism and tribal gods and seek communion with the whole. While Worgul believes the imagination enables one to apprehend real presence in all of life,

---

[37] *Ibid.*, 204.
[38] *Ibid.*, 207.

as a sacramental theologian he applies his provocative theory to the central paradigm of communion in Christendom and to the premier sacrament of the Catholic Church: the Eucharist. The Roman Catholic tradition has affirmed and defended the Eucharist as the real presence of Jesus the Christ in space and time. Worgul's creative theological program situates the theology of real presence within the theoretical scheme of root metaphors, ritual and imagination. He believes that the Church's affirmation of eucharistic real presence appears to concretely match contemporary theories of ritual and symbol systems. He summarizes and embraces a rather traditional theological position: "The affirmation of eucharistic presence claims that the whole person of the resurrected Jesus is historically present to the worshipping community in and through a variety of symbols and the faith horizon of the community."[39]

Let me briefly outline how Worgul's program interprets a theology of real presence within the context of ritual studies and the structured imagination. Presenting Christ's eucharistic presence as a presence through celebration, Worgul makes the following case: First, any authentic celebration presumes that the reality-event being celebrated is already present to the extent that celebrations function symbolically. Second, all symbols have as their a priori condition of possibility the reality that they are making present through symbolization. Third, the Christian celebration of the Eucharist thus presumes Christ's presence. Fourth, the actual celebrating of the Eucharist by the community intensifies and deepens this presence. Fifth, it is the imagination that acts as a catalyst for the apprehension of the presence of Christ in the celebration. Finally, through directionality the imagination, both individually and collectively, enables the celebrating community to recognize

---

[39] Worgul, "Imagination, Ritual and Eucharistic Real Presence," 208.

the presence of Christ in and through ritual symbols and symbolic activity.[40]

Worgul's theology of presence is careful to clarify that the eucharistic presence of Christ can only be judged real by an imagination which operates and is intrinsically conditioned by the root metaphor and culture of Christianity. "Faith," he writes, "as a commitment to the cultural metaphor and horizon of Christianity is the environment of presence."[41] For Worgul, the objectivity of eucharistic presence is always conditioned by the subjective situation.

George Worgul's sacramental theology moves religious and theological reflection from magic to metaphor as it presents eucharistic presence not as magical or even imaginary, but as a reality within a sophisticated understanding of human imagination and symbol systems. His program is catholic and ecumenical in the best sense as he grounds theological 'fact' in the fact of human existence and experience. His clear statement that eucharistic presence does not imply the physical presence of the historical Jesus in the biological sense, nor is it to be understood as merely mental recall of the memory of historical fact, opens up important possibilities for ecumenical dialogue, understanding and cooperation.

THE LORD'S TABLE AS A TESTIMONY TO A SACRAMENTAL VIEW OF THE UNIVERSE: SOME ECUMENICAL REFLECTIONS ON REAL PRESENCE

Commenting on the poverty of symbolic understanding that accompanies the rationalism of the Enlightenment project, Piet Fransen has correctly observed that the assertion "... 'It is only a symbol' is probably the most silly and disastrous statement one hears so

---

[40] *Ibid.* I have summarized and outlined Worgul's position as it appears on pages 207-209 of the above-cited article.

[41] *Ibid.*, 209.

frequently."[42] I am a pastor and theologian in a tradition which has historically resisted any doctrine of sacramental real presence by insisting, 'It is only a symbol!' This position came not from the Enlightenment but from the Radical Reformation of the sixteenth century.[43]

The Radical Reformation tradition, under the influence of Zwingli, Grebel, Simons and others, has traditionally given little attention to sacramental theology. In fact the three public symbols celebrated in a worship service, baptism, communion and feet-washing, are referred to as ordinances rather than sacraments. Historically, and I believe correctly, the radical reformers perceived the Lutheran and Roman Catholic understandings of the sacraments to be too close to magic and superstition and not close enough to faith, the Word of God, Christian ethical experience and life outside the sanctuary doors. Further, the radicals challenged the late-medieval church's claim to exclusive control of religious symbols and the representational arena. Clearly, the Radical Reformation was a response to a crisis within the sacramental system of the late-medieval church.

In recent years many sons and daughters of Conrad Grebel and Menno Simons, influenced by both their interreligious encounters and their humanistic studies in literature, linguistics, semiotics, anthropology and the arts, have called their pastors and theologians to shorten the distance between the signifier and the signified by taking another look at sacramental theology. They are suggesting that the poverty of ritual and symbol that characterizes the typical

---

[42] From Fransen's foreword in *From Magic to Metaphor*, xiv.

[43] For one of the best historical treatments of this movement and tradition, see George Huntson Williams, *The Radical Reformation* (Philadelphia, PA: Westminster Press, 1962) and for one of the better theological overviews, Walter Klaassen, *Anabaptism:Neither Catholic nor Protestant* (Waterloo, Ont.: Conrad Press, 1981).

Radical Reformation, Anabaptist or free church worship service may be the result of both an underdeveloped or even mistaken theory of ritual and an overemphasis on the narrative quality and structure of human existence.

In most Anabaptist congregations the ordinances of the church are celebrated only quarterly. Virtually all worship services therefore give precedence to the Word-Event or the preached Word of God. The sermon is both the center and the climax of the worship experience except on those rare occasions when it is Communion Sunday on the church calendar. The elevation of the Word-Event is reflected in the central position of the pulpit in free church architecture. On the wall behind the pastor hangs an empty cross; below the pastor's pulpit is the communion table. An astute critic might conclude from this symbolism that the pastor is the only 'sacrament' present in the typical free church sanctuary. Mourning this problematic 'pastor as functional sacrament' symbolism in the tradition, one Anabaptist scholar has concluded, "It is not surprising that in recent years some Anabaptist pastors have left their pastorates to enter the Episcopal priesthood in part because they would prefer to step aside and point to the sacrament rather than be it."[44]

Scores of my theological ancestors and forebears were beaten, imprisoned, and executed because they refused to submit their lives to what they considered to be the superstitious and oppressive sacramentology of the late-medieval church. Not only was this

[44] Stephen Boyd made this observation and other insightful reflections of the problem or the pastor as sacrament in the free church tradition in an unpublished presentation at the Believers' Church Conference at Bethany Theological Seminary in Chicago, Sept. 2-5, 1987. Boyd has published an interesting revisionist Anabaptist article on the sacraments in which he locates sacramental presence not in the pastor, nor in the host, nor even in the Word, but in the gathered community. Stephen B. Boyd, "Community as Sacrament in the Theology of Hans Schlaffer," *Anabaptism Revisited*, ed. Walter Klaassen (Scottdale, PA: Herald Press, 1992) 50-64.

perceived magical theology an offence to reason and their human experience, it provided a polemic and a representational control of 'reality' that effectively oppressed the poor, the powerless and the nonconformists of the age. With the blood of Anabaptist martyrs dripping from late-medieval eucharistic cups and the voices of drowned Mennonites crying out from the waters of high church baptismal fonts, a revisionary Anabaptist sacramentology will understandably not enter the church through the classic theological tomes and dogmas which have called Rome, not Zurich, home.

If contemporary Anabaptists and other low church Protestants are to develop a theory of symbol and ritual that has the potential of leading their communities to what Paul Ricœur terms a 'second naivete' relative to religious symbolism, it will not be through studying the theological arguments of conventional sacramentologists, but through discovering how symbolic activity is co-natural with the human person. George Worgul's theological method and program can be quite helpful and instructive in this regard. His validation of the sacraments move them from superstition and magic to metaphor as his thesis carefully demonstrates their connection to and emergence from ordinary human experience. Human life is by its very nature symbolic and ritualistic whether in the sanctuary or in the street. Worgul's clear defense of the anthropological dimension of the sacraments provides what I see as the only method of reflection by which an Anabaptist or a Protestant from another communion can regain a much needed second naivete concerning religious symbols at the end of the twentieth century.

As an Anabaptist pastor and professor, I can affirm Professor Worgul's revisionist and metaphorical sacramental theology of real presence.[45] Presenting a theology of presence that is connected to

---

[45] Sallie McFague has suggested that the Catholic tradition's *analogia entis* theological paradigm tends to see similarity, connection, harmony and continuity

and emerging from ordinary slices of life, the Lord's Table becomes a testimony to a sacramental view of the universe. Even as we gather in the sanctuary to eat the flesh of the Son of Man and drink his blood, we participate in the agony of his crucifixion and the glory of his resurrection as we set the banquet table of peace, justice, and celebration in the center of life's brokenness, violence and despair. We gather hoping, praying, believing beyond belief that wherever two or three are gathered in his name, there he is present; and where Christ is present, there is grace and truth and liberation. Consciousness does indeed precede being; and it is in and through a real presence that we all live and move and have our being.

We now move on to a more general look, through selected case studies, at how under the gaze of the inspired, incarnate imagination, art, ritual, and religion as co-extensive dimensions of the evolution of human consciousness give rise to a sacramental theology.

---

between God and creation and thus has preferred 'symbols' over 'metaphors'. In contrast, she suggests that the Protestant sensibility tends to see dissimilarity, distinction and tension, and hence stresses the transcendence of God and the finitude of creation. Thus, this tradition prefers metaphor over symbol because of the clear 'it is' and 'it *is not*' signifying character of the metaphor. She has identified a problem. Often the analogical imagination is tempted to collapse the otherness of the Other into its own limited reality. I believe Worgul's linking of symbol, metaphor and ritual can hold together the inherent tensions between the analogical and dialectical imaginations. *Metaphorical Theology*, 17.

WHEN ART AND RITUAL EMBRACE AND KISS:
TOWARD A SACRAMENTAL THEOLOGY

*As the theological retrieval of the symbolic imagination continues
on several fronts — on the realities of images, myths, metaphors,
analogies, stories, and rituals — we may well find an increased
interest among theologians for adding aesthetic criteria as a major
component in the present post-modern determination of theological
criteria. Indeed, such a possibility seems, at least to me, one of the
most promising in the present revival of interest in the symbolic
imagination and in linguistic, sociological, and anthropological
studies. If that does in fact continue to occur then the ever delicate
attempt of post-modernity to unite both critique and tradition, both
emancipation and fidelity, both ritual and reflection, in a truly
critical fashion can succeed*

David Tracy

INTRODUCTION

This study of the narrative turn in theology has considered how the
symbolic, metaphorical or poetic imagination turns toward the body
and performance. Returning to the thought of Andrew Greeley, it
could be said that the religious imagination is "an aesthetic and an
incarnate imagination." Perhaps not surprisingly, the most constructive and creative exploration of this claim by David Tracy was
written for the Andrew Greeley *Festschrift, The Incarnate Imagination: Essays in Theology, the Arts and Social Sciences in Honor
of Andrew Greeley*.[1] In Tracy's essay, he places Greeley in the long

---

[1] Ingrid H. Shafer, *The Incarnate Imagination: Essays in Theology, The Arts
and Social Sciences in Honor of Andrew Greeley, A Festschrift* (Bowling Green,
OH: Bowling Green University Press, 1988).

tradition of storytellers, poets and priests who understand that good theology must be informed by both a religious and aesthetic sensibility. These thinkers, Tracy argues, understand the rich "tradition" of the faith not as *tradita* (a reified, dogmatic, unquestioned, inherited system) but as *traditio* (the living, liberating, imaginative and intellectual retrieval of the faith's major narratives, rituals and symbols for the radical historicity of our social selves). Such a *traditio*, Tracy suggests, continues to speak to our postmodern condition, not in the literal or plain sense of text, but rather in a symbolic language capable of inviting a "second naivete" towards the resources of religious traditions once dismissed by the modern turn to the discourses of rational or scientific positivisms.[2]

Such a symbolic language, Tracy argues, is the language of possibility. It is not the language of proposition but of metaphor, analogy and ritual. Tracy has suggested that we are currently seeing a post-modern revival of symbolic language in culture and in the academy inviting us to rethink theology in light of the classical categories of the "beautiful, the good and the true." I will return to a consideration of Tracy's evolving thoughts on an "aesthetic criteria" for contemporary theology as I continue to make the case in this chapter that a constructive sacramental theology can signify and embody both narrative and performance as well as both art and ethics. First, however, I want to turn to two case studies that illustrate a public and primordial hunger for ritual and dramatic performance in the quest to understand and tell the human story: The *Funeral of a Princess* and *Waiting for Godot* in Sarajevo.

---

[2] See Tracy's contribution to the above Greeley *Festschrift*, "Theology and the Symbolic Imagination: A Tribute to Andrew Greeley," 235-247.

THE FUNERAL OF A PRINCESS

The Sunday morning just after the announcement of the tragic death of Princess Diana of Wales, I was quite surprised by how many members of my suburban Pittsburgh congregation — young and old — wanted to talk (and even pray) about her life and death. Likewise, I was somewhat surprised by how closely they followed the week's ceremonies leading up to and within her funeral. It was certainly in part because this was a media event and thus constantly before them. Yet I think it was much more. I think it captured their hearts and minds because as a root metaphor it was both a human event and a ritual event.

Despite the postmodern claims about the "incommensurability" of different and diverse narratives, Diana's death signified something universal about human love, longing and loss. The poet-priest John Donne understood this metaphorical movement of the human soul well when he wrote, "No man is an Iland, intire of it selfe; every man is a peece of the Continent, a part of the maine ... any man's death diminishes me, because I am involved in Mankinde." Donne continues, "And therefore never send to know for whom the bell tolls; *it tolls for thee.*"[3] Writers as diverse as John Donne, Ernest Hemingway and Johann Baptist Metz have understood intuitively and intellectually how the ritual funeral bell tolls for us all and thus unites us all in the rich plurality and ambiguity of the human story.

Ritual theorist Ronald Grimes was asked by the American Academy of Religion to reflect on the significance of Diana's funeral as

---

[3] This Donne poem is of course a modern classic and may be found in any number of Donne collections as well as in poetry anthologies. It was called to my memory recently as the epigraph in Hemingway's novel, *For Whom the Bells Toll* (New York: Charles Scribner's Sons, 1940).

a public, media event.[4] While conceding that it was a media event and that great international interest was indeed "created" by the media, Grimes suggested that the ceremony around the death of the princess also intersected with a deep and often neglected human ritual desire. He noted how virtually all of the media commentators could only offer "a protestant" analysis of the ceremonies. They could comment on the words of Diana's brother's eulogy. They could offer commentary on how Elton John changed the words of his "Candle in the Wind" to speak no longer of the death of Marilyn Monroe but now of the Princess. Grimes observed how in the media coverage there was either an awkward silence or a strange, embarrassing stammering around the ritual performance behind, around and beyond the word-events of the ceremony. Grimes commented:

> That Diana's funeral was a media event no one doubts. But it was also a ritual event, and this utterly basic fact went almost unrecognized and certainly unanalyzed ... I would not like to hear analysis of the rites during those rites, but afterwards, surely someone needs to think about the cadence of the walk, the tones of the voice, the mediation of public and sacred space, the effect of dressing up and dressing down, and the relationship between ceremonial traditions and spontaneous actions.[5]

Perhaps most interestingly, Grimes, himself a Canadian, focused on a remark made by the sometimes sage-like Canadian CBC radio commentator, Michael Enright, "We kept distracting ourselves with ceremony." While Enright meant to imply that the ritual around Diana's death seemed to most sophisticated moderns a mere "distraction" from the tragic realities of what actually happened and from the difficult emotions and thoughts around it all, Grimes

---

[4] Ronald Grimes, "Diana's Funeral: A Ceremonial Distraction?," *AAR Religious Studies News* Vol. 12, No. 14 (November 1997) 21.

[5] *Ibid.*

suggested that Enright was in fact partly right but also very wrong. Grimes, an astute ritual critic, explained. Funerals do in part distract. In the midst of cognitive chaos and confusion, emotional conflict, inarticulate pain and unspeakable loss they "create a countervailing order." According to Grimes, a funeral ritual, like other rites of passage, erects a safety net that allows participants to fall emotionally and intellectually — but only so far. After the free fall, the ritual net catches the participant and "yanks him or her up just short of hitting the ground at too high a velocity." As such, it can be a profound "distraction" from the harsh realities of pain, suffering and death.

Yet Grimes argued in his AAR reflections that the funeral ceremony was much more than a distraction. It also performed the opposite function. Grimes explained, "The funeral took us to a place where it hurt, even if it did not need to, and even if we never knew the woman." The work of Ron Grimes contends that rites of passage like this funeral not only connect us with more deeply with our own aching humanity and the humanity of others, they also train us or educate us in the art of expressing inarticulate feelings, impressions and movements of thought. Indeed, they aid us in enacting and interpreting the human story. His ritual theory makes the case that one of the reasons that human beings enact funeral rites is to "train us in the art of grieving." The expression of grief, like all human expressions, is taught and learned in the human community. To say this is to say that grief is cultural.

Grimes insists that such a cultural understanding is not to suggest that grief is not also biological, psychological and spiritual. For Grimes, a textured, not merely a "textual," understanding of culture must read all human phenomena carefully, critically and compassionately. To assert that all is cultural is not to suggest with some postmodernists that "it is all about language games in the end." On the contrary, according to Grimes, it is to acknowledge that all physical activity "from breathing to eating to defecating to weeping is choreographed." Grimes further argues that all embodied acts — from eating to praying to weeping to kissing — no mater how natural (and he would freely add, or supernatural), "are also canvases on which traditions put their stamp."[6] It is important to note here that Grimes deliberately uses the terminology of "art, choreography and canvas" and not merely the language of writing to describe this complex cultural process.[7]

The latest work of anthropologist Clifford Geertz likewise strongly emphasizes the importance of reading or viewing all human action as a kind of text beyond mere modern understandings of the priority of written texts and narratives.[8] A similar movement of emphasis can be seem in the final works of anthropologist and ritual theorist Victor Turner. Turner became convinced of the important aesthetic relationships between religious ritual, theater or drama, and transformative social action. Working out of a parallel understanding of ritual, drama and social change, Susan Sontag perplexed and annoyed many political peace activists when she "waited for Godot in Sarajevo."

Waiting for Godot in Sarajevo

Carl Rollyson's and Lisa Paddock's new biography, *Susan Sontag: The Making of an Icon*, reminds us of Susan Sontag's impressive career as an international public intellectual.[9] From her early

---

[6] *Ibid.*

[7] The development of this kind of analysis can be found in Ronald L. Grimes, *Reading, and Ritualizing: Ritual in Fictive, Liturgical, and Public Places* (Washington, DC: The Pastoral Press, 1993).

[8] Clifford Geertz, *Works and Lives: The Anthropologist as Author* (Stanford, CA: Stanford University Press, 1988).

[9] Carl Rollyson and Lisa Paddock, *Susan Sontag: The Making of an Icon* (New York: Norton, 2000).

days of bringing the latest French literature and philosophy to America, to her insightful work on *Illness as a Metaphor* during her own battle with cancer, through her cosmopolitan criticism, political commentary and historical fiction, Sontag's work is a witness to a life critically and creatively engaged with culture. She once called herself, "a wandering Jew whose grandparents came to America from Poland. And then I wander all over the world..."[10]

Susan Sontag's wandering took her from the comforts of her New York City home to Sarajevo several times in 1993 as the city was besieged and battered from one of this century's bloodiest civil wars. Alarmed by what she saw as a failure of the United States and western European powers to firmly intervene in the face of Serb fascism and by "the decay of any notion of international solidarity" among her intellectual friends and colleagues, she traveled to Sarajevo to in some small way become involved. She was especially distressed by those who simply dismissed the bloody ethnic cleansings with historical cliches such as, "The Balkins is a place of eternal conflict. After all, haven't they always been slaughtering each other?" Sontag remembered and lamented a similar response by other intellectuals when warned of the realities of Auschwitz, "You know, anti-Semitism is just an ancient story in Europe."[11]

Sontag learned to know the city of Sarajevo as she worked with elementary school children, broadcast on the radio, and appeared in documentaries produced by SAGA, Sarajevo's film production company. Then one day while talking to a theatre director, upon an impulse, she asked if he might be interested in her directing a play. He said, "Yes," and she announced that she would like to do *Waiting for Godot*. Sontag later wrote that, "... There was one obvious play for me to direct. Beckett's play, written over forty years ago,

---

[10] *Ibid.*, 210.
[11] Susan Sontag, "A Lament for Bosnia," *The Nation* (December 25, 1995) 819.

seems written for, and about, Sarajevo."[12] There was much criticism from journalists in both the United States and Europe that she would direct a play in a situation that now seemed more like a concentration camp than a cultured city. Yet she explained that she would direct it as "an act of solidarity," a "small contribution" to a city that refused to capitulate to "Serb fascism."

Others critiqued her choice of *Godot*. It seemed to them a depressing choice, a choice without a political message of hope or liberation. It was pessimistic. After all, wasn't the play's opening line, "Nista ne moze da se uradi." (Nothing to be done.)? But to Sontag the play seemed just right because the characters persisted in spite of their despair, just as Sarajevans waited and waited for deliverance from some Godot — from God, from the West, from Clinton, from somewhere or someone. *Nista ne moze de se uradi.* Despite the criticisms and unconventional venue, Sontag reported that the play, produced on a stage as spare as the city stripped bare from war, spoke in a genre more powerful than any mere political or ethical commentary could offer:

> Waiting for Godot opened with twelve candles on stage, on August 17. There were two performances that day, one at 2:00 PM and the other at 4:00 PM. In Sarajevo there are only matinees; hardly anybody goes out after dark. Many people were turned away ... I think it was at the end of the third performance — on Wednesday, August 18 at 2:00 PM — during the long tragic silence of the Vladimirs and the Estragons which follows the messenger's announcement that Mr. Godot isn't coming today, but will surely come tomorrow, that my eyes began to sting with tears. Velibor was crying too. No one in the audience made a sound. The only sounds were coming from the outside of the theater: a UN APC thundering down the street and the crack of sniper fire.[13]

[12] *Susan Sontag: The Making of an Icon*, 291.

[13] For a complete account of her production in Sarajevo see Susan Sontag, "Godot Comes to Sarajevo," *New York Review of Books* (October 21, 1993) 52-59.

Susan Sontag was warmly thanked by the people of Sarajevo and the city's mayor came onstage after a performance to declare her an honorary citizen, the only foreigner so honored other than the United Nations commander, Lieut. Gen. Phillipe Morillon. Yet the criticisms from western Europe and America continued. One journalist asked bluntly, "Isn't putting on a play [in Sarajevo] like fiddling while Rome burns?" Sontag's response merits reflection. Writing about her experience in an essay in the *New York Review of Books*, she said that in Sarajevo she discovered, "There are more than a few people who feel strengthened and consoled by having their sense of reality affirmed and transfigured by art."[14] Let me briefly turn to Susan Sontag's other work to further reflect upon this claim.

Many philosophers and a few theologians first became acquainted with Sontag through what her biographers call her signature essay, "Against Interpretation." It is indeed a brilliant piece on criticism and hermeneutics.[15] Respectful of the discipline of hermeneutics, Sontag nevertheless argues that, "In place of a hermeneutics we need an erotics of art."[16] What does this mean?

The hermeneutics of David Tracy have said much the same thing. For example, Nathan Scott, Tracy's former colleague at Chicago, learning from his formal study of religion and literature and his Episcopal liturgy, argued that we need "a poetics of religion more than a hermeneutics."[17] Likewise, Andrew Greeley, whose work we have considered, continues to remind us that we must "think of religion much like we think of poetry" or its nearest

---

[14] *Ibid.*, 52.

[15] Susan Sontag, "Against Interpretation," *A Susan Sontag Reader*, with an introduction by Elizabeth Hardwick (New York: Vintage Books, 1983) 95-105.

[16] *Ibid.*, 105.

[17] Nathan Scott, "The Rediscovery of Story in Recent Theology and the Refusal of Story in Recent Literature," in Robert Detweiler, *Art/Literature/Religion: Life on the Borders* (Chico, CA: Scholars Press, 1987) 139-155.

analogue, art.[18] For Sontag, "Against Interpretation" does not overthrow hermeneutics but calls one to be more attentive to "the
erotics" or the sensory experience giving rise to the narrative text
or the work of art. She explains that hermeneutics or interpretation
tends to take the sensory experience of a work of art or a writing
for granted, and then proceeds from there. She suggests that the
kind of reductionism or hyper-textualism and over-interpretation
of our modern age have dulled our senses. She argues that we do
not need to "assimilate Art into Thought." She writes, "What is
more important now is to recover our senses. We must learn to *see*
more, to *hear* more, to *feel* more."[19] I am reminded here of critic
John Ruskin's declaration, "To see clearly is poetry, prophecy and
religion — all in one."[20]

An engaging intellectual like Sontag is not calling for an irra-
tionalism. After all, she can be counted in the company of New
York intellectuals like Lionel Trilling who, paraphrasing Matthew
Arnold, declares that one has "the moral obligation to be intelligent."[21] Instead, she is calling for a more embodied, erotic, if you
will, style of reasoning that enables one to see more, hear more, feel
more, and indeed think more. In Sarajevo she experimented with her
belief that dramatic art could perhaps aid in this kind of knowledge
more than either an explicit political manifesto or act of protest.
The final work of Victor Turner argues much the same thing.

Turner's *From Ritual to Theatre* as well as *The Anthropology of
Performance*, apart from making important links between ancient

---

[18] Andrew M. Greeley, *Religion as Poetry* (New Brunswick: Transaction Publishers, 1996).

[19] "Against Interpretation," 104.

[20] Robert Hewison, *John Ruskin: The Argument of the Eye* (Princeton, NJ:
Princeton University Press, 1976) 7.

[21] Lionel Trilling, *The Moral Obligation to be Intelligent: Selected Essays*,
ed. by Leon Wieseltier (New York: Farrar, Straus & Giroux, 2000).

religious ritual and modern theater, argue that dramatic performance expresses meaning inaccessible to everyday observation and reasoning:

> For me, the anthropology of performance is an essential part of the anthropology of experience. In a sense, every type of cultural performance, including ritual, ceremony, carnival, theatre, and poetry is an explanation of life itself, what is normally sealed up, inaccessible to everyday observation and reasoning, in the depths of sociocultural life, is drawn forth — Dilthey uses the term *Ausdruck*, "an expression," from *ausdrucken*, literally "to press or squeeze out." "Meaning" is squeezed out of an event which has either been directly or indirectly experienced by a dramatist or poet, or cries out for penetrative, imaginative understanding (Verstehen).[22]

For Turner, an experience is not complete until meaning it is squeezed out in some performative way. He turns to the etymology of "performance" to further explain this. Performance is not primarily about "form" but derives from the Old French *parfournir*, "to complete or carry through completely." A performance is the proper finale of an experience.

Turner looks to Wilhelm Dilthey's philosophy of consciousness to validate his own anthropology on this point. Dilthey wrote of units of experience or in German, *Erlebnis*, literally, "what has been lived through." According to Dilthey, at least five "moments" of *Erlebnis* can be identified in a kind of procession.[23] (1) Experience has a perceptual core of pain or pleasure that may be felt more intensely than mundane, routinized life may allow. (2) Images of past experiences may be evoked with unusual clarity of outline,

---

[22] Victor Turner, *From Ritual to Theatre: The Human Seriousness of Play* (New York: PAJ Publications, 1982) 13. Also see Victor Turner's posthumous collection, *The Anthropology of Performance* (New York: PAJ Publications, 1987).

[23] See *From Ritual to Theatre*, 12-15 and *The Anthropology of Performance*, 72-98.

strength of sense, and energy of projection. (3) But past events remain inert unless the feelings bound up with them can be revived. (4) Meaning is generated by "feelingly" thinking about the interconnections between past and present events. Here Dilthey accents the formal structure of experience as holding unity and multiplicity, likeness and difference, whole and part. (5) Most importantly for Victor Turner, Dilthey stresses that an experience is never complete until it is expressed, communicated or performed in terms intelligible to others. Experience, to be complete, must be expressed.

For the purposes of our consideration of art, ritual and religion, it is important to note that Turner is most interested in locating the possibilities of "expression" in social dramas, religious rituals and theatrical performances. He believes the poet, the artist, the dramatist or priest can aid persons in moving to that place of completion in depth experience (*Erlebnis*) "where life grasps life." Susan Sontag, like Victor Turner, believes that art, both making it and beholding it or experiencing it, can assist in the expression and thus completion of experience. Let us return to her statement that in Sarajevo "people need to have their sense of reality affirmed and transfigured through art."

Sontag's critics failed to understand that good art, like good religion, both affirms and transfigures or transforms. Both art and religion are necessarily both world-confirming and world-disconfirming when the movements of the analogical and dialectical imaginations are allowed full play. *Godot* was and was not about Sarajevo. The production of *Godot* in Sarajevo did indeed affirm the people's sense of reality — "Nothing to be done" — and brought a certain dark comfort and consolation. Yet even skeptical observers noted that it did something more; as it affirmed the solidarity of suffering it led to a fiercer solidarity of resistance to fascism. The art, in providing a deep sense of incarnation or connection with historical reality, also invited transcendence as the people

in solidarity continued to resist and waited, waited, waited —
knowing despair too well while transcending or transfiguring it.[24]
The critics of Sontag who worried that doing art in a city under
siege was ethically or politically insensitive at worst or ineffective
at best tended to display typical misunderstandings about art as
simply adornment and entertainment or art as mere beauty. Sontag
in Sarajevo understood that art, though pleasurable to the senses,
can also be disturbing to the senses. Art is about "the beautiful"
only if beauty is not understood as simply "the pretty." A profound
sense of beauty includes what the religious seer, poet and artist
William Blake called a "fearful symmetry." Remember Blake's
Tyger:

> Tyger! Tyger! Burning bright
> In the forest of the night,
> What immortal hand or eye
> Could frame thy fearful symmetry?[25]

Blake then asks the Tyger and in so doing also the immortal hand
or eye, "Did he who made the Lamb make thee?" The "beauty"
of art presents or re-presents life in expressions that testify to both
a lovely *and* a fearful symmetry.

Both the funeral of a princess and the brooding play in Sarajevo
are cultural case studies in ritual and dramatic art but they are much
more. I would suggest that they teach us something quite profound
about narrative and performance and about word and sacrament.
To explore this further it is helpful to survey what appear to be

---

[24] The postmodern theologian David Toole uses the example of Sontag's play
in Sarajevo rather differently than the interpretation I am offering here. For Toole
this is an interesting emblem of postmodern nihilism, tragedy and apocalypse. See
Toole, *Waiting for Godot in Sarajevo* (Boulder, CO: Westview Press, 1998).

[25] William Blake, *The Complete Poetry and Prose of William Blake*, ed. David
V. Erdman, commentary by Harold Bloom (Berkeley, CA: University of California Press, 1982) 24.

important movements in theological, religious and critical studies during the past decade or so. It is a movement of thought and experience through narrative, aesthetics, ritual and sacrament.

NARRATIVE, AESTHETICS, RITUAL, SACRAMENT

When I began to research and write about narrative theology well over a decade ago, the famous "linguistic turn" in philosophy, critical theory and theology which had been inspired by postmodernism or deconstructionism had become a full blown narrative turn. My office soon became filled with books and journals on the various dialogues and debates within narrative circles: Yale School vs. Chicago School, intratextuality vs. intertextuality, the pure narrative of the old, New Critics vs. the impure stories of Bakhtin's literary disciples, narrative as a kind of grammar vs. narrative as life's story, and the list continues on and on. Soon, as I have noted earlier in this study, the narrative turn intersected with both the themes of "body" and "aesthetics."

The movement from story to aesthetics and the body is of course quite natural. Narrative certainly has something to do with art, and art or aesthetics involves a sensual perception and experience of reality. The explosion in publication of "body books" and articles preceded the publication of many important new studies in aesthetics. In fact, my book shelves are sagging and sighing from the weight of actually too many volumes on the body as it relates to narrative, literary theory, philosophy and theology. This publication explosion is a testimony to the fact that in telling the human story one must be attentive to both "the body and the book," or to both language and behavior. As I have indicated, my own thought has been moving from the standard treatments of narrative, body and aesthetics on to ritual studies and then into sacramental theology.

In theological language, this movement returns us to the classical categories of Word and sacrament. This seems to be a necessary and "a natural movement" in hermeneutics, if one takes artful embodiment seriously and if, indeed as Ricœur has taught us, the *symbol* gives rise to thought and returns back to symbol again in the hermeneutical circle.

In the remainder of this chapter, with David Tracy's theology of the analogical imagination in view, I would like to consider some of the best current work on aesthetics, ritual and sacramental theology to demonstrate their connection and even convergence within a theory and theology of *the imagination.*

AESTHETICS AND THE IMAGINATION

In the contemporary political and churchly outcry about "a moral breakdown" in society we hear almost nothing about "an aesthetic breakdown." In fact, few politicians, clergy or ethicists seem to see art as at least part of the remedy for the moral and spiritual aimlessness of our age. Liturgist Catherine Madsen has observed that few who agitate for prayer in the schools (or at high school football games) have a concern for the quality of prayer in the churches and few contemporaries who advocate a high morality seem interested in what has long been called the beauty of holiness. Madsen, in a growing company of theological thinkers, argues that moral language alone rarely *attracts* the listener to the ethical life and that the manifestation of the moral life has much to do with the delicate relationship between the aesthetic and the ethical.[26]

The word "aesthetic" generally conjures thoughts of "the beautiful" in the popular imagination but aesthetics originally had much

---

[26] Catherine Madsen, "Liturgy for the Estranged: The Fascination of What's Difficult," *Cross Currents* 46 (1996-97) 471-486.

to do with sense perception, indeed, it signified the expression and education of our sensory perceptions. Only later did it become more narrowly associated with a philosophy of the beautiful. As such, the *aesthetic* was seen as an education and critical articulation of human feeling in converse of the *anesthetic*. The new, massive *Encyclopedia of Aesthetics* uses an earlier, inclusive understanding of aesthetics as "critical reflection on art, culture and nature."[27] It is not mere experiential-expressivism. As any good artist knows, art critically conceals even as it reveals and thus has learned the discipline of both expression and restraint. It thus has everything to with an education of the senses and is therefore another path to the ethical. In this sense, the beauty of the aesthetic knows not only the pretty or even the lovely but the symmetry of educated feelings, emotions and perceptions in face of life's many binary oppositions.

The Chronicle of Higher Education recently declared, "Beauty is Back!" as a header line for a lengthy article examining a renewed interest in aesthetics in American colleges and universities.[28] The author of the article, Scott Heller, notes that after many years of literary and cultural studies in the academy in which all work has been criticized and deconstructed in an attempt to interrogate the political or ethical implications or core under all texts' artful prose and poetry, many academics are now seeing that beauty, art or aesthetics might in fact lead one to a good life. The chasm between art and ethics, politics and poetry, may not be as great as some earnest critics have assumed. Many important studies

[27] Michael Kelly (ed.), *The Encyclopedia of Aesthetics*, 4 vols. (Oxford: Oxford University Press, 2000).

[28] Scott Heller, "Wearying of Cultural Studies, Some Scholars Rediscover Beauty," *The Chronicle of Higher Education* 14, no.15 (December 4, 1998) 14-15.

in diverse disciplines are now underway to explore the almost forgotten links between the beautiful, the good and the true.[29]

Art is also back in theology. Several new works could be cited
here but I have found the work of Fordham theology professor
Richard Viladesau most insightful. Viladesau's two new works take
seriously David Tracy's claim that art and religion are closely
related. Viladesau, a theologian and Catholic priest, has produced
both a volume of theological aesthetics in the genre of foundational
theology and a second volume that brings aesthetics into very productive conversations with both systematic and practical theologies.[30] Richard Viladesau observes that the neglect of the aesthetic
in much contemporary theology is related to a certain "logocentrism" — a preoccupation with the verbal and especially written
word that has dominated the modern study of Christianity. He notes
that this logocentric emphasis is understandable for two reasons.
First, the tradition has insisted upon the normativity of the "Word"
contained in scripture, and second, the textual-centered emphasis on
truth and meaning is generally characteristic of Western intellectual
culture and scholarship. This emphasis itself of course derives, in
part, from the Judeo-Christian tradition of scriptural study.

---

[29] Dozens of recent titles could be noted here. See especially: Jerrold Levinson (ed.), *Aesthetics and Ethics: Essays at the Intersection* (Cambridge: Cambridge University Press, 1998), Bill Beckley and David Shapiro (eds.), *Uncontrollable Beauty: Toward a New Aesthetics* (New York: Allworth Press, 1998),
Elaine Scarry, *On Beauty and Being Just* (Princeton, NJ: Princeton University
Press, 1999), Alejandro Garcia-Rivera, *The Community of the Beautiful: A Theological Aesthetics* (Collegeville,MN: The Liturgical Press, 1999), John Dykstra
Eusden and John Westerhoff III, *Sensing Beauty: Aesthetics, the Human Spirit,
and the Church* (Cleveland, OH: United Church Press, 1998).

[30] Richard Viladesau, *Theological Aesthetics* (Oxford: Oxford University
Press, 1999) and *Theology and the Arts: Encountering God Through Music, Art
and Rhetoric* (New York: Paulist Press, 2000).

Viladesau understands that while the postmodern critique of logocentrism tends to remained locked into thick and theoretical texts, it has nevertheless led many to consider all of material culture (language, behavior, root metaphors, art, etc.) as a "text" to be read and interpreted. This is returning art to theology according to Viladesau. He is quite fond of the nineteenth-century art and literary critic John Ruskin, who of course informed and inspired many of his contemporary Anglican priests and theologians. Ruskin wrote:

> Great nations write their autobiographies in three main manuscripts — the book of their deeds, the book of their words, and the book of their art. Not one of these books can be understood unless we read the two others; but of the three the only quite trustworthy one is the last.[31]

Viladesau argues that what is true of great nations is also true of great religions. His work illustrates how faith communities constitute and communicate themselves not only through the texts of their scriptural and theological writings but likewise through their institutions, ethical practices or behaviors, rituals, poetry, painting, music, sculpture and architecture. All of these expressions of the inspired human imagination must be read and interpreted in an attempt to understand the story of religion. One cannot understand one of these "books" — words, deeds, art — without bringing it into conversation with the other two.

David Tracy agrees with Viladesau's assessment. Thus, he sees value in considering classic expressions of the human imagination in light of the convertibility of the beautiful, the good, and the true. This suggests, for example, that the consideration of "aesthetic criteria" for religion can aid the theologian in the quest for ethical criteria in theology. We will consider Tracy's thought on the aesthetic

---

[31] Cited in Viladesau, *Theology and the Arts*, 124.

criteria for religion and theology but first we must briefly revisit his theory of the classic for it is key in understanding this possible convertibility of the beautiful, the good and the true.

According to Tracy, every major religious tradition composes classics —"understood as those texts, events, images, persons, rituals and symbols which are assumed to disclose permanent possibilities or meaning and truth."[32] The theologian's work is to interpret those classics in such a way that they might become disclosive of truth and transformative of the individual and society. When theologians do this well, "they perform a genuinely public function for both society and academy analogous to the philosopher's interpretation of the classics of philosophy or the literary critic's interpretation of the classics of literature."[33] In this context Tracy contends that religious classics become cultural classics and as such enter the public realm and become available to all inquirers, whatever their religious tradition might be.

By the term "classic," of course, Tracy does not merely mean the classics of Greek or Latin literature or the great classical music of Bach or Beethoven. He is referring more generally to "those certain expressions of the human spirit [which] so disclose a compelling truth about our lives that we cannot deny them some kind of normative status."[34] These disclosures both comfort and challenge, soothe and shock, reveal and conceal, center and de-center us as they transcend the historical and cultural context in which they originated. In asserting this, Tracy is not claiming that the particular contextual origin is insignificant or erased. On the contrary, in art as in religion, the particular takes on a more universal significance. Most good artists understand that one does not begin

---

[32] Tracy, *The Analogical Imagination*, 68.
[33] *Ibid.*
[34] *Ibid.*, 108.

with a generic vision but with a very particular perspective in producing fine work. Likewise, most good ethicists or theologians understand that it is only when one lives out one's life in a committed particularity that one's life begins to take on universal significance.

For Tracy, the primary analogue for the classic, any classic, is the work of art, and for him, art is not a mere matter of taste or décor; it has the possibility of manifesting truth. He writes, "That the work of art discloses an event not merely of taste, genius or beauty, but truth — only a philistine, even an 'aesthetic' one will finally deny."[35] It should be noted that Tracy does distinguish a religious classic from an artistic classic in that the religious classic seeks in more deliberate ways to speak of "the whole." He explains that "explicitly religious classic expressions will involve a claim to truth as the event of a disclosure-concealment of the whole of reality *by the power of the whole* — as, in some sense, a radical and gracious mystery."[36] Yet in both art and religion, it is the symbolic imagination, Tracy argues, that composes and constructs classics.

David Tracy is careful to remind the reader, however, that critical reason must be employed on all our symbols. His theory of aesthetics, like his hermeneutics, is greatly funded by Paul Ricœur's work: "The symbol gives rise to thought, but thought always returns to and is informed by the symbol."[37] For Tracy, this means that rigorous and reflective thought must interrogate our symbols and that our symbolic articulations in art, ritual and religion must likewise inform and form a more robust notion of reason. This refers to all symbols, of course, yet as we have seen, both Tracy and Ricœur devote most of their attention to linguistic symbols.

[35] *Ibid.*, 115.

[36] *Ibid.*, 163.

[37] Paul Ricœur, *The Symbolism of Evil* (New York: Harper and Row, 1967) 347-357.

With this in mind, we now turn to David Tracy's "aesthetic criteria" for interpreting religion and even theology. This means, for Tracy, criteria that are both religious and aesthetic.

In interpreting the possibilities of the symbolic imagination, Tracy turns to the "symbolic-as-analogical vision" of Thomas Aquinas. He admits that, for some, Aquinas might seem like an unlikely conversation partner, since scholars have looked to his highly conceptual system to find metaphysical or ethical criteria for theology, not aesthetic criteria. Yet Tracy sees some convertibility here and suggests that the Thomistic theological use of analogical language nicely parallels the aesthetic figure of speech, the metaphor. Mining both Thomistic analogy and modern theories of metaphor, Tracy offers three aesthetic criteria.[38]

First, the non-reducibility of any truly symbolic reality, whether linguistic as in metaphor, or non-linguistic as in ritual, to merely literal meanings. Here Tracy insists that metaphors (and/or rituals) are not merely rhetorical devices in the sense of decorative substitutions for true-as-literal meaning. There is a surplus of meaning in the metaphor that cannot be expressed in any other way. Tracy turns to the literary genre of the Biblical parable and their "Kingdom of God" language to expand this point. He notes that in older styles of scholarship, both liberal and conservative, there was a temptation to reduce the parables' sense and reference to moral truths or doctrinal teachings. Tracy argues that in the parable, the metaphor or the ritual there is always an excess that manifests to the awake imagination a more-than-literal meaning and truth.

Second, in the employment of metaphorical or symbolic language, a new meaning, never expressible without loss in literal terms, emerges from the interaction of words not ordinarily used conjunctively. Here Tracy reminds us that good metaphor or good

---

[38] David Tracy, "Theology and the Symbolic Imagination," 241-244.

poetry cannot be learned by formulating rules. Following Aristotle on poetry and Aquinas on the language of analogy, Tracy again insists that the capacity to recognize similarity in dissimilarity is the mark of poetic genius. Although Tracy's focus is largely on words or language here, he also writes, "Good ritual, we might add, demands the same power of religious and aesthetic discrimination."[39]

The third criterion Tracy considers most important. It is a recognition of what Ian Ramsey has called the "odd logic" of religious language and what Tracy and Ricœur have called a "symbolic limit-language." Since we have already considered Tracy's limit language earlier in this study, I will only summarize his notion of a limit-language here. Tracy explains that a genuinely religious use of any symbolic form involves a limit character wherein "precisely by *stating* a limit-to the ordinary use of language, also *shows* and *partly states* a symbolic language expressive of an imagined 'limit-of' possibility, some vision of expressing a final meaningfulness to human life in relationship to the whole."[40]

David Tracy indicates that these three proposed criteria are not meant to overthrow the philosophical use of ethical and metaphysical criteria in the quest for both meaning and truth. Rather, they are meant to accent and further investigate the analogies between art and religion and to further explore the classical claim that there is both a connection and convergence in the beautiful, the good and the true for those who have an artful, analogical imagination.

---

[39] *Ibid.*, 241.
[40] *Ibid.*, 242.

(A PARENTHETICAL INTERRUPTION ON ETHICS AND AESTHETICS)

Before I move from the above consideration of aesthetics and the imagination to a look at ritual and imagination, a parenthetical interruption on ethics and aesthetics seems necessary. Tracy's analogical imagination is informed by the dictum of Thomas Aquinas that grace presupposes nature; it does not destroy it but completes it. Thus, at least until his most recent work, he has spoken freely of a sacramental universe. Therefore, it seems that he understands well that for life to be ethical it must likewise be graceful and artful, for in a sacramental universe there is a convertibility between the beautiful, the good and the true. Yet in our postmodern, post-Holocaust age, the great yet terrible haunting voice of the master of suspicion, Friedrich Nietzsche, returns:

> For a philosopher to say, "the good and the beautiful are one," is infamy: if he goes on to add, "also the true," one ought to thrash him. Truth is ugly. We possess art lest we perish of the truth.
>
> *The Will to Power*[41]

There is something disruptive, de-centering and disorienting in Nietzsche's bold proclamation. There is something hard and harsh, true and ugly. It makes even the unapologetic aesthete uneasy about cultured correlations of the good and the beautiful, the good and the true. Happily, a theologian as smart as Tracy admits that the beautiful does not always mean the pretty. Especially in his most recent work, there is more attention to brokenness, alienation, disharmony, distance, fragmentation and anguish in the human condition. The reality of a dark aesthetic is recognized. Yet the tone and texture of the theoretical use of Aquinas on analogy,

---

[41] Cited and discussed within the context of Nietzsche's aesthetics in Leslie Paul Thiele, *Friedrich Nietzsche and the Politics of the Soul: A Study in Heroic Individualism* (Princeton,NJ: Princeton University Press, 1990) 119-138.

integrity and correlation must raise critical questions in light of the terrors of history.

Allow me to return briefly to those cages outside the cathedral. Both postmodern and Anabaptist critics must ask about the possibility of integrity, correlation and coherence in a comparative reading of the *Summa Theologica* and the *Martyrs Mirror*. The *Martyrs Mirror*, also known as the *Bloody Theater*, is a martyrology of early Anabaptist and other dissenting Christians, many of whom were put to death by the magisterial defenders of Christendom.[42] Until recent years, it rested near the family Bible in many Amish, Mennonite, Brethren and Free Church or Anabaptist homes. It is not easy to move from the Thomistic, or perhaps more accurately neo-Thomistic system, of integrity, analogy, harmony and brightness to the dark and discordant witnesses on the stage of that bloody theater of free church and dissenting church history. In fact, the suspicious critic must ask if there is not a disturbing correlation between a system or metaphysics guided by a desire for integrity/perfection, harmony and brightness and the purging or punishment of a dissonance or contrast that fails to cohere with the meta-aesthetic of the beautiful, the good and the true? Prophetic, dialectical religion knows that truth is often ugly, and that the strong, awake and alive soul is marked more by mystery, plurality and ambiguity than by brightness and clarity. We have art (and religion) lest we perish of the "truth"? Perhaps. Because nature *is* our home but not our *only* home; culture — art and religion — is also our home. Good art and religion are indeed embodied, incarnate, yet they give us an imaginative re-presentation and interpretation of our human, historical existence. They are imaginative discourses of possibility.

David Tracy has noted that in his reading, the classical modern Thomists have tried to systematize a single Thomistic doctrine of

[42] Thieleman J. van Braght, *The Bloody Theater or the Martyrs Mirror of the Defenseless Christians* (Scottdale, PA: Herald Press, 1997).

analogy out of what a close and careful reading of Aquinas reveals to be a highly pluralistic use of analogical language.[43] Tracy understands well that good religious language is symbolically precise yet conceptually imprecise, inviting a conflict of interpretations, and hopefully a productive, humane and imaginative conversation around life's plurality and ambiguity. Good religion, like good art, both conceals and reveals, resisting narrative closure and always inviting further investigations around the beautiful, the good and the true. For one with an analogical imagination, the greatest heresy is perhaps to stop the conversation.

It is in this context that I have been arguing in my own work and in this study, admittedly moving beyond David Tracy's hermeneutical proposals, that "aesthetics precedes ethics." This claim is grounded in my understanding of the productive imagination, but also emerges from an ongoing quarrel with my Anabaptist tradition and its dialectical imagination. I ask the reader's permission to write personally here in this small slice of this study for I believe it will help elucidate several of the arguments in this thesis around aesthetics and the theological imagination.

One of my old teachers, John Howard Yoder, combining the negative dialectics of his Mennonite heritage with his mentor Karl Barth's dialectical theology of the Word-Event, declared, "The church precedes the world epistemologically ... as well as axiologically."[44] In such a theology revelation becomes limited to the Word, not the world; the category of church eclipses the wonder of creation; and the story of the disciple erases the narrative of the human. Such a theology also underwrites and enforces what Yoder called "social ethics as Gospel." That is, the Jesus story read through the lens of such a positivism of revelation enforces an

---

[43] David Tracy, "Theology and the Symbolic Imagination," 242.

[44] John Howard Yoder, *The Priestly Kingdom: Social Ethics as Gospel* (Notre Dame, IN: University of Notre Dame Press, 1984) 11.

ethics of the Word that utters only a thundering "No" to the invitation of aesthetic innovation in the realms of belief and behavior. Because my intellectual and spiritual journey led me *more in the direction of imagination than mimesis in theological and ethical composition*, I could not follow Yoder's direction although we remained friendly conversation partners until his untimely death.

What am I suggesting by aesthetic innovation? Let me turn to a life story rather than to a theory for illustration and thus to the practice of biography as theology. When Dietrich Bonhoeffer traveled from Berlin to New York City to study theology as a post-doctoral fellow, he was rather Barthian in his theological method. We are only now beginning to understand how important Bonhoeffer's year in New York was for his final resistance to European totalitarianism. New York taught him as much about aesthetics as ethics, indeed, an art of resistance.[45]

While in New York Bonhoeffer read many of the works of the Harlem Renaissance. He read and worked with James Weldon Johnson's *Autobiography of an Ex-Colored Man*, *The Souls of Black Folks* by W. E. D. Dubois, and the collected poetry of Langston Hughes and Countee Cullen. He spent a year teaching Sunday school and worshipping in Harlem at the senior Adam Clayton Powell's black Baptist Church. There he not only picked up the notions of "cheap and costly grace," which found their way into his most famous book, but he also learned and embraced a musical metaphor that was to later blend into theology and ethics.

As a classical pianist, it is likely that Bonhoeffer was already acquainted with the term "polyphony." Yet in Harlem within the context of the improvisation of jazz, the contingency of the blues and the rhythms of gospel music, the profound meaning of

[45] For a more complete account of the aesthetic turn in Bonhoeffer's thought see my, "First We Take Manhattan, Then We Take Berlin: Bonhoeffer's New York," in *Cross Currents* 50 (Fall 2000) 369-382.

polyphony came alive for Bonhoeffer as an aesthetic reality and later even as a theological metaphor. A *polyphony* is not a neat harmony or even a traditional symphony but a rather complicated musical piece in which two or more very *different* melodies come together in a satisfying way. To ears trained in the integrity, harmony and clarity of Wagner's symphonies, the new Negro art, literature and music of Harlem must have first seemed as disharmonious and disruptive as a Nietzschean prophetic aphorism. But it gradually came together for Bonhoeffer and helped form and inform his ethics of resistance to fascist totalitarianism.

The move from a moral (*Nachfolge*) to a musical (polyphony) metaphor for theology and ethics is seen in the evolution of Bonhoeffer's work and life. He had become a rather committed pacifist as he struggled with the call and cost of discipleship or *Nachfolge* — following after the peaceful way of Jesus. Yet the terrors of history and his emerging aesthetic approach to understanding and action led to his growing sense that "Jesus was a man for others," not simply the Christ of the church, and to his active involvement in a plot to kill Adolf Hitler. I would suggest that we see in Bonhoeffer's thought an openness to aesthetic innovation. He spoke of the situation in his country under Hitler as a time of both "black storm-cloud and brilliant lightening-flash," a time in which "reality lays itself bare." He wrote that, "Shakespeare's characters walk in our midst ... They emerge from primeval depths and by their appearance they tear open the infernal or divine abyss from which they come and enable us to see for a moment into mysteries of which we had never dreamed."[46]

At a time with reality laid bare and saints and villains from the divine or infernal abyss playing their parts in the dramas of history, Bonhoeffer concluded, "What is worse than doing evil is being

---

[46] Dietrich Bonhoeffer, *Ethics*, trans. Neville Horton Smith (New York: Macmillan, 1963) 64-65.

evil. It is worse for a liar to tell the truth than a lover of the truth to lie."[47] With such an insight written in his notebook "on ethics," Bonhoeffer gave himself to the secret plan to assassinate Hitler. He was never able to complete his improvisational *Ethics*. He was imprisoned and hanged by the Nazis at Flossenberg Concentration Camp at the age of thirty-nine only days before its liberation by the Allied Forces.

I am interested in the Bonhoeffer story because of this notion of an artful innovation of the ethical and because of its great, and I would add "beautiful," virtue. But my interests are also quite personal. Several of the young men in my family's Ohio Anabaptist congregation put on the military uniform, in violation of churchly ethics and the pacifist politics of Jesus, during the Second World War. My father flew American B-24 Liberators in bombing missions over the Reich and his younger brother, the artist and intellectual of the Holland family, for whom I was named, fell in Germany late in the war during the Allied push to liberate the camps. A German sniper's bullet took him down. According to family stories, my fallen uncle insisted that his decision to transgress our church's understanding of the teachings (ethics) of Biblical pacifism had "more to do with his art than ethics." Ethics as rules, principles, and fidelity to the inscribed Word would have prevented his aesthetic innovation in belief and behavior on behalf of the other during that horrific period of Holocaust when Shakespeare's characters returned to walk the earth, demanding a dramatic response. The accent on art rather than ethics was able to address life's binary oppositions and polyphonies in the difficult quest for a "fearful symmetry."

Interestingly, both David Tracy and Paul Ricœur approach this kind of aesthetic understanding in some of their more marginal remarks. Tracy does include the manifestive power of classic persons

---

[47] *Ibid.*

or characters and the witness of their lives in his list of the "classics." He has suggested that just as a hermeneutical theologian like Gerhard Ebeling can interpret the Protestant Reformation as a "Word-Event," in a similar manner the Catholic hermeneutical theologian can interpret the Catholic Reformation as an "Image-Event." Tracy writes, "My own belief is that the classics of Catholicism in the Tridentine and immediately post-Tridentine period are less likely to be found in the explicitly theological works of the period than in the works of art and the use of imagery in spirituality (recall Ignatius of Loyola's innovations here and Trent's decree on images) and in the manifestive power of classic persons, the extraordinary saints and mystics of the sixteenth and seventeenth centuries."[48] Tracy believes that the developers and commentators on the Scholasticism of the period were indeed impressive Catholic theologians, but in his view far less expressive of the religious manifestation orientation of Catholic Christianity than were the classic saints and artists of the period.

The fine book of Catholic theologian William Thompson, *Fire and Light: The Saints and Theology*, models this method of doing theology in conversation with the classic witness of lives well lived, indeed, it is an example of theology done in communion with the saints.[49] Paul Ricœur, in a recent series of autobiographical interviews, has likewise reflected upon the aesthetics of testimony or how the beauty of a life witness might manifest a reciprocal relationship between ethics and aesthetics.[50]

---

[48] David Tracy, *The Analogical Imagination*, 222, note 27.

[49] William M. Thompson, *Fire and Light: The Saints and Theology* (New York: Paulist Press, 1987).

[50] Paul Ricœur, trans. by Kathleen Blamey, *Critique and Conviction: Conversations with Francois Azouvi and Marc de Launay* (New York: Columbia University Press, 1998).

Ricœur begins this reflection on testimony by first considering art proper. He is interested in the possible universality of a work of art beyond its fidelity to what might be considered formal rules of composition. He argues that the "universality" to which great art aspires is possible only "through the intermediary of its extreme singularity." He uses the example of nonfigurative painting in modern art to make the point. He suggests that it is truly the nakedness of the singular experience that is communicated without the mediation of rules susceptible to being recognized within a tradition and without the elements of normativity that nevertheless allows this art it to touch something more general in the human imagination, even as it breaks the "weak" rules of generality. Ricœur believes this aesthetic principle applies to both nonfigurative and figurative art. He writes:

> This is why I think that, already in figurative art, the beauty of a given work, the success of a given portrait belonged not to the quality of representation, not to the fact that it resembled a model, not even to its conforming to allegedly universal rules, but to a *surplus* in relation to any representation and to any rule; the work could represent an object or a face with close resemblance, it could agree upon rules agreed upon in advance, but if it deserves to figure today in our imaginary museum, it is because *in surplus* it is perfectly matched up to its genuine object, which was not the fruit bowl or the face of the young girl in the turban but the singular grasp of Cezanne or Vermeer of the singular question posed to them.[51]

Ricœur believes this same aesthetic principle can be transported into the realm of human action or ethics as one considers the art of testimony. He suggests that like works of art, "persons are also single conjunctions — a face in which features are assembled in a single manner, a single time; like works, they cannot be substituted for one another."[52]

[51] *Ibid.*, 181.
[52] *Ibid.*, 182.

As Ricœur moves from art to ethics, he suggests that the work of art with its conjunction of singularity and communicability can be a model for thinking about a poetics of testimony. He argues that apart from predictable rules, a beauty emerges specific to the acts we admire in a life well lived. He has in mind the particularity of testimony given by exemplary lives. Ricœur contends that these testimonies speak "by a sort of short circuit to the absolute, to the fundamental, without there being any need for them to pass through the interminable degrees of our laborious ascensions; [to] see the beauty of certain devoted, or as we say, consecrated, faces."[53]

Paul Ricœur does in fact have specific examples in mind about the art of testimony. He has in mind the many faces of testimony that resisted Nazi totalitarianism and murder. He notes, for example, the men and women whose testimonies Marek Halter collected in his film *Tseddek*. When asked why they broke the law, violated inherited moral principles (from telling lies to plotting violence) and risked their lives to rescue Jews, their answers are lovely in their singularity, "What else could we do? It was the only thing to do in that situation." Ricœur suggests that even as a painter is solving a particular problem he is confronting, he and he alone, so the actions of those who resisted Fascism manifest a parallel art. He observes, "And from the solitude of the sublime act we are led directly to its communicability by a prereflective grasp of its relation of agreement with the situation: in this given case, here and now, we are certain that *this* is exactly what had to be done, in the same way that we consider a given painting to be a masterpiece because right away we have the feeling that it realizes the perfect adequation of the singularity of solution to the singularity of the question."[54]

---

[53] *Ibid.*
[54] *Ibid.*

For Ricœur, in this context, this focus on the solitary decision, the sublime act, the singularity of the testimony and the reality of the face, one's own face and the face of the other, invites him to use the language of aesthetics on the way to a more profound ethics. In fact, could one not also make the case that even in the fiercely ethical system of a philosopher like Emmanuel Levinas, because of his brilliant and beautiful attention to "the face," we have an ethics that is likewise called into being, indeed beyond being, by a more primordial and primary aesthetics?[55] This question must await a further study. For now, let us move from this consideration of aesthetics, ethics and the imagination to a brief examination of ritual and the imagination.

RITUAL AND THE IMAGINATION

In his book, *Deeply into the Bone*, Ronald Grimes offers his most comprehensive cross cultural study of how rites and rituals facilitate the difficult passages in a human life. He has chosen the title because his lifelong study has convinced him that ritual lodges in the bone, in its very marrow.[56] The metaphorical title struck him when an archaeologist was explaining to him at a dig how certain

[55] Emmanuel Levinas, trans. by Alphonso Lingis, *Totality and Infinity: An Essay on Exteriority* (Pittsburgh, PA: Duquesne University Press, 1961). Levinas was certainly rightly suspicious of an aesthetics inspired by the Heideggerian poetics of philosophy. Yet he did value poets such as Paul Celan whose imaginations disclosed a being present to and for the other. In fact, Celan's poetics, presented in his Buchner Prize acceptance speech, only recently published as *Der Meridian*, in many ways parallels the philosophy of Levinas. For Celan, a poem is lonely and in motion, moving towards the other, whom or which the poem requires for its existence. Paul Celan, *Der Meridan* (Frankfurt: Suhrkamp, 2000).

[56] Ronald L. Grimes, *Deeply into the Bone: Reinventing Rites of Passage* (Berkeley, CA: University of California Press, 2000).

values and social practices can be inferred from bone matter. For example, by studying bone composition an archaeologist can deduce that the men of a particular society consumed more protein than the women. Likewise, by studying bone shape, size and structure it can be concluded that women in some cultures did more physically demanding work than men. Archaeologists have learned that social practices and values are literally inscribed in the bones. Grimes makes the point that "even though we tend to imagine bone as private, and deeply interior to the individual body, it is also socially formed."[57]

The same is true, metaphorically, about ritual. Ritual, according to Grimes, is inscribed in our bones. Social practices and values carried in ritual are as much a part of our human constitution as the marrow of our bones and our body's lifeblood. Following and extending his previous work in ritual case studies, Grimes illustrates that "ritual, like art, is the child of the imagination, but the ritual imagination requires an invention, a constantly renewed structure, on the basis of which a bodily and communal enactment is possible."[58] Grimes explains that unlike some other expressions of human creativity or imagination, ritual imagining cannot stay in the head and heart but must be embodied and performed socially. However, the many ritual case studies of Ronald Grimes also demonstrate that if rituals are not to become empty rites and dead metaphors, the process and performance of imagination and innovation must never cease. Since rituals go deep into the bone, they must live and breathe and grow and change with all that is the human.

This new book by Grimes also highlights the dramatic increase of interest in ritual in the past decade or so, both in the academy and in society. Both professionally and personally, many want to

[57] *Ibid.*, 4.
[58] *Ibid.*

reconsider the meanings conveyed and composed in ritual and related expressions of human performance and practice. Grimes notes that this interest is not only theoretical but also practical, even spiritual.

On a recent trip to France, I was prepared to talk with my university hosts at Strasbourg about Derridian deconstruction and other textual matters that I considered proper for educated conversation in France. My hosts told me that Derrida is much more popular in America than in France and that there, "Pierre Bourdieu is the rage!" When I asked why, I was told, "Because he works with real sociology, real anthropology, real practice."

Bourdieu is a sociologist and his work, *The Logic of Practice* and other related studies, draws from his own fieldwork and from many ethnographic, sociological and anthropological studies.[59] He is especially critical of what he terms, "scholastic reason." This is not to be simply equated with Scholasticism proper, although it is not unrelated. Bourdieu argues that scholastic thought, which can be roughly translated as "academic thought" or highly theoretical thought, tends to become detached from the logic of practice in the social and historical world. His work outlines three forms of what he calls "the scholastic fallacy."[60] First, Bourdieu argues that practical reason is collapsed into theoretical reason leading scholars, especially philosophers, to neglect the "embedded and embodied logic of practice." Second, this form of reasoning displays certain temptations toward the universalizing of ethics and thus tends to suppress the social, political and economic conditions of access and thus exclude those who are deprived of the means of realizing such a "universal." Third, Bourdieu insists that scholastic reason

[59] Pierrie Bourdieu, *The Logic of Practice* (Stanford, CA: Stanford University Press, 1980).

[60] Pierrie Bourdieu, *Pascalian Meditations* (Stanford, CA: Stanford University Press, 1997).

overlooks the extent to which both ethical and aesthetic judgments are rooted in and emerge from historical and cultural fields, not from theoretical texts.

My European university hosts suggested that perhaps, at least on the Continent, the once celebrated movement from existentialism to language philosophy, the great "linguistic turn," neglected the body and society as texts. "The social sciences are returning to philosophy," my hosts gladly reported. I was happy to report that the social sciences are back in theology.

Nathan Mitchell at the University of Notre Dame is doing some of the finest work in the country of bringing the social sciences — sociology, anthropology and ritual studies — into conversation with theology, especially liturgical and sacramental theology. Before I make some more explicit remarks about imagination and ritual, it seems in order to at least summarize what Mitchell is teaching us about ritual and its relationship to theology. Mitchell's work considers what is both a "prevailing consensus" in ritual studies and also what is becoming a new category in the study of ritual, "emerging ritual," which is really a look at ritual expression in our postmodern, pluralistic age.[61] First let me list verbatim Mitchell's summary of the "prevailing consensus:"

- Ritual is neither an obsessive neurosis nor an artificial construct imposed on life from the outsider; rather, ritual is expressive, formalized, traditional, authoritative, nonutilitarian, symbolic, invariable, repeatable behavior whose remote roots are closely linked to the ontogenetic development of the human person.
- Although individuals may engage in idiosyncratic "rituals" of their own devising, the term is best reserved for actions that are public, social and collective (rather than strictly personal or private) in nature.

---

[61] Nathan D. Mitchell, *Liturgy and the Social Sciences* (Collegeville, MN: The Liturgical Press, 1999).

- Ritual embodies and transmits vital cultural information and processes (meanings, values, categories, classifications, contradictions) that support the collective identity and social cohesion of participants.
- Ritual does not merely enforce already existing symbols and social structures: it may also generate or promote the emergence of new, transformative structures.
- Ritual is often (but not only) linked to social transitions (to rites of passage or life-crisis events).
- While its primary intention is to promote social cohesion and identity, ritual may sometimes encourage or legitimate social change and adaptation.
- Rituals preserve and represent archaic acts, ancestral memories and so provide access to the historic past — hence, a community without rituals is a community without memory.
- A ritual's power is rooted in repetition and familiarity rather than unexpected novelty or innovation.
- Rituals are rehearsals both of who a community is (in its present life) and what it means to become (in its eschatological future).
- Ritual orders and regulates social life, and thus it characteristically resists radical change, experimentation or improvisation.[62]

Nathan Mitchell explains that the above list is his summary of the classic consensus among scholars of what ritual is and what ritual does. However, Mitchell also explains that in our postmodern, pluralistic age we are seeing a new category of "emerging ritual." Ritual specialists such as Victor Turner and Ronald Grimes have given much attention to emerging ritual beyond the classic consensus. What is emerging ritual? Let us again follow the careful and concise work of Mitchell:

Rituals grow more elaborate — not less so — as cultures become more complex and diverse. Mitchell notes that in multicultural societies like the United States, family affiliation is chosen rather than

---

[62] *Ibid.*, 25.

imposed. Genetics and ethnicity alone do not determine the social or ritual significance of kinship. Thus, looser seasonal or life-cycle rites (Thanksgiving dinner or the celebration of Grandmother's birthday, for example) become the essential means of creating bonds among extended family members. Mitchell observes that such rituals and rites can indeed be elaborate.

Rituals create and confirm membership in a group (e.g., a family). They may thus generate social solidarity even in the absence of a shared belief. Mitchell illustrates this by pointing to the celebration of the Passover seder in Jewish families and the Christmas dinner and exchange of gifts in Christian families. Many American Jews celebrate the traditional seder with their families, even if all around the table do not agree on the religious meaning of the ritual. Likewise, many who gather ritually with their Christian families on December 25th may or may not share a belief in the mystery of the incarnation but ordinary life is nevertheless transfigured into something deeper and more magical or hopeful in these focused events. Mitchell contends that "in the absence of shared beliefs, ritual may be more important, not less so."[63]

Rituals encourage us to interpret and enact reality in very specific ways. Here Mitchell uses the example of the sense of ritual place and placement of furniture as well as characters at a formal dinner. For example, the hosts preside in the "presidency chairs," the guests practice social graces perhaps more deliberate or exaggerated than around their own kitchen tables. There is a certain social script that is followed even in the midst of friendly and comfortable social discourse. Mitchell's argument is that we interpret and perform many dimensions of our social lives in the rubrics of ritual. The notion of social drama is essential to understanding how ritual works in groups of people.

---

[63] *Ibid.*, 39.

Rituals link smaller groups (e.g. families) to larger ethnic or cultural ones. In short, what Mitchell is suggesting here is that the rites and rituals that provide family identity (ways of talking and relating around a meal, for example) are not separate from more public rites that help provide ethnic and cultural identities.

Religious rituals are the products of family rites — not vice versa. Mitchell builds upon the previous point and reminds us that many anthropologists, following Freud, surmise that the first "religious" ritual may have been a family dinner. He contends that *theological* and *sacerdotal* interpretations of secular rites emerged *later*, when the need arose to justify existing social arrangements by linking the historical present to a sacred past. "The family celebration came first; the theological rationale followed"[64]

Rituals may be potent vehicles for social change. Nathan Mitchell's program is most interested, it seems, in the way rituals become innovative, imaginative vehicles for social change and even transformation. This can be the case, Mitchell insists, even when the rituals do not represent a clear, shared belief or the general consensus of a community. It is here that Mitchell — following Grimes and the later work of Turner — departs somewhat from the classic consensus of linking rituals to their specific cultural-linguistic communities of origin. He uses the example of Martin Luther King's leadership in the civil rights movement and the amazing "ritual potency" embodied there. He notes how on the streets of Selma to the Washington Mall in front of the Lincoln Memorial, in ritual and hopeful rhetoric, whites and blacks, Protestants, Catholics and Jews, the religious and the not so religious joined in enacting a movement of solidarity leading to the landmark civil rights legislation of 1965. King's intuitive and imaginative use of "emerging ritual" did not require participants to hold a specific religious affiliation

---

[64] *Ibid.*, 41.

or communal membership yet he was profoundly effective in offi-
ciating over "public rituals" leading to social transformation.
Therefore, Mitchell posits, ritual potency does not necessarily
derive from a structured belief system, a unified narrative, or a
bounded cultural-linguistic community.

Nathan Mitchell concludes that ritual is coming to be viewed
more and more as a fully cultural, historical and embodied process.
As such, it is characterized by a remarkable amount of inventive-
ness, innovation, creativity, change and variability. *It is a process
and product of the imagination.* At this point a few more comments
on ritual and the theological imagination are in order.

Gordon Kaufman's book on theological method begins with a
wonderful quotation from George Bernard Shaw's play *Saint
Joan.*[65] Joan of Arc insists, "I hear voices telling me what to do.
They come from God." Baudricourt scoffs, "They come from your
imagination!" Joans responds, "Of course. That is how the mes-
sages of God come to us." Like David Tracy, Kaufman locates theology in the productive imagination. I cite both Kaufman and Tracy
together here because they have both been so influential in my own
intellectual development. In my contribution to a *Festschrift* for
Gordon Kaufman, I recall how as a very young pastor in Pittsburgh
I had almost lost interest in "academic, scribal theology."[66] It was
putting my mind and soul to sleep. I was preaching and minister-
ing under a heavy "Barthian and biblical burden." Then, in 1981,
I walked from my chaplain's office on the campus of the University of Pittsburgh to the Pitt Book Store and ordered two new
books: Tracy's *The Analogical Imagination* and Kaufman's *The*

---

[65] Gordon D. Kaufman, *An Essay on Theological Method* (Missoula, MT:
Scholars Press for the AAR, 1975). See the epigraph page before the Introduction.

[66] See my "Einsbildungskraft: The Power to Form into One," *Mennonite Theology in Face of Modernity: Essays in Honor of Gordon Kaufman,* ed. Alain Epp
Weaver (Newton, Kansas: Mennonite Press, 1996) 244-254.

Theological Imagination.[67] Both books, although quite different from one another in tone and method gave me a passion for the imaginative possibilities of God-talk.

The late Father Edward Murray of Duquesne University gave much of his scholarly attention to the phenomenology of the human imagination. He often turned to the German word for imagination to more fully define and discuss its integrative function: *Einbildungskraft*, literally, "the power to see or form into one." As a phenomenological psychologist, Murray accented imagination's "unity-building power within the person."[68] As we saw in the previous chapter, George Worgul's important, interdisciplinary work in sacramental theology likewise views imagination as the unity-building power within the human person actively seeking and composing connection, convergence, communion, intimacy and integration with the whole of reality. With David Tracy, Worgul agrees that imagination, above all else, defines the human. In fact, even as Kaufman and Tracy led me to a deeper understanding of the imagination and God-talk, Worgul led me to a new and transformative understanding of theology and God-practice in and through ritual.

Since we have already considered at length Worgul's satisfying theology and theory of how the imagination leads to the apprehension and attainment of real presence in ritual performance within a gathered community we will not review that work here. However, let me return to Worgul's claim that, "Every practical

---

[67] Gordon Kaufman, *The Theological Imagination: Constructing the Concept of God* (Philadelphia, PA: Westminster Press, 1981). In recent years I have found the work of Richard Kearney on the imagination quite helpful. See both his *Poetics of Modernity: Toward A Hermeneutic Imagination* (New Jersey: Humanities Press, 1995) and *Poetics of Imagining: Modern to Post-modern* (New York: Fordham University Press, 1998).

[68] Edward L. Murray, *Imaginative Thinking and Human Existence* (Pittsburgh, PA: Duquesne University Press, 1986) 62.

presence of a reality or a person is at the same time analogically a presence of the whole." While some postmodern critics would certainly charge that such a claim is hopelessly Romantic, it is important to recognize that the work of Worgul is addressing *every practical presence of a reality or person.* This includes not only experiences or expressions of desire and bliss, but also the realities of death and suffering. Indeed, according to Worgul, this claim is also about the inescapable reality and presence of "hard times." He argues that binary oppositions are "the stuff of life." Life, even life lived imaginatively in a sacramental universe, is about "hard times."[69] The dance of light-darkness, life-death, holy-profane, self-other, joy-sorrow, hope and despair truly define the human experience. In the language of this study, this returns us again to David Tracy's emphasis on both the analogical and dialectical movements of the imagination.

The theological imagination is no stranger to these binary oppositions of life. In fact, the theologian believes these tensions find resolution, redemption and transformation (never elimination) through the diverse practices of the faith community. Indeed, the sacramental imagination knows Eucharist to signify not only thanksgiving and real presence, but also the trace of torture and the cry of absence: *Eli, Eli, lema sabachthani?* We will explore this as we turn now to sacramental theology and the imagination.

SACRAMENTAL THEOLOGY AND THE IMAGINATION

As we have seen in this study, David Tracy's hopeful, analogical imagination is able to declare that we live in a sacramental universe.

---

[69] For Worgul's own treatment of how ritual works using the case study of a funeral see his, "Death, Sacraments, and Christianity Spirituality," *Studies in Formative Spirituality* 2 (1981) 231-246.

Although such a vision of a world of grace and a natural theology is evident in theologians from Irenaeus to Karl Rahner, it seems that it was first used boldly and explicitly by Archbishop William Temple in his Gifford Lectures.[70] Anglican scholars have speculated that Temple gleaned the imagery and language of a "sacramental universe" from one of his long departed brother priests, George Herbert. Herbert's poems and hymns spoke of the material world as an outward and visible sign of an immanent and transcendent grace. Other great poets dear to Temple presented a parallel vision of creation. Consider Elizabeth Barrett Browning:

> Earth's crammed with heaven,
> And every common bush afire with God;
> But only he who sees takes off his shoes,
> The rest sit round and pluck blackberries.[71]

William Temple's Gifford Lectures celebrated the goodness and grace of an earth crammed with heaven, a *sacramental universe* in his words.[72]

As Temple was preparing his lectures the year was 1939. Continental theology, in his view, was too dominated by Karl Barth's dialectical theology of the Word-Event. His bold declaration of creation as "a sacramental universe" sought to overcome the Barthian exaggerated stress on God's transcendence. Temple was interested in a greater accent on the immanence of God and thus on the possibility of a natural theology, which Barth of course resisted. He

---

[70] See John Macquarrie, *A Guide to the Sacraments* (New York: Continuum, 1997) 1-11. Temple's Gifford Lectures were published under the title, *Nature, Man and God* (London: Macmillan, 1940).

[71] Cited in Macquarrie, *A Guide to the Sacraments*, 8.

[72] For a good discussion of the emergence of the notion of world and sacrament or sacramental universe see Geoffrey Wainwright: *Worship with One Accord: Where Liturgy and Ecumenism Meet* (New York: Oxford University Press, 1997) 85-104.

attempted to balance transcendence and immanence or we might say dialectics and analogy when he began his lecture on "The Sacramental Universe" with this explanation: "Our argument has led us to the belief in a living God who, because he is such, is *transcendent* over the universe, which owes its origin to his creative act, and which he sustains by his *immanence* in it."[73]

Archbishop Temple compared God to an artist to further illustrate his understanding of God's relationship to the world. Even as an artist transcends his or her work, so God transcends the creation. Nevertheless, the artist has poured his or her creativity, energy and genius into the work and through the work we can know something of the artist. The artist is not his work but his imprint or presence is certainly there. Likewise, God is the artist who is both in yet beyond and above the creation. Because of this understanding of creation, which is further validated and affirmed in the Incarnation, Temple proclaimed that "Christianity is the most avowedly materialistic of all the great religions."[74]

The material, worldly and bodily importance of theology has likewise been affirmed by many great modern and postmodern sacramental theologians since Temple. Within the past two years I have attended the lectures of three internationally recognized sacramental theologians, each of whom emphasized both the materiality or corporeality of theology and its artfulness or reliance on the imagination. I can only note their projects here. They are Louis-Marie Chauvet, Jean-Luc Marion, and David Power. Both Chauvet and Marion would be considered postmodern in their approach to sacramental theology and Power is a contemporary sacramental theologian in conversation with the best from the classical, modern and postmodern sources of thought and practice.

[73] *Ibid.*, 7.
[74] *Ibid.*, 6.

Louis-Marie Chauvet moves from metaphysics to what he terms the symbolic.[75] He views the entire order of salvation from the perspective of the "symbolic" of sacramental practice. He uses the category of symbolic rather than symbol to avoid the temptation of taking any symbol as an adequate expression of the divine or the desire to elevate the symbol itself above the one who comes to humanity in and through the symbolic. There is both an intimacy and a distanciation in the symbolic, an immanence and a transcendence, an analogy and a dialectic. The symbolic imagination for Chauvet is an embodied imagination. It looks to what he identifies as a symbolic articulation (*symbole* = articulation) in and through at least four "bodies": the individual body as the story of the person's desires, the ancestral body of tradition, a social body of culture and a cosmic body of nature. As one considers the work of Chauvet, although his arguments are often thick and theoretical, one could make the case that the closet analogue to his sacramental theology, funded as it is by the symbolic, is art. It is an art that blends theology, philosophy and the social sciences in an articulation of sacramental presence.

However, because of his engagement with postmodernism in the way that a preceding generation of Catholic theologians engaged existentialism, Chauvet does bring deconstruction's language of "the trace" into his project. To avoid the notion of any reified language of representation, Chauvet explains that God acts in time but what is left is a mere trace of divine action. Continuing in the genre of postmodern thought, Chauvet asserts that working from the traces the church "writes itself" through its preaching, theology, ritual and ethics. At this reading, this seems to be an unfortunate

---

[75] Louis-Marie Chauvet, *Symbol and Sacrament: A Sacramental Reinterpretation of Christian Existence*, trans. Patrick Madigan, S.J., and Madeleine Beaumont (Collegeville, MN: The Liturgical Press, 1995).

concession to the colonizing and all too correct anti-representational rhetoric of deconstructionism. One must ask, if the classical language of symbol and metaphor — presence and absence, is and is not, immanence and transcendence — is not a more linguistically robust and truly embodied way of rendering God's name in history. Further, Chauvet's emphasis on God's acts in time and narrative, at this reading, seriously neglects a strong articulation of the possibility of God's epiphany in space.

This study has been arguing that every story *takes place*. Narratives happen some*where* and in some*body* as well as some*time*. In the sacramental imagination, the earth is not merely crammed with stories of heaven. Stories of the burning bush and traces of an ancient but now extinguished flame, traced only in the telling of the tale, will move few to take off their shoes. At this reading, Chauvet's use of the symbolic is far too Protestant in its limit-language and fails to consider the ways in which even the postmodern story has a body. A critic might protest, "Certainly you are not suggesting that common bushes are *really* ablaze with the presence of God?" A careful reader of this study will understand why I must answer, "Yes!"

In the same manner as Chauvet, the highly philosophical work of Jean-Luc Marion engages postmodern thought. Marion's work relative to sacramental theology is far too rich and complex to adequately summarize here.[76] I cite Marion, however, because David Power has characterized his entire project as "an aesthetics of love."[77] Marion moves beyond metaphysics and beyond the category of Being in his naming of God. He fears that such language

---

[76] Jean-Luc Marion, *God Without Being*, trans. Thomas Carlson (Chicago, IL: University of Chicago, 1991).

[77] David N. Power, O.M.I., "Sacramental Theology: A Review of the Literature," *Theological Studies* 55 (1994) 688-689.

risks idolatry by fixing the divine in systems of human perception. His project relies on an ongoing openness to "the iconic." For Marion, the "iconic" of divine Love, never an idol of mere Being or human perception, is revealed as *agape*, as gift, incarnate in the Word and embodied in Church in the central and primary hermeneutic site of the Eucharist. In Marion's theology, the *sacramentum* — *mysterion* — mystery of the Eucharist becomes the hermeneutic site for the interpretation of revelation. Much more could be said about this "aesthetics of love," but it does indeed suggest much not only about the gift of the divine sacrament but also about the artful, iconic human imagination.

Finally, the recent work of sacramental theologian David Power follows the interdisciplinary approach of earlier, influential studies such as the work of George Worgul. Power blends the research of traditional and contemporary theology, the behavioral sciences, narrative study and ritual study in his hermeneutics of "sacrament as the language of God's giving."[78] Power demonstrates that one must utilize all "languages" in approaching the divine and in articulating a theology of God, self, other and world: careful and creative verbal, textual language of course, but also the "language" of bodily performance in ritual. As Power writes of the sacramental imagination, he turns to the language of poetic possibility and the "projection of life into the world." Citing with pleasure his fellow countryman Seamus Heaney's Nobel Lecture, Power highlights the movement of the poetic imagination.

Heaney writes that poetic language has a "double adequacy."[79] It has an ability to address the harsh, historical realities of life as

---

[78] David N. Power, *Sacrament: The Language of God's Giving* (New York: Crossroad Publishing Company, 1999).

[79] *Ibid.*, 63. See Seamus Heaney, *Crediting Poetry: The Nobel Lecture* (New York: Farrar, Straus & Grioux, 1995).

it is lived. To this end it is adequate. Yet it also has an adequacy to what is larger and greater and truer than what factually is. It is the projection of life into the world. This movement of the poetic imagination not only illuminates the hard times of the human, historical situation, but also helps resolve their tensions and even transform their possibilities. In this way the poetic and the sacramental imaginations are quite parallel.

This chapter has been extending the claim through case studies, theory and theology that was made earlier in this study: in the evolution of the primal imagination, art, ritual and religion were coextensive with the invention of language and thus with culture. Thus, we should not be surprised that in the best examples of sacramental theology, art and ritual not only appear as essential expressions of religious consciousness, indeed, they join the Word made flesh and embrace and kiss on the holy altar. I began this chapter with two case studies. I would like to conclude with some reflections on a case study that takes us to the place Marion contends is the primary hermeneutic site for understanding the holy in history: the Eucharist.

Across North America, in this season of economic boom and relative optimism, Catholic priests and Protestant ministers, following the instructions of their respective denominations' offices for liturgy, are reminded to not merely officiate at Communion or Eucharist but to truly "celebrate it!" Although the word "celebrate" is indeed a rich concept, the current advice from these liturgical offices tends to accent celebration as the festive, joyful invitation to come freely to a banquet of love and there eat and drink the gift of God's grace and generosity. Perhaps reacting against an excessive historic emphasis in some communions on the memory of a suffering savior or on a meal marked by bloody sacrifice, in these good times the contemporary emphasis on the festivity and feast of love is understandable. Priests, preachers, and parishioners leave the bounty of the Lord's Table and return home blessed to full tables of their own. This accent on positive presence seeks to fill all empty spaces with only the finest bread and wine. As a modern American cleric, I too have carried this spirit of great analogical optimism to the Table. Yet a guest Salvadorian pastor and theologian at my seminary this year tells a different story of a Eucharistic celebration. It is a story that has become a contemporary classic in the theological imaginations of both Catholics and Protestants in his country.[80]

Pastor Miguel Thomas Castro tells this story. A priest stands at the altar in a small chapel in the company of only a few worshippers. He blesses and elevates the host and then blesses and raises the cup. The presence of God, grace, gift and love are signified and celebrated but a gun shot breaks the silence. The chief liturgist of El Salvador falls and the blood of Christ mingles with his own at the altar signifying terror, torture, absence and death. Archbishop Oscar Romero was murdered. The cry of absence, "My God, my God, why have you forsaken me?" was on the lips of many who loved the bishop that dark day. The Reverend Castro insists that this too must be understood as the story of Communion. He reports that in Salvador this classic story or root metaphor of the sacrament in current history and of a contemporary saintly life is now celebrated by Catholics and Protestants alike as "The Feast of Oscar Romero." Castro reports that the many binary oppositions of life — suffering

---

[80] Miguel Thomas Castro is a Baptist pastor and theologian from San Salvador who took his sabbatical leave in 2000-2001 at Bethany Theological Seminary and Earlham School of Religion. He is at work on a book about "the contemporary martyrs of El Salvador." I am indebted to the Revered Castro for some of these reflections on Archbishop Oscar Romero. I am also indebted to an excellent article on Romero by liturgical theologian Rowena Hill, "Poured Out for You: Liturgy and Justice in the Life of Archbishop Romero," *Worship* 74 (2000) 414-432.

and celebration, death and desire, absence and presence, oppression and liberation, despair and hope — are addressed in this narrative and ritual commemoration and celebration of the co-mingling of Christ's blood and the Bishop's blood on the altar. This signifies, according to Castro and other Salvadorian theologians, the link between the church's liturgy and social justice.

Much could be said about this and happily many fine studies linking the liturgy and the performance of public ethics or social justice are now in progress or have been recently been published. This is important because the link is almost absent in earlier theological reflections.[81] For example, the papal encyclicals addressing social justice such as *Rerum Novarum* and *Centesimus Annus* do nothing to unite the questions of social justice with liturgy and the sacraments. Protestants have likewise neglected this interconnection. However, those who view the very well done film *Romero*, or study the Archbishop's life and writings, will see that his death at the altar was not lightly coincidental; there was an inseparable link between his office as chief liturgist in Salvador and his passionate commitment to the poor, the oppressed, the marginalized and the persecuted. He became a voice for the voiceless.

His Eucharistic liturgies were as threatening to the politics of injustice as his public pronouncements on social justice. This is not because he politicized the sacraments. He did not. In fact, he carefully guarded his liturgies from any ideological captivity, whether to the right or the left and was at times criticized by some liberation theologians for not bringing more explicit political pronouncements into the liturgy and celebration of the sacraments.

---

[81] In addition to Hill's study cited above, see James R. Brockman, *Romero: A Life* (Maryknoll, NY: Orbis Books, 1989). The most provocative and engaging book on the relationship of worship to social justice I have read is William T. Cavanaugh's *Torture and Eucharist: Theology, Politics and the Body of Christ* (Oxford: Blackwell Publishers, 1998).

It seems that Oscar Romero understood well that the Christian faith, even in times of great social, cultural and political distress, is not a mere ideology for social ethics, but is rather *a doxology against all idolatry*, even the idols of ethics and political action. Romero understood that the rich symbolism of the Christian faith contained a surplus capable addressing matters "political" without bringing partisan or ideological politics proper into the poetics of worship. His theological imagination resisted both political and spiritual reductionism. He wrote, "In our circumstances this danger of reductionism as far as evangelism is concerned can take two forms. Either it can stress only the transcendent elements of spirituality and human destiny, or it can go to the other extreme, selecting only those immanent elements of a kingdom of God that ought to be already beginning on this earth."[82] Doxology invites and inspires both analogical and dialectical movements of the imagination.

Doxology also both consoles and transforms. Romero understood that something happens in the ritual performance of the Eucharist that transcends mere ethical, political or doctrinal instruction. This was apparent in his funeral mass of a priest and four young boys who joined the long list of contemporary martyrs in El Salvador. As we know, Romero was passionately committed to human dignity and echoed in his life and work the classical affirmation, "*Gloria Dei, vivens homo* — the glory of God is the living person." He saw too much defacing of the living person in Salvador as they were stripped of their dignity, which for some even ended in a literal defacing and death. He wrote in his diaries how the National Guard not only murdered but often defaced or mutilated their victims. When his friend Father Octavio and four boys were killed at a Catholic retreat center in 1979, Bishop Romero discovered that

---

[82] Oscar Romero, *Voice of the Voiceless: The Four Pastoral Letters and Other Statements* (Maryknoll, NY: Orbis Books, 1985) 130.

he had been defaced, "Fr. Octavio's face was very disfigured; it looked like it had been run over and flattened by something heavy."[83]

The funeral mass celebrated by Bishop Romero presented the deaths of these five modern martyrs as mirrors of the Pascal Mystery celebrated in the Eucharist. He connected their deaths with the dangerous memory of the crucified God.[84] He presented them as witnesses to the crucifixion and resurrection of Jesus. Commenting on this service, liturgical theologian Rowena Hill writes:

> The deaths of these five people point to the meaning of the Mass and the Mass illuminates the significance of their deaths. No longer faceless, these corpses have become witnesses to the Pascal Mystery in which the Body of Christ participates in the Eucharist. At this funeral mass, bodies damaged and dishonored, are transformed into apostles of the joy of the resurrection. The suffering that they endured, and that their friends and relatives still endure, is in no way diminished, but by being placed into relationship with the suffering of Christ, theirs has gained meaning.[85]

In this way Romero understood both the consoling and transformative power of the sacrament of Eucharist.

In some of his writings Romero compares this transformative experience to the biblical narratives about transcendence and even transfiguration. Writing in a doxological manner of the theology

---

[83] Rowena Hill comments on this matter of defacing in El Salvador and the significance of Romero's attention to it. See "Poured Out for You," 416. See Oscar Romero, *Archbishop Oscar Romero: A Shepherd's Diary* (Cincinnati: St. Anthony Messenger Press, 1993) 131. Cited by Hill.

[84] In connecting the Eucharist to human suffering we see the strongest parallels in the Catholic theology of J. B. Metz cited earlier and in the Protestant theology of Jurgen Moltmann's *The Crucified God* (New York: Harper and Row, 1974). Metz and Moltmann together authored *Meditations on the Passion* (New York: Paulist Press, 1974).

[85] Hill, "Poured Out for You," 417.

underwriting the sacraments, the Bishop declares, "When we leave the Mass, we ought to go out the way Moses descended Mt. Sinai: with his face shining, with his heart brave and strong to face the world's difficulties."[86] Worship that invites the full range of the incarnate imagination transforms and transfigures, both one's own face, and how one then sees the face of the other. With these reflections on doxology before us, let us now bring this lengthy exploration of "how stories save us" to a conclusion as we consider with David Tracy why the theologian, in the attempt to name himself and the other as well as render God's name in history, should in fact pray.

[86] Oscar Romero, *The Church is All of You* (Minneapolis, MN: Winston Press, 1984) 86. Cited by Hill, "Poured Out for You," 417.

EPILOGUE: WHY THEOLOGIANS SHOULD PRAY

*It is not sufficient any longer to listen at the end of a wire to the
rustlings of the galaxies; it is not enough even to examine the
great coil of DNA in which is coded the very alphabet of life.
These are our extended perceptions. But beyond lies the great
darkness of the ultimate Dreamer, who dreamed the light and
the galaxies. Before act was, or substance existed, imagination
grew in the dark.*

Loren Eiseley

Is postmodernism at its best returning us to mystery and imagination? Is the deconstruction of the positivisms of science and logic opening even the skeptical mind to a new interest in deep symbols, spiritual metaphors and the revival of religion, indeed, in the return of God? Is the suspicion about the grand-narrative of Western thought returning us to the stories of God? Scholars of seventeenth-century literature, linguistics and rhetoric such as Stanley Fish and Ian Robinson have noted a shift in post-Reformation and Enlightenment writing from the passionate and speculative to the rational and didactic.[1] They suggest that passion, tragedy, ecstasy and great beauty became unfit subjects, too large and uncanny, for an emerging rational speech marked more by a smooth, systematic quest for logical organization than by the unruly thoughts and emotions of self-doubt and self-examination. With the new, enlightened rhetoric of science, commerce and scholarship some things entangled in

---

[1] Ian Robinson, *The Establishment of Modern English Prose in the Reformation and Enlightenment* (New York: Cambridge University Press, 1996); Stanley Fish, *Self-Consuming Artifacts: The Experience of Seventeenth-Century Literature* (Berkeley, CA: University of California Press, 1972).

transcendent mystery and the human imagination became impossible to articulate. Thus, the large and uncanny slices of life were either dismissed or domesticated by a prosaic discourse stripped of the deep symbols capable of carrying both tragedy and ecstasy. Yet, at least for some, the collapse of the grand narrative of modernism in its most reified forms — scientism and rationalism — is inviting a return of the ultimate Dreamer and the paradoxical truths of the imagination.

According to David Tracy, a separation of theology and spirituality really began in and certainly became more pronounced after medieval scholasticism and intensified even more with the advent of modern thought from the seventeenth century onward. Tracy is very uneasy with this split between theory and practice, and in an interview addressing the recent shifts in his own work, he calls for an end to the separation of theology and spirituality. This epilogue to the study will attempt to collect but never close many of the themes explored thus far by bringing them into conversation with three of Tracy's more recent, occasional pieces. All reflect his "large, unwritten God-book," and all appeared in *Cross Currents* journal.[2]

David Tracy confesses that the dilemmas of modernity itself and the postmodern turn or critique of modernity have led him to rethink the question of God. For the past decade he has been at work on a large manuscript on God which will likely be titled, *The Post-Modern Naming of God as Incomprehensible and Hidden.* This is not volume three of his projected trilogy of *Blessed Rage*

---

[2] David Tracy, "The Post-Modern Naming of God as Incomprehensible and Hidden," *Cross Currents* 50 (2000) 240-247. David Tracy, "The Hidden God: The Divine Other of Liberation," *Cross Currents* 46 (1996) 3-16. David Tracy, Todd Breyfogle and Thomas Livergood, "Conversation with David Tracy," *Cross Currents* 44 (1994) 293-316.

for Order, The Analogical Imagination, and a planned third volume on practical theology. Although a book on practical theology would seem like the next reasonable step for a thinker interested in closing the gap between theory and practice (after the detour of *Plurality and Ambiguity* to name the epistemological challenges of postmodernity and *Dialogue with the Other* to engage a central concern of postmodern thought: alterity). Why not now turn to practical theology or theological ethics? Yet Tracy sensed that he needed to first address the gap between theology and spirituality by returning to the question of God proper.

In entering this intellectual quest, Tracy is interested in recovering the spirit of Jean Leclercq's famous book, *The Love of Learning and the Desire for God*. Lecercq critiques the scholastic and especially neoscholastic tendency and temptation to split knowledge and desire, theory and praxis, and theology and spiritual practices.[3] Tracy worries that too much of contemporary academic theology — whether Catholic or Protestant — is really neoscholastic in style and substance because it is quite "modern," not postmodern or premodern. In its theoretical management of the mystical and through its polite, prosaic glosses over the prophetic it tames and tutors human agony and ecstasy as well as Divine terror and wonder. In these contemporary, scholastic approaches to theology, the *logos* of modernity seems tempted to domesticate the awful and awesome presence of *Theos*. Tracy is therefore interested in recovering classical and alternative traditions for rethinking the problem of God.

However, he insists that this project, this rethinking, this re-imagining, must follow a path that joins theory and practice. Pierre

---

[3] "Conversation with David Tracy," 296. See Jean Leclercq, *The Love of Learning and the Love for God: A Study of Monastic Culture* (New York: Fordham University Press, 1982).

Hadot in the College de France has alerted him to the realization
that modern Western culture is peculiar among cultures in having
developed such a sharp split between theory and spiritual practices.
For example, in the classical company of philosophers, if one were
a Stoic he would engage in practices every day to make himself
more in tune to the relationship between his logos or reason and the
logos of the universe. Likewise, the Epicurean would enter practices to help him yield to the nature of reality. Platonists, Aris-
totelians, Buddhists and many other ancient thinkers would engage
in behaviors — meditative disciplines and even ritual practices —
to aid in the development of composing and living out a philosophy or theology.

David Tracy was asked in a *Cross Currents* interview to put a
face on this insight or assertion about theory and practice or theology and spirituality. What people did he know or has he known
who achieved an admirable synthesis of intellectual reflection and
spiritual life? He named Karl Rahner, his old mentor Bernard Lonergan, Rowan Williams (the Anglican theologian and Archbishop
of Canterbury), Gustavo Gutierrez, and the monk Sebastian More,
whose spiritual theology, *The Fire and the Rose Are One*, Tracy
considers a remarkable work of integration.[4] More's title is of
course taken from an intricate and complex stanza in T. S. Eliot's
Four Quarets, "And all manner of thing shall be well/ When the
tongues of flame are in-folded/ Into the crowned knot of fire/ and
the fire and the rose/ are one."[5]

Tracy is profoundly interested in this kind of integration, yet one
must not assume that his God-book, so long in meditative production, will read like an Eliot poem. Neither will it read like most
books written in the genre of spiritual theology or spirituality. His

---

[4] *Ibid.*, 295.
[5] T.S. Eliot, *Four Quartets* (New York: Harcourt, Brace, Jovanovich, 1971) 55.

evolving work, informed by the spiritual life, nevertheless follows Tracy's familiar, rigorous hermeneutical method. He is drawn to the symbol, but before the symbol of the rose and the fire become one, they must give rise to critical thought! Two companion essays give us in broad, brush strokes the work that has obsessed Tracy in recent years. I will summarize each here for they give us a window not only into David Tracy's thought, but into tongues of flame, and into what the poet declared about the life of passionate engagement: "We can only live, only suspire/ consumed either by fire or fire" (T. S. Eliot).

One essay seeks to recover for theology and spiritual life the Hidden God of the Protestant tradition and the other piece recovers the Incomprehensible God of the Catholic traditions of apophatic mysticism and love mysticism. The rich theological program of David Tracy, always attentive to both the analogical and dialectical movements of the imagination, in its beginning expressed this full range of the imagination in terms of manifestation/proclamation, later in terms of the mystical/prophetic, and now in the recovered classical language of the Hidden-Revealed God and the Comprehensible-Incomprehensible God.

The essay, "The Hidden God," returns us to Martin Luther's God. Yet before Tracy takes us to Luther he offers a thundering prophetic word against the modern story. He begins his essay with these words, "The real face of our period, as Emmanuel Levinas saw with such clarity, is the face of the other: the face that commands, 'Do not kill me'. The face insists: Do not reduce me to your narrative."[6] Thus, we are reminded by Tracy that the minor literatures and unfamiliar stories of the other and the different now come from the margins to the center as categories, indeed faces, that cannot be denied or simply domesticated in all the major

---

[6] "The Hidden God," 5.

disciplines, including theology. According to Tracy, they come as "God's shattering otherness, the neighbor's irreducible otherness and the othering reality of 'revelation' (not the consoling modern notion of 'religion'). They come transgressing liberal pieties and the all too ordered economy of modern thought. This unexpected and uninvited revelation of the other, essays Tracy, "disrupts the continuities, the similarities, the communalities of all modern 'religion'." Tracy continues:

> God enters contemporary history not as a consoling "ism" but above all as an awesome, often terrifying, hope-beyond-hope. God enters history again not as a new speculation — but as an unpredictable, liberating, Hidden God. For this God reveals Godself in hiddenness: in the cross and negativity, above all in the suffering of those others whom the grand narrative of modernity has set aside as non-peoples, non-events, non-memories, in a word, non-history.[7]

How and where will we see this revelation? Tracy answers that we see this kind of disturbing return of the Divine as Gustavo Gutierrez tells the story of God speaking out of Job's whirlwind, as African American theologians sing with both joy and lamentation in prophetic resistance to mere modern theological speculations, and as Elizabeth Johnson dares to name this God, "She Who Is." We will see the return of this Hidden-Revealed God especially in the suffering of those ignored, marginalized, and colonized by the grand narrative of modernity. Tracy announces, "The Hidden God returns to undo the power of the modern *logos* over 'God' in many modern theologies."[8]

David Tracy is fascinated by how this dialectical return of God was named and known in the classical, protesting theology of Martin Luther. The theology of Luther brings the cross into conflict

[7] *Ibid.*, 8.
[8] *Ibid.*

with any optimistic narrative of creation, for there is an awefulness in both history and nature. This Lutheran theology of the cross likewise brings 'revelation' into tension with 'religion'. In Luther, the sacramental imagination turns its gaze from the categories of nature and reason to the cross: God is understood in Christ *sub contrariis* in and through Christ's cross, and in all the terrible hiddenness of the cross, and through the suffering caused by the violence of both secular and religious history. Tracy explains his attraction to the Lutheran prophetic corrective:

> The heart of Luther's original insight into God is that God's revelation is principally through hiddenness — i.e., God discloses Godself to sinful humans *sub contrariis*: life through death, wisdom through folly; strength through abject weakness. A hidden God is not merely humble but humiliated: *deus incarnatus, deus absconditus in passionibus.* God is found at the limit of the relentless dialectical logic of Hegel — that quintessentially Lutheran thinker — and in the political theology of Moltmann — that contemporary Lutheran *manque.* The Hidden God is *deus crucifixus,* the Crucified God. That is the God implicit in much liberation and political theology.[9]

For Tracy, this God is returning not merely in the highly personal form of the earliest Lutheran thinkers nor in the brooding existentialism of so many modern Lutherans from the theology of Tillich to the art of Ingmar Bergman. The return of God through the hiddenness of suffering, violence, negativity and the cross is now being rendered in historical-political terms. Now, with all who suffer in view, we must rethink our response to the question: "Does God lead history — or disrupt it? Appear at its center — or at its margins?"

Even as the postmodern appropriation of Luther's Hidden God invites the silenced and suffering to speak, so Tracy believes a recovery of the Incomprehensible God of the classical Catholic

---

[9] *Ibid.,* 9.

mystics can bring the repressed stories of the marginalized, the hysterics, the dissenters, the fools, the martyrs, the mystics and the avant-garde artists back into the theological conversation. When they are invited to speak in their own terms they utter otherness, difference, transgression and excess as an alternative discourse to "the deadening sameness and totalizing systems of modernity." With Levinas, Tracy knows that the desire for totality "is the concealed wish and death-dealing fate of modern reason."[10] Thus, of the four classical expressions of mysticism, Tracy, along with many postmodern thinkers, is interested in returning to the love mystics and the apophatic mystics in the experiment of re-imagining God for our times.

Tracy's essay on the return of the mystics only begins to sketch their importance for contemporary theology. The love mystics in their striking use of erotic as well as transgressive and even violent imagery subvert the modern notions of love as well- measured relationality and the pre-modern or neo-Platonic notions of love as emanation. Love is presented as transgression, excess and gift. Such a vision of love overthrows the possibility for totality not only in theology but in any encounter or relationship with an other. Not only does the face of the other declare, "Do not kill me," but also, "You cannot possess me, for I am other."

Closely related to the undomesticated spirit of transgression, excess and gift in the love mystics is the appeal to incomprehensibility by the apophatic mystics like Meister Eckhart and his Godhead beyond God. David Tracy is especially interested in how the recent work of Jacques Derrida and John Caputo make truly interesting and important use of the apophatic traditions.[11] Unlike

---

[10] "The Post-Modern Re-Naming of God," 244.

[11] Jacques Derrida and Gianni Vattimo (eds.), *Religion* (Stanford, CA: Stanford University Press, 1998). See Derrida's "Faith and Knowledge: The Two

modern existentialist thinkers such as Paul Tillich and Thomas Merton who viewed the apophatic as the emblem of a disturbing dark night of the soul, these postmoderns do not mourn the eclipse of comprehensive knowledge nor fear its shadows. Instead, they see the *positive reality* of the radical incomprehensibility of God and the resulting void of full presence or totality. The postmodern return of the apophatic refers not only to the problem of human finitude and lack of knowledge, but rather to incomprehensibility as a positive affirmation of the possibility of God's reality. We name with language yet beyond language, indeed even beyond the God clothed in the Word, what God perhaps is by conceding what God likely is not; for the postmodern Christian theologian, the Incomprehensible God is the most adequate naming of the Reality of God as mystery.

In the incomparable evolving work of David Tracy, God is returning with a new force in the company of mystics and prophets and in the stories of difference once too politely edited and censored or impolitely exiled and silenced by modern sensibilities. Yet Tracy, as a public theologian, does not simply commune with Christian mystics and prophets in his wide-ranging spiritual imagination. We are, after all, living in a sacramental universe. When asked a rather whimsical question, that if he could have dinner with any three people from the ages, with whom he would choose to eat, drink and talk, he answered quickly: "Plato without hesitation, Augustine without hesitation ... and probably either Kierkegaard or Nietzsche."[12]

What would he talk with them about? After a moment's reflection Tracy answered: *"My guess is that there would be a good*

Sources of 'Religion' at the Limits of Reason Alone," 1-78. John D. Caputo, *More Radical Hermeneutics: On Not Knowing Who We Are* (Bloomington, IN: Indiana University Press, 2000).

[12] "A Conversation with David Tracy," 312.

deal of conversation about the relationship between, for want of a
better word, beauty and truth. And the need to articulate that relationship in different forms and even different styles."[13] A theologian engaging postmodernism with the complex classical sensibilities of Tracy understands how the urgent need to heal the tear
between theory and praxis and to re-imagine the relationship
between theology and spiritual practices is profoundly related to
the question of beauty and truth, for the truth of religion, like the
truth of its nearest analogue, art, is primordially a truth of manifestation.

This truth, according to Tracy, is manifested in the many stories
of this large life disclosed in texts, events, images, persons, rituals
and symbols. In the quest for a well-integrated life, one must
thoughtfully, prayerfully and imaginatively consider all these
sources as one seeks to name oneself and render God's name in history. How do these stories save us? Living into them and through
them is only part of the answer. The rabbis are right; we tell a story
in order to find yet another story. Resisting narrative closure, and
yielding to Infinity rather than to a tempting historical totality, in
good religion as in good art, narratives lead to other narratives,
metaphors encourage new metaphors, practices invoke more practices and conversations invite more conversations.

Because theology is not mere God-talk in the end but also practice attentive to the true, the good and the beautiful, David Tracy
believes the theologian should indeed pray, for only the healing of
the modern split between theory and spiritual practice can help heal
this blessed fallen world. The modern critical philosopher undoubtedly sees an incommensurable divide between David Tracy's office
at the University of Chicago's Swift Hall and his chapel at Calvert
House, the Roman Catholic university chaplaincy two short blocks

---

[13] *Ibid.*

away. In Professor Tracy's book-cluttered office the critic might find copies of the works of Plato, Derrida, Augustine, Nietzsche, Eckhart and Freud open together on his large, oaken work table. And at a weekly Mass at Calvert House, the visitor observes a priest with the Gospel lesson open on the pulpit near him and the bread and cup on the ritual table in front of him. Following the ancient liturgical rhythms of Word and sacrament, Father David Tracy faithfully elevates and blesses the host, then he elevates and blesses the cup. The visiting philosopher likely shakes his skeptical head, but the poet, indeed, a favorite poet of the celebrating priest, has found language as real as the body and blood:

> All manner of thing shall be well
> When the tongues of flame are in-folded
> Into the crowned knot of fire
> And the fire and the rose
> Are one.[14]

---

[14] T.S. Eliot, *The Four Quartets*, 55. David Tracy discusses the work of Eliot in "Fragments: The Spiritual Situation of Our Times," *God, the Gift, and Post-modernism*, ed. John D. Caputo and Michael J. Scanlon (Bloomington, IN: Indiana University Press, 1999) 170-184.

GENERAL BIBLIOGRAFPHY

Allen, Douglas. *Structure and Creativity in Religion: Hermeneutics in Mircea Eliade's Phenomenology.* The Hague: Mouton, 1978.

Alter, Robert and Frank Kermode (eds.) *The Literary Guide to the Bible.* Cambridge, MA: Harvard University Press, 1987.

Altizer, Thomas J.J., et. al. (eds.) *Deconstruction and Theology.* New York: Crossroad Press, 1987.

Aristotle, *Poetics,* trans. W. Hamilton Fyfe. Cambridge: Harvard, 1960.

—. *The Basic Works of Aristotle,* ed. Richard McKeon. New York: Random House, 1941.

Auerbach, Erich. *Mimesis: The Representation of Reality in Western Literature.* Princeton, NJ: Princeton University Press, 1953.

Bakhtin, Mikhael. *The Problems of Dostoyevsky's Poetics,* ed. and trans. Caryl Emerson. Minneapolis, MN: University of Minnesota Press, 1984.

Bal, Mieke. *Reading Rembrandt: Beyond the Word-Image Opposition.* Cambridge: Cambridge University Press, 1991.

Ballinger, Phillip A. *The Poem as Sacrament: The Theological Aesthetics of Gerard Manley Hopkins.* Leuven/Grand Rapids, MI: Peeters Press/Eerdmans, 2000.

Baum, Frank. *The Wonderful Wizard of Oz.* London: British Film Institute, 1992.

Baudrillard, Jean. *America.* London: Verso, 1989.

Beckley, Bill and David Shapiro (eds.) *Uncontrollable Beauty: Toward a New Aesthetics.* New York: Allworth Press, 1998.

Bell, Richard H. (ed.) *The Grammar of the Heart: New Essays in Moral Philosophy.* New York: Harper and Row, 1988.

Bellah, Robert N. "Is There a Common American Culture?," *Journal of the American Academy of Religion* 66 (Fall 1998).

—. *Beyond Belief.* New York: Harper and Row, 1970.

Betz, Hans Dieter (ed.) *The Bible as a Document of the University.* Chico, CA: Scholars Press, 1981.

Bishop, Jonathan. *Some Bodies: The Eucharist and Its Implications.* Macon, GA: Mercer University Press, 1992.

Bly, Robert (ed.) *News of the Universe: Poems of Twofold Consciousness.* San Francisco, CA: Sierra Club Books, 1995.

Bogue, Ronald. *Deleuze and Guattari.* New York: Routledge, 1989.

Bonhoeffer, Dietrich. *Ethics*, trans. Neville Horton Smith. New York: Macmillan, 1963.

Bourdieu, Pierrie. *Pascalian Meditations.* Stanford, CA: Stanford University Press, 1997.

—. *The Logic of Practice.* Stanford, CA: Stanford University Press, 1980.

Brandt, Di. *Dancing Naked.* Stratford, Ont.: The Mercury Press, 1996.

Brockman, James R. *Romero: A Life.* Maryknoll, NY: Orbis Books, 1989.

Browning, D.S. and F.S. Fiorenza (eds.) *Habermas, Modernity and Public Theology.* New York: Crossroad, 1992.

Browning, D.S. (ed.) *Practical Theology: The Emerging Field in Theology, Church and World.* New York: Harper and Row, 1983.

Brunette, Peter and David Wells (eds.) *Deconstruction and the Visual Arts.* London: Cambridge University Press, 1994.

Burnham, Frederich B. (ed.) *Postmodern Theology: Faith in a Pluralistic World.* San Francisco, CA: Harper and Row, 1989.

Butler, Judith. *Bodies That Matter: On the Discursive Limits of Sex.* New York: Routledge, 1993.

Cairns, Scott. *Recovered Body.* New York: George Braziller Publisher, 1998.

Callahan, Sidney. *In Good Conscience: Reason and Emotion in Moral Decision Making.* San Francisco, CA: Harper, 1991.

Capps, Walter H. *Ways of Understanding Religion.* New York: Macmillan, 1972.

Caputo, John D. *More Radical Hermeneutics: On Knowing Who We Are.* Bloomington, IN: Indiana University Press, 2000.

—. *The Prayers and Tears of Jacques Derrida: Religion Without Religion.* Bloomington, IN: Indiana University Press, 1997.

Caputo, John D. and Michael J. Scanlon (eds.) *God, the Gift and Postmodernism.* Bloomington, IN: Indiana University Press, 1999.

Cassarella, Peter and George P. Schner, S.J. (eds.) *The Thought of Louis Dupre: Christian Spirituality and the Culture of Modernity.* Grand Rapids, MI: Eerdmans, 1988.

Cassirer, Ernst. *Kant's Life and Thought*, trans. James Haden. New Haven, CT: Yale University Press, 1985.

Cavanaugh, William T. *Torture and Eucharist: Theology, Politics and the Body of Christ*. Oxford: Blackwell Publishers, 1998.

Celan, Paul. *Der Meridan*. Frankfurt: Suhrkamp, 2000.

Chauvet, Louis-Marie and Francios Kabasele Lumbala (eds.) *Liturgy and the Body. Concilium*. Maryknoll, NY: Orbis, 1995.

—. *Symbol and Sacrament: A Sacramental Reinterpretation of Christian Existence*, trans. Patrick Madigan, S.J. and Madeleine Beaumont. Collegeville, MN: The Liturgical Press, 1995.

Christ, Carol. *Laughter of Aphrodite*. San Francisco, CA: Harper and Row, 1987.

Clayton, Jay and Erie Rothstein (eds.) *Intertextuality and Influence in Literary History*. Madison, WI: University of Wisconsin Press, 1991.

Comstock, Gary L. "Two Types of Narrative Theology," *Journal of the American Academy of Religion* 55 (Winter 1987) 687-717.

—. "Truth or Meaning: Ricœur versus Frei on Biblical Narrative," *Journal of Religion* 66 (Winter 1986) 117-140.

Coffin, William Sloane. *The Heart is a Little to the Left: Essays on Public Morality*. Hanover, NH: Dartmouth/University Press of New England, 1999.

Countryman, L. William. *The Poetic Imagination: An Anglican Spiritual Tradition*. Maryknoll, NY: Orbis Press, 1999.

Cousineau, Phil (ed.) *Soul: An Archaeology: Readings from Socrates to Ray Charles*. San Francisco, CA: Harper, 1994.

Cousins, Ewert. *Bonaventure and the Coincidence of Opposites*. Chicago, IL: Franciscan Herald, 1978.

Critchley, Simon. *The Ethics of Deconstruction: Derrida and Levinas*. London: Blackwell Publishers, 1992.

Crites, Stephen. "The Narrative Quality of Experience," *Journal of the American Academy of Religion* 39 (September 1971).

Crossan, John Dominic. *The Dark Interval: Towards a Theology of the Story*. Sonoma, CA: Polebridge Press, 1988.

—. *Paul Ricœur on Biblical Hermeneutics*. Missoula, MT: Scholars Press, 1975.

Damaiso, Antonio. *The Feeling of What Happens: Body and Emotion in the Making of Consciousness*. New York: Harcourt Brace & Company, 1999.

Damisch, Hubert. *The Judgement of Paris*. Chicago, IL: University of Chicago, 1996.

Deleuze, Gilles and Felix Guattari, *Kafka: Toward a Minor Literature*. Minneapolis, MN: University of Minnesota Press, 1986.

de Mann, Paul. *Allegories of Reading: Figural Language in Rousseau, Nietzsche, Rilke and Proust*. New Haven, CT: Yale University Press, 1979.

Derrida, Jacques and Gianni Vattimo (eds.) *Religion*. Stanford, CA: Stanford University Press, 1998.

Derrida, Jacques. *Writings and Difference*, trans. Allan Bass. Chicago, IL: University of Chicago Press, 1978.

Detwiler, Robert. *Uncivil Rites*. Champaign, IL: University of Illinois Press, 1996.

—. *Art/Literature/Religion: Life on the Borders*. Chico, CA: Scholars Press, 1987.

— (ed.) *Derrida and Biblical Studies* (*Semeia* 23). Chico, CA: Scholars Press, 1982.

—. *Story, Sign and Self*. Philadelphia, PA: Fortress Press, 1978.

Devaney, Shelia Greeve (ed.) *Theology at the End of Modernity*. Philadelphia, PA: Trinity Press International, 1991.

Dewey, John. *Characters and Events*. New York: Holt, Rinehart and Winston, 1929.

Di Censo, James J. *Hermeneutics and the Disclosure of Truth: A Study in the Work of Heidegger, Gadamer and Ricœur*. Charlottesville, VA: University of Virginia, 1990.

DiPasquale, Theresa M. *Literature and Sacrament: The Sacred and the Secular in John Donne*. Pittsburgh, PA: Duquesne University Press, 1999.

Dissanayake, Ellen. *Homo Aestheticus: Where Art Comes From and Why*. Seattle: University of Washington Press, 1992.

Driver, Tom F. *The Magic of Ritual: Our Need for Liberating Rites That Transform Our Communities*. San Francisco, CA: Harper San Francisco, 1991.

Dudley, Guilford III. *Religion on Trial: Mircea Eliade and His Critics*. Philadelphia, PA: Temple University Press, 1978.

Eagleton, Terry. *The Ideology of the Aesthetic*. Cambridge: Blackwell, 1990.

Ebert, Teresa. *Ludic Feminism and After: Postmodernism, Desire and Labor in Late Capitalism.* Ann Arbor, MI: University of Michigan, 1996.

Edmundson, Mark. *Literature Against Philosophy, Plato to Derrida: A Defence of Poetry.* New York: Cambridge University Press, 1995.

Eliade, Mircea. *Ordeal by Labyrinth: Conversations with Claude-Henri Racquet,* trans. Derek Coltman. Chicago, IL: University of Chicago Press, 1982.

——. (ed.) *The Encyclopedia of Religion.* Vol. 14. New York: Macmillan Publishing Company, 1987.

——. *Myth and Reality.* New York: Harper Torch Books, 1963.

——. *The Myth of the Eternal Return.* New York: Harper and Row, 1959.

Eliot, T.S. *Four Quartets.* New York: Harcourt, Brace, Jovanovich, 1971.

——. *George Herbert.* London: The British Council and the Book League by Longmans, Green 7 Co. 1962.

Espada, Martin (ed.) *Poetry Like Bread: Poets of the Political Imagination.* Willimanic, CT: Curbstone Press, 1994.

Eusden, John Dykstra and John Westerhoff III. *Sensing Beauty: Aesthetics, the Human Spirit, and the Church.* Cleveland, OH: United Church Press, 1998.

Fiorenza, Elizabeth Schüssler. *In Memory of Her: A Feminist Theological Reconstruction of Christian Origins.* New York: Crossroad, 1984.

——. *Bread Not Stone: The Challenge of Feminist Biblical Interpretation.* Boston, MA: Beacon Press, 1984.

Fiorenza, Francis Schüssler. *Foundational Theology: Jesus and the Church.* New York: Crossroad, 1985.

Fish, Stanley. *Self-Consuming Artifacts: The Experience of Seventeenth Century Literature.* Berkeley, CA: University of California Press, 1972.

Forche, Carolyn (ed.) *Against Forgetting: Twentieth-Century Poetry of Witness.* New York: W.W. Norton, 1993.

Frei, Hans. *Types of Christian Theology.* New Haven, CT: Yale University Press, 1992.

——. *The Identity of Jesus Christ.* Philadelphia, PA: Fortress Press, 1975.

——. *The Eclipse of Biblical Narrative.* New Haven, CT: Yale University Press, 1974.

Gadamer, Hans Georg. *Truth and Method.* ed. and trans. Garrett Barden and John Cumming. New York: Crossroad, 1988.

Garcia-Rivera, Alejandro. *The Community of the Beautiful: A Theological Aesthetics.* Collegeville, MN: The Liturgical Press, 1999.

Gates, Henry Louis Jr. *Loose Canon: Notes on the Culture Wars.* New York: Oxford University Press, 1992.

Geertz, Clifford. *Works and Lives: The Anthropologist as Author.* Stanford, CA: Stanford University Press, 1988.

—. *Interpretation of Cultures.* New York: Basic Books, 1973.

—. *Islam Observed.* New Haven, CT: Yale University Press, 1968.

Gerhart, Mary and Anthony C. Y. *Morphologies of Faith: Essays in Religion and Culture in Honor of Nathan A. Scott, Jr. (AAR Studies in Religion,* 59). Atlanta, GA: Scholars Press, 1990.

Gerhart, Mary and James G. Williams (eds.) *Genre, Narrative and Theology: (Semeia,* 43). Atlanta, GA: Scholars Press, 1988.

Gilkey, Langdon. *Gilkey on Tillich.* New York: Crossroad, 1990.

—. *Naming the Whirlwind: The Renewal of God Language.* New York: Bobbs-Merrill, 1969.

Girardot, Norman J. and Mac Linscott Ricketts (eds.) *Imagination and Meaning: The Scholarly and Literary Worlds of Mircea Eliade.* New York: Seabury Press, 1982.

Goldberg, Michael. "God, Action and Narrative: Which Narrative? Which Action? Which God?" *Journal of Religion* 68 (January 1988).

—. *Theology and Narrative: A Critical Introduction.* Nashville, TN: Abingdon, 1981.

Greeley, Andrew M. *The Catholic Imagination.* Berkeley, CA: University of California Press, 2000.

—. *Religion as Poetry.* New Brunswick: Transaction Publishers, 1995.

—. "Theology and Sociology: Validating David Tracy," *Journal of the American Academy of Religion* 59 (Winter 1991) 643-652.

Green, Garrett (ed.) *Scriptural Authority and Narrative Interpretation.* Philadelphia, PA: Fortress Press, 1987.

Griffin, David Ray with William A. Beardslee and Joe Holland. *The Varieties of Postmodern Theology.* Albany, NY: SUNY Press, 1989.

Grimes, Ronald L. *Deeply Into the Bone: Reinventing Rites of Passage.* Berkeley, CA: University of California Press, 2000.

—. "Diana's Funeral: A Ceremonial Distraction?" *AAR Religious Studies News* 12 (November 1997).

—. *Reading and Ritualizing: Ritual in Fictive, Liturgical, and Public Places.* Washington DC: The Pastoral Press, 1993.

——. *Ritual Criticism: Case Studies in Its Practice, Essays on Its Theory.* Columbia, SC: University of South Carolina Press, 1990.

——. "Of Words the Speaker, of Deeds the Doer," *The Journal of Religion* 66 (1986).

——. *Beginnings in Ritual Studies.* Lanham, MD: University Press of America, 1982.

Grosz, Elizabeth. *Space, Time, and Perversion: Essays on the Politics of Bodies.* New York: Routledge, 1995.

Grumbach, Doris. *The Presence of Absence: On Prayer and an Epiphany.* Boston, MA: Beacon Press, 1999.

Guerriere, Daniel (ed.) *Phenomenology of the Truth Proper to Religion.* Albany, NY: SUNY Press, 1990.

Harper, Ralph. *On Presence: Variations and Reflections.* Philadelphia, PA: Trinity Press International, 1991.

Hauerwas, Stanley, Nancy Murphy and Mark Nation (eds.) *Theology Without Foundations: Religious Practice and the Future of Theological Truth.* Nashville, TN: Abingdon Press, 1994.

Hauerwas, Stanley. *Unleashing the Scriptures: Freeing the Bible from Captivity to America.* Nashville, TN: Abingdon, 1993.

——. *After Christendom: How the Church is to Behave if Freedom, Justice, and a Christian Nation are Bad Ideas.* Nashville, TN: Abingdon Press, 1991.

Hauerwas, Stanley with William Willimon. *Resident Aliens: Life in the Christian Colony.* Nashville, TN: Abingdon Press, 1989.

Hauerwas, Stanley and Gregory L. Jones (eds.) *Why Narrative? Readings in Narrative Theology.* Grand Rapids, MI: Eerdmans, 1989.

Heaney, Seamus. *Crediting Poetry: The Nobel Lecture.* New York: Farrar, Straus & Grioux, 1995.

Hein, Hilde and Carolyn Korsmeyer (eds.) *Aesthetics in Feminist Perspective.* Bloomington, IN: Indiana University Press, 1993.

Heller, Scott. "Wearying of Cultural Studies, Some Scholars Rediscover Beauty," *The Chronicle of Higher Education* 14 (December 4, 1998).

Hemingway, Ernest. *For Whom The Bells Toll.* New York: Charles Scribner's Sons, 1940.

Herbert, George. *George Herbert: The Country Parson, The Temple,* ed. John N. Wall, Jr. (Classics of Western Spirituality). New York: Paulist Press, 1981.

Hewison, Robert. *John Ruskin: The Argument of the Eye*. Princeton, NJ: Princeton University Press, 1976.

Hill, Rowena. "Poured Out for You: Liturgy and Justice in the Life of Archbishop Romero," *Worship* 74 (September 2000).

Himes, Michael J. and Kenneth R. Himes, O.F.M. *Fullness of Faith: The Public Significance of Theology*. New York: Paulist Press, 1993.

Hoekema, David A. and Bobby Fong (eds.) *Christianity and Culture in the Crossfire*. Grand Rapids, MI: Eerdmans, 1997.

Holland, Scott. "First We Take Manhattan, Then We Take Berlin: Bonhoeffer's New York," *Cross Currents* 50 (Fall, 2000).

—. "How Do Stories Save Us?" *Louvain Studies* 22 (1997).

—. "Theology is a Kind of Writing: The Emergence of Theopoetics," *Cross Currents* 47 (Fall 1997).

—. "So Many Good Voices in my Head," *Soundings* 79 (Spring/Summer 1996).

—. "Communal Hermeneutics as Body Politics or Disembodied Politics?," *Brethren Life and Thought* (Spring 1995).

—. "Dialogue with the Other," *Conrad Grebel Review* 12 (Spring 1994).

—. "Signifying Presence: The Ecumenical Sacramental Theology of George Worgul," *Louvain Studies* 18 (1993).

—. "The Problems and Prospects of a Sectarian Ethic: A Critique of the Hauerwas Reading of the Jesus Story," *Conrad Grebel Review* 10 (Spring 1992).

Hollander, John. *Melodius Guile: Fictive Patterns in Poetic Language*. New Haven, CT: Yale University Press, 1988.

Hollywood, Amy, "On the Materiality of Air: Janet Kauffman's 'Bodyfictions'" *New Literary History* 27 (1996).

Holmer, Paul. *The Grammar of the Heart: New Essays in Moral Philosophy*, ed. Richard H. Bell. New York: Harper and Row, 1978.

Holquist, Michael. *Dialogism: Bakhtin and his World*. New York: Routledge, 1990.

— (ed.) *The Dialogic Imagination: Four Essays by M. M. Bakhtin*, trans. Caryl Emerson and Michael Holquist. Austin, TX: University of Texas Press, 1981.

Hoopes, James (ed.) *Pierce on Signs: Writings on Semiotic by Charles Sanders Pierce*. Chapel Hill, NC: University of North Carolina Press, 1991.

Hooks, bell. *Teaching to Transgress: Education as the Practice of Freedom*. New York: Routledge, 1994.

Iser, Wolfgang. *The Act of Reading: A Theory of Aesthetic Response*. Baltimore, MD: Johns Hopkins University Press, 1978.

Janzen, Jean. *Snake in the Parsonage*. Intercourse, PA: Good Books, 1995.

Jasper, David. *Rhetoric, Power and Community*. Louisville; KY: Westminster/John Knox Press, 1993.

— (ed.) *Postmodernism, Literature and the Future of Theology*. New York: St. Martin's Press, 1993.

Jauss, Hans Robert. *Toward an Aesthetic of Reception*, trans. Timothy Bahti. Minneapolis, MN: University of Minnesota Press, 1982.

Jeanrond, Werner G. and Jennifer L. Rike (eds.) *Radical Pluralism and Truth: David Tracy and the Hermeneutics of Religion*. New York: Crossroad, 1991.

Jeanrond, Werner and Claude Geffre. *Why Theology* (*Concilium* 6). Maryknoll, NY: Orbis, 1994.

Jeanrond, Werner G. *Theological Hermeneutics: Development and Significance*. New York: Crossroad, 1991.

—. *Text and Interpretation as Categories of Theological Thinking*. New York: Crossroad, 1988.

Kant, Immanuel. *Observations on the Feeling of the Beautiful and Sublime*, trans. John T. Goldthwait. Berkeley, CA: University of California Press, 1960.

Kaufman, Gordon. Review of *The Nature of Doctrine*, in *Theology Today* 42 (July 1985).

—. *The Theological Imagination: Constructing the Concept of God*. Philadelphia, PA: Westminster Press, 1981.

—. *An Essay on Theological Method*. Missoula, MT: Scholars Press, 1975.

Kearney, Richard. *The Poetics of Imagining: Modern to Post-modern*. New York: Fordham University Press, 1998.

—. *Poetics of Modernity: Toward a Hermeneutic Imagination*. New Jersey: Humanities Press, 1995.

Kelly, Michael (ed.) *The Encyclopedia of Aesthetics*. 4 vols. Oxford: Oxford University Press, 2000.

Kemp, Peter T. and David Rasmussen (eds.) *The Narrative Path: The Later Works of Paul Ricœur.* Cambridge: MIT Press, 1989.

Kermode, Frank. *The Genesis of Secrecy: On the Interpretation of Narrative.* Cambridge, MA: Harvard University Press, 1979.

Klassen, Walter (ed.) *Anabaptism Revisited.* Scottdale, PA: Herald Press, 1992.

—. *Anabaptism: Neither Catholic nor Protestant.* Waterloo, Ont.: Conrad Press, 1981.

Kort, Wesley A. *Text and Scripture: Literary Interests in Biblical Narrative.* University Park, PA: Penn State University Press, 1979.

Kreiswirth, Martin. "Trusting the Tale: The Narrative Turn in the Human Sciences," *New Literary History* 23 (Summer 1992) 629-657.

Kristeva, Julia. *Strangers to Ourselves,* trans. Leon S. Roudiez. New York: Columbia University Press, 1991.

—. *Desire in Language: A Semiotic Approach to Literature and Art,* ed. Leon S. Roudiez, trans. Thomas Gora, Alice Jardine and Leon S. Roudiez. New York: Columbia University Press, 1980.

Küng, Hans and David Tracy (eds.) *Paradigm Change in Theology.* New York: Crossroad, 1989.

Lakoff, George and Mark Johnson. *Philosophy in the Flesh: The Embodied Mind and Its Challenges to Western Thought.* New York: Basic Books, 1999.

—. *Metaphors We Live By.* Chicago, IL: University of Chicago Press, 1980.

Lakoff, George and Mark Turner. *More Than Cool Reason: A Field Guide to Poetic Metaphor.* Chicago, IL: University of Chicago Press, 1989.

Langer, Monika M. *Merleau-Ponty's Phenomenology of Perception.* Tallahassee, FL: Florida State University Press, 1989.

Leclercq, Jean. *The Love of Learning and the Love for God: A Study of Monastic Culture.* New York: Fordham University Press, 1982.

Leitch, Vincent B. *Deconstructive Criticism: An Advanced Introduction.* New York: Columbia University Press, 1983.

Levinas, Emmanuel. *Totality and Infinity: An Essay on Exteriority.* Pittsburgh, PA: Duquesne University Press, 1961.

Levinson, Jerrold (ed.) *Aesthetics and Ethics: Essays at the Intersection.* Cambridge: Cambridge University Press, 1998.

Lindbeck, George A. "Scripture, Consensus and Community," *This World: A Journal of Religion and Public Life* 23 (Fall 1988) 5-24.

—. *The Nature of Doctrine: Religion and Theology in a Postliberal Age.* Philadelphia, PA: Westminster Press, 1984.

Lisher, Richard. "The Limits of the Story," *Interpretation* 38 (January 1984).

Lonergan, Bernard J.F. *Insight: A Study of Human Understanding.* New York: Harper and Row, 1978.

—. *Method in Theology.* New York: Seabury Press, 1972.

Lyotard, Jean-Francios. *Toward the Postmodern.* New Jersey: Humanities Press, 1992.

—. *The Postmodern Condition: A Report on Knowledge,* trans. Geoff Bennington and Brian Massumi. Minneapolis, MN: University of Minnesota Press, 1989.

MacDonald, Diane Prosser. *Transgressive Corporeality: The Body, Post-structuralism, and the Theological Imagination.* Albany, NY: SUNY, 1995.

Macquarrie, John. *A Guide to the Sacraments.* New York: Continuum, 1997.

Madsen, Catherine. "Intellectual Light," *Cross Currents* 49 (Fall 1999).

—. "Liturgy for the Estranged: The Fascination of What's Difficult," *Cross Currents* 46 (1996-97) 471-486.

Magnus, Bemd, Stanley Stewart, and Jean-Pierre Mileur, *Nietzsche's Case: Philosophy As/And Literature.* New York: Routledge, 1993.

Mahan, B. and L.D. Richesin (eds.) *The Challenge of Liberation Theology: A First World Perspective.* Maryknoll, NY: Orbis Books, 1981.

Mariani, Philomena (ed.) *Critical Fictions: The Politics of Imaginative Writing.* Seattle: Bay Press, 1991.

Marion, Jean-Luc. *God Without Being,* trans. Thomas Carlson. Chicago, IL: University of Chicago, 1991.

Marshall, Bruce D. (ed.) *Theology and Dialogue: Essays in Conversation with George Lindbeck.* Notre Dame, IN: University of Notre Dame Press, 1990.

Marty, Martin E. *The Public Church.* New York: Crossroad, 1981.

Maslow, Abraham H. *Religions, Values and Peak Experiences.* New York: Viking, 1970.

May, Melanie. *A Body Knows: A Theopoetics of Death and Resurrection.* New York: Continuum, 1995.

McConnell, Frank (ed.) *The Bible and the Narrative Tradition.* New York: Oxford University Press, 1986.

McFague, Sallie. *Metaphorical Theology: Models of God in Religious Language*. Philadelphia, PA: Fortress Press, 1982.

McKeon, Richard (ed.) *The Basic Works of Aristotle*. New York: Random House, 1941.

McKnight, Edgar V. *Post-Modern Use of the Bible: The Emergence of Reader-Oriented Criticism*. Nashville, TN: Abingdon Press, 1988.

Merleau-Ponty, Maurice. "La Conscience et l'acquisition du langage," *Bulletin de psychologie* 18 (1964).

—. *Phenomenology of Perception*, trans. Colin Smith. London: Routledge and Kegan, 1961.

Metz, Johann Baptist. "In the Pluralism of Religious and Cultural Worlds: Notes Toward a Theological and Political Program," *Cross Currents* 49 (Summer 1999) pp.???.

—. *A Passion for God: The Mystical-Political Dimension of Christianity*. New York: Paulist Press, 1998.

Metz, Johann Baptist and Jürgen Moltmann, *Meditations on the Passion*. New York: Paulist Press, 1974.

Michelfelder, Diane P. and Richard Palmer. *Dialogue and Deconstruction: The Gadamer-Derrida Encounter*. Albany, NY: SUNY Press, 1989.

Miller, Richard. *Causitry and Modern Ethics: A Poetics of Practical Reasoning*. Chicago, IL: University of Chicago Press, 1996.

Mitchell, Nathan D. *Liturgy and the Social Sciences*. Collegeville, MN: The Liturgical Press, 1999.

Moltmann, Jürgen. *The Crucified God*. New York: Harper and Row, 1974.

Mudge, L. S. and J. N. Poling (eds.) *Formalism and Reflection: The Promise of Practical Theology*. Philadelphia, PA: Fortress, 1987.

Murphy, Nancey and James Wm. McClendon, Jr. "Distinguishing Modern and Postmodern Theologies," *Modern Theology* 5 (April 1989).

Murphy, Nancy. *Beyond Liberalism and Fundamentalism: How Modern and Postmodern Philosophy Set the Theological Agenda*. Valley Forge, PA: Trinity Press International, 1996.

Murray, Edward L. *Imaginative Thinking and Human Existence*. Pittsburgh, PA: Duquesne University Press, 1986.

Neruda, Pablo. *Love: Ten Poems by Pablo Neruda from the Movie The Postman*, comp. Francesca Gonshaw, trans. Alastair Reid. New York: Hyperion Miramax Books, 1996.

—. *Song of Protest*, trans. Miguel Algarin. New York: Murrow, 1976.

Norris, Kathleen. *Amazing Grace: A Vocabulary of Faith*. New York: Riverhead Books, 1998.

Nussbaum, Martha C. *Poetic Justice: The Literary Imagination and the Public Life*. Boston, MA: Beacon Press, 1995.

—. *Love's Knowledge: Essays on Philosophy and Literature*. New York: Oxford University Press, 1990.

Ogden, Schubert. *On Method*. San Francisco, CA: Harper and Row, 1986.

—. *Faith and Freedom: Toward a Theology of Liberation*. Nashville, TN: Abingdon, 1979.

O'Meara, Thomas A., O.P. and Celestin D. Weisser, O.P. (eds.) *Paul Tillich in Catholic Thought*. Dubuque, IA: The Priory Press, 1964.

Ormistom, Gayle L. and Alan D. Schrift. *The Hermeneutic Tradition: From Ast to Ricœur*. Albany, NY: SUNY Press, 1990.

Ottati, Douglas F. *Hopeful Realism: Reclaiming the Poetry of Theology*. Cleveland, OH: The Pilgrim Press, 1999.

Patrick, Anne E. "The Linguistic Turn and Moral Theology," *CTSA Proceedings* 42 (1987).

Patton, Paul (ed.) *Deleuze: A Critical Reader*. Cambridge: Blackwell, 1996.

Pauck, Wilhelm and Marion. *Paul Tillich: His Life and Thought*. Vol. I. New York: Harper and Row, 1976.

Peperzak, Adriaan T. (ed.) *Ethics as First Philosophy*. New York: Routledge, 1995.

Pepper, Stephen. *World Hypothesis*. Berkeley, CA: University of California Press, 1942.

Pickstock, Catherine. *After Writing: On the Liturgical Consummation of Philosophy*. Oxford: Blackwell, 1998.

Placher, William C. *Unapologetic Theology: A Christian Voice in a Pluralistic Conversation*. Louisville, KY: Westminster/John Knox Press, 1989.

—. "Hans Frei: The Bible as Realistic Story," *The Christian Century* 106 (May 24-31, 1989).

—. "Paul Ricœur and Postliberal Theology: A Conflict of Interpretations?," *Modern Theology* 4 (October 1987).

—. "Revisionist and Postliberal Theologies and the Public Character of Theology," *The Thomist* 49 (1985).

Plato, *The Republic*, trans. Francis McDonald Cornford. London: Oxford University Press, 1941.

Poland, Lynn M. *Literary Criticism and Biblical Hermeneutics: A Critique of Formalist Approaches*. Chico, CA: Scholars Press, 1985.

Power, David N. *Sacrament: The Language of God's Giving*. New York: Crossroad Publishing Company, 1999.

—. O.M.I. "Sacramental Theology: A Review of the Literature," *Theological Studies* 55 (1994).

Rappaport, Roy A. *Ritual and Religion in the Making of Humanity*. Cambridge: Cambridge University Press, 1999.

Ray, Allan. *The Modern Soul: Michael Foucault and the Theological Discourse of Gordon Kaufman and David Tracy*. Philadelphia, PA: Fortress Press, 1987.

Reynolds, Frank E. and Sheryl L. Burkhalter (eds.) *Beyond the Classics? Essays in Religious Studies and Religious Education*. Atlanta, GA: Scholars Press, 1990.

Ricœur, Paul. *Critique and Conviction: Conversations with Francois Azouvi and Marc de Launay*. New York: Columbia University Press, 1998.

—. *Oneself as Another*. Chicago, IL: University of Chicago Press, 1992.

—. *From Text to Action: Essays in Hermeneutics, II*,. trans. Kathleen Blamey and John B. Thompson. Evanston, IL: Northwestern University Press, 1991.

—. *Soi-Meme comme un autre*. Paris: Éditions du Seuil, 1990.

—. *Time and Narrative*. Vol. III, trans. Kathleen Blamey and David Pellauer. Chicago, IL: University of Chicago Press, 1988.

—. "Life: A Story in Search of a Narrator," in M.C. Doeser and J.N. Kraay (eds.) *Facts and Values*. Boston, MA: Martinus Nijhoff Publishers, 1986.

—. *Time and Narrative*. Vol. II, trans. Kathleen McLaughlin and David Pellauer. Chicago, IL: University of Chicago Press, 1985.

—. *Time and Narrative*. Vol. I, trans. Kathleen McLaughlin and David Pellauer. Chicago, IL: University of Chicago Press, 1984.

—. *Essays on Biblical Interpretation*, ed. Lewis S. Mudge. Philadelphia, PA: Fortress Press, 1980.

—. "Naming God," *Union Seminary Quarterly Review* 34 (1979).

—. "Manifestation and Proclamation," *Journal of the Blaisdall Institute*

12 (Winter 1978) 13-35.

—. "Can Fictional Narratives Be True?," in Anna-Teresa Tymieniecka, *The Phenomenology of Man and of the Human Condition*. Dordrecht: D. Reidel Publishing Company, 1978.

—. *The Rule of Metaphor: Multi-disciplinary Studies of the Creation of Meaning in Language*, trans. Robert Czerny. Toronto: University of Toronto Press, 1977.

—. "History of Religious Ideas," *Religious Studies Review* 1 (1976).

—. *Interpretation Theory: Discourse and the Surplus of Meaning*. Fort Worth, TX: Texas University Press, 1976.

—. "Philosophy and Religious Language," *Journal of Religion* 54 (1974).

—. "Creativity of Language," *Philosophy Today* 17 (1973).

—. *The Symbolism of Evil*. Boston, MA: Beacon, 1967.

Robinson, Ian. *The Establishment of Modern Prose in the Reformation and Enlightenment*. New York: Cambridge University Press, 1996.

Rollyson, Carl and Lisa Paddock. *Susan Sontag: The Making on an Icon*. New York: Norton, 2000.

Romero, Oscar. *Archbishop Oscar Romero: A Shepherd's Diary*. Cincinnati: St. Anthony Messenger Press, 1993.

—. *Voice of the Voiceless: the Four Pastoral Letters and Other Statements*. Maryknoll, NY: Orbis Books, 1985.

—. *The Church is All of You*. Minneapolis, MN: Winston Press, 1984.

Rorty, Richard. *Contingency, Irony, and Solidarity*. New York: Cambridge University Press, 1989.

—. "Philosophy as a Kind of Writing: An Essay on Derrida," *New Literary History* 10 (Autumn 1978).

Ruf, Frederick J. *Entangled Voices: Genre and the Religious Construction of the Self*. New York: Oxford University Press, 1997.

Sacks, Oliver. "The Lost Mariner," *New York Review of Books* 31 (1984).

Sanks, T. Howland, S.J. "David Tracy's Theological Project: An Overview and Some Implications," *Theological Studies* 54 (1993).

Scarry, Elaine. *On Beauty and being Just*. Princeton, NJ: Princeton University Press, 1999.

Schrag, Calvin O. *The Self After Postmodernity*. New Haven, CT: Yale University Press, 1997.

—. *The Poetics of Belief*. Chapel Hill, NC: University of North Carolina Press, 1985.

Shafer, Ingrid H. *The Incarnate Imagination: Essays in Theology, the Arts and Social Sciences in Honor of Andrew Greeley, A Festschrift.* Bowling Green, OH: Bowling Green University Press, 1988.

Simonson, Rick and Scott Walker (eds.) *The Greywolf Annual Five: Multi-Cultural Literacy.* Saint Paul: Greywolf Press, 1988.

Skarmeta, Antonio. *The Postman,* trans. Katherine Silver. New York: Hyperion Mirimax Books, 1995.

Smith, Huston. *Forgotten Truth: The Common Vision of the World's Religions.* San Francisco, CA: Harper and Row, 1992.

Sontag, Susan. "A Lament for Bosnia," *The Nation* (December 25, 1995).

—. "Godot Comes to Sarejevo," *New York Review of Books* (October 21, 1993).

—. *A Susan Sontag Reader.* New York: Vintage Books, 1983.

Stacy, George J. *Nietzsche and Emerson: An Elective Affinity.* Athens: Ohio University Press, 1992.

Steiner, George. *Real Presences.* Chicago, IL: University of Chicago Press, 1989.

Swidler, Leonard (ed.) *Consensus in Theology: A Dialogue with Hans Kung and Edward Schillebeeckx.* Philadelphia, PA: Westminster Press, 1980.

Tanner, Kathryn. "Respect for Other Religions: A Christian Antidote to Colonial Discourse," *Modern Theology* 9 (January 1993).

—. *The Politics of God: Christian Theologies and Social Justice.* Minneapolis, MN: Fortress Press, 1992.

Taylor, Mark C. (ed.) *Critical Terms for Religious Studies.* Chicago: University of Chicago Press, 1998.

—. *Erring: A Postmodern A/theology.* Chicago, IL: University of Chicago Press, 1984.

—. *Deconstructing Theology.* New York: Crossroad, 1982.

Temple, William. *Nature, Man and God.* London: Macmillan, 1940.

Theil, John E. *Nonfoundationalism.* Minneapolis, MN: Fortress Press, 1994.

—. *Imagination and Authority: Theological Authorship in the Modern Tradition.* Minneapolis,MN: Fortress Press, 1991.

Thiele, Leslie Paul. *Friedrich Nietzsche and the Politics of the Soul: A Study in Heroic Individualism.* Princeton, NJ: Princeton University Press, 1990.

Thiemann, Ronald F. *Constructing A Public Theology: The Church in a Pluralistic Culture.* Louisville, KY: Westminster/John Knox Press, 1991.

Thompson, William M. *Fire and Light: the Saints and Theology.* New York: Paulist Press, 1987.

Tillich, Paul. *The Relevance and Irrelevance of the Christian Message.* Cleveland, OH: The Pilgrim Press, 1996.

—. *Systematic Theology.* 3 vols. Chicago, IL: University of Chicago Press, 1951.

Tilley, Terrence W. *Story Theology.* Wilmington, DE: Michael Glazier, 1985.

—. "Incommensurability, Intertextuality and Fideism," *Modern Theology* 5 (January 1979).

Toole, David. *Waiting for Godot in Sarejevo.* Boulder, CO: Westview Press, 1998.

Toulmin, Stephen. *An Examination of the Place of Reason in Ethics.* Cambridge: Cambridge University Press, 1950.

Trilling, Lionel. *The Moral Obligation to be Intelligent: Selected Essays,* ed. Leon Wieseltier. New York: Farrar, Straus & Giroux, 2000.

Turner, Victor. *An Anthropology of Performance.* New York: PAJ Publications, 1987.

—. *From Ritual to Theatre: The Human Seriousness of Play.* New York: PAJ Publications, 1982.

Valdes, Mario J. (ed.) *A Ricœur Reader: Reflection and Imagination.* Toronto: University of Toronto Press, 1991.

van Braght, Thieleman. *The Bloody Theater or the Martyrs Mirror of the Defenseless Christians.* Scottdale, PA: Herald Press, 1997.

Vanhoozer, Kevin J. *Biblical Narrative in the Philosophy of Paul Ricœur: A Study in Hermeneutics and Theology.* New York: Cambridge University Press, 1990.

Viladesau, Richard. *God Through Music, Art and Rhetoric.* New York: Paulist Press, 2000.

—. *Theological Aesthetics.* Oxford: Oxford University Press, 1999.

Wainwright, Geoffrey. *Worship with One Accord: Where Liturgy and Ecumenism Meet.* New York: Oxford University Press, 1997.

Wall, James M. *Theologians in Transition.* New York: Crossroad, 1981.

Wallace, Mark I.. *Fragments of the Spirit.* New York: Continuum, 1996.

—. *The Second Naivete: Barth, Ricœur, and the New Yale Theology.* Macon, GA: Mercer University Press, 1990.

Weaver, Alain Epp. *Theology in Face of Modernity: Essays in Honor of Gordon Kaufman.* Newton, Kansas: Mennonite Press, 1996.

Wilder, Amos N. *The Bible and the Literary Critic.* Minneapolis, MN: Fortress Press, 1991.

—. *The Language of the Gospel: Early Christian Rhetoric.* New York: Harper and Row, 1964.

Williams, George Huston. *The Radical Reformation.*Philadelphia, PA: Westminster Press, 1962.

Winterson, Jeanette. *Art Objects: Essays on Ecstasy and Effrontery.* New York, Knopf, 1996.

Worgul, George. "Ritual, Power, Authority and Riddles: The Anthropology of Rome's Declaration on the Ordination of Women," *Louvain Studies* 14 (1989).

—. "Ritual as the Interpreter of Tradition," *Louvain Studies* 10 (1984).

—. "Death, Sacraments, and Christianity Spirituality," *Studies in Formative Spirituality* 2 (May 1981).

—. "Imagination, Ritual and Eucharistic Real Presence," *Louvain Studies* 9 (1982).

—. *From Magic to Metaphor: A Validation of the Christian Sacraments.* New York: Paulist Press, 1980.

Wyschogrod, Edith. *Saints and Postmodernism: Revisioning Moral Philosophy.* Chicago, IL: University of Chicago Press, 1990.

Yeats, William Butler. *Selected Poems and Four Plays*, ed. M. L. Rosenthal. New York: Scribner paperback Poetry, 1996.

Yoder, John Howard. *The Priestly Kingdom: Social Ethics as Gospel.* Notre Dame, IN: University of Notre Dame Press, 1984.

BIBLIOGRAPHY FOR DAVID TRACY

Prepared by the author from David Tracy's Working Bibliography compiled by David Tracy and Stephen Webb

Books

On Naming the Present: God, Hermeneutics and the Church. Maryknoll, NY: Orbis, 1994.

Dialogue With The Other, The Inter-Religious Dialogue. Based of the Dondeyne Lectures, University of Leuven. Leuven/Grand Rapids, MI: Peeters Press/Eerdmans, 1990.

Plurality and Ambiguity: Hermeneutics, Religion, Hope. San Francisco, CA: Harper and Row, 1987.

A Catholic Vision. With Stephen Happel. Philadelphia, PA: Fortress Press, 1984.

A Short History of the Interpretation of the Bible. With Robert Grant. Second edition. Philadelphia, PA: Fortress Press, 1984.

Talking About God: Doing Theology in the Context of Modern Pluralism. With John Cobb. New York: Seabury, 1983.

The Analogical Imagination: Christian Theology and the Culture of Pluralism. New York: Crossroad, 1981.

Blessed Rage for Order: The New Pluralism in Theology. New York: Seabury, 1975.

The Achievement of Bernard Lonergan. New York: Herder & Herder, 1970.

Articles, Chapters, and Papers

"The Post-Modern Re-Naming of God as Incomprehensible and Hidden," *Cross Currents* 50 (Spring/Summer 2000) 240-247.

"Writing," *Critical Terms for Religious Studies*, ed. Mark C. Taylor. Chicago, IL: University of Chicago Press, 1998.

"The Hidden God: The Divine Other of Liberation," *Cross Currents* 46 (Spring 1996) 5-16.

"Conversation with David Tracy," *Cross Currents* 44 with Todd Breyfogle and Thomas Livergood (Fall 1994) 293-315.

"Charity, Obscurity, Clarity: Augustine's Search for True Rhetoric," *Morphologies of Faith: Essays in Religion and Culture in Honor of Nathan A. Scott, Jr. (AAR Studies in Religion*, 59). Atlanta, GA: Scholars Press, 1990.

"On Reading the Scriptures Theologically," *Theology and Dialogue: Essays in Conversation with George Lindbeck*, ed. Bruce Marshall. Notre Dame, IN University of Notre Dame Press, 1990.

"Hermeneutics and the Tradition," *Proceedings of the American Catholic Philosophical Association* 62 (1990).

"God, Dialogue and Solidarity: A Theologian's Refrain," *The Christian Century* (October 10, 1990) 900-904.

"Hermeneutical Reflections in the New Paradigm," *Paradigm Change in Theology*, ed. Hans Kung and David Tracy. New York: Crossroad, 1989.

"The Uneasy Alliance Reconceived: Catholic Theological Method, Modernity, and Postmodernity," *Theological Studies* 50 (1989) 548-570.

"Argument, Dialogue and the Soul in Plato," *Witness and Existence: Essays in Honor of Schubert M. Ogden*, ed. Phillip E. Devenish and George L. Goodwin. Chicago, IL: University of Chicago Press, 1989.

"Hermeneutics," Article in *International Encyclopedia of Communication*. New York: Oxford university Press, 1989.

"Afterword: Theology, Public Discourse, and the American Tradition," *Religion and Twentieth-Century American Intellectual Life*. Cambridge: Cambridge University Press, 1989.

"On the Origins of Philosophy of Religion: The Need for a New Narrative of its Founding," *Myth and Philosophy*, vol. 1 of *Toward a Comparative Philosophy of Religion(s)*, ed. Frank Reynolds and David Tracy. Albany, NY: SUNY, 1989.

"Mystics, Prophets, Rhetorics: Religion and Psychoanalysis," *The Trial(s) of Psychoanalysis*, ed. Francoise Meltzer. Chicago, IL: University of Chicago Press, 1988.

"Can Virtue be Taught? Education, Character and the Soul," *Theological Education* 24, Supplement 1 (1988) 33-52.

"The Christian Understanding of Salvation-Liberation," *Face to Face: An Interreligious Bulletin*, Anti-Defamation League of B'nai B'rith, 19 (Spring 1988) 35-40.

"Theology and the Symbolic Imagination: A Tribute to Andrew Greeley," *The Incarnate Imagination, Essays in Honor of Andrew Greeley*, ed. Ingrid H. Schafer. Bowling Green, OH: Bowling Green State University Popular Press, 1988.

"Models of God: Three Observations, *(reply to Sallie McFague),"* *Religion and Intellectual Life* 5 (1988) 24-28.

"The Problem of Comparative Religion." Metaphysic nach Kant?, ed. Dieter Henrich and Rolf-Peter Horstmann. Publication of the 1987 Stuttgart Hegel Conference. Klett-Cotta, 1988.

"The Question of Criteria for Inter-Religious Dialogue: A Tribute to Langdon Gilkey," *The Whirlwind in Culture*, ed. Donald W. Musser and Joseph L. Price. Bloomington, IN: Meyer-Stone, 1988.

"Author's Response," In "Review Symposium on *Plurality and Ambiguity," Theology Today* 44 (January 1988) 513-519.

"Comparative Theology," *The Encyclopedia of Religion*. Vol. 14, ed. Mircea Eliade. New York: Macmillan, 1987: 446-455.

"Christianity in the Wider Context: Demands and Transformations," *Worldviews and Warrants: Plurality and Authority in Theology*, ed. William Schweiker and Per M. Anderson. Lanham, MD: University Press of American, 1987. Also published in *Religion and Intellectual Life* 4 (Summer 1987) 7-20.

"Practical Theology in the Situation of Global Pluralism," *Formation and Reflection, The Promise of Practical Theology*, ed. Lewis S. Mudge and James N. Poling. Philadelphia, PA: Fortress Press, 1987.

"The Christian Understanding of Salvation-Liberation," *Journal of Buddhist-Christian Studies* 7 (1987) 129-138.

"Exodus: Theological Reflection," *Exodus, A Lasting Paradigm. (Concillium* 189), ed. Bas Van Iersel and Anton Weiler. Edinburgh: T & T Clark, 1987.

"Particular Classics, Public Religion, and the American Tradition," *Religion and American Public Life*, ed. Robin Lovin. New York: Paulist Press, 1986.

"The Dialogue of Jews and Christians: A Necessary Hope," *Christian Theological Seminary Register* 76 (Winter 1986) 20-28.

"Religious Studies and its Community of Inquiry," *Criterion* 25 (Autumn 1986) 21-24.

"Hermeneutics as Discourse Analysis: Sociality, History, Religion," *Archivo Di Filosofia* 54 (1986) 261-184.

"Lindbeck's New Program for Theology: A Reflection," *The Thomist* 49 (July 1985) 460-472.

"Tillich and Contemporary Theology," *The Thought of Paul Tillich*, ed. J. Adams, W. Pauck and R. Shinn. San Francisco, CA: Harper and Row, 1985.

"Correlation between Theology and Catholic Charities," *Social Thought* 11 (Winter 1985) 24-31.

"Analogy, Metaphor and God-language: Charles Hartshorne," *Modern Schoolman* 62 (May 1985) 249-64.

"Is a Hermeneutics of Religion Possible?" *Religious Pluralism*, ed. L. Rouner. Notre Dame, IN: University of Notre Dame Press, 1984.

"Levels of Liberal Consensus," *Commonweal* 111 (August 10, 1984) 426-431.

"Existential Trust," *Commonweal* 111 (August 10, 1984) 429

"To Trust or Suspect," *Commonweal* 111 (October 5, 1984) 532-534.

"Karl Rahner, S.J, All is Grace," *Commonweal* 111 (April 20, 1984) 230.

"The Role of Theology in Public Life: Some Reflections," *Word & World: Theology for Christian Ministry* 4 (1984) 230-239.

"The Holocaust as Interruption and the Christian Return to History," With Elizabeth Schussler Fiorenza. *The Holucaust as Interruption. (Concillium* 1975), ed. with Elizabeth Schussler Fiorenza. Edinburgh, Scotland: T & T Clark, 1984.

"A Thoughtful Life, (review of Aurthur A. Cohen's *An Admirable Woman),*" *Commonweal* 111 (Feb. 10, 1984) 92-93.

"Creativity in the Interpretation of Religion: The Question of Radical Pluralism," *New Literary History* 15 (1983-1984) 289-309.

"On Thinking with the Classics (389th Convocation address at the University of Chicago)," *Criterion* 22 (Autumn 1983) 9-10. Also published in *The University of Chicago Record* 18 (April 20, 1984) 40-41.

"Religion and Human Rights in the Public Realm," *Daedalus* 112 (1983) 237-254.

"The Questions of Pluralism: The Context of the United States," *Mid-Stream: An Ecumenical Journal* 22 (1983) 273-285.

"Project X: Retrospect and Prospect," *Twenty Years of Concillium. (Concillium* 170), ed. P. Brand, E. Schillebeeckx and A. Weiler. New York: Seabury, 1983.

"Schubert M. Ogden: Doctor of Humane Letters," *Criterion* 22 (Autumn 1983) 3-4.

"Editorial," Cosmology and Theology (*Concillium* 166) With Nicholas Lash. New York: Seabury, 1983.

"The Foundations of Practical Theology," *Practical Theology*, ed. Don Browning. San Francisco, CA: Harper & Row, 1983.

"Foreword," *Edward Schillebeeckx: In Search of the Kingdom of God.* By John S. Bowden. New York: Crossroad, 1983.

"The Necessity and Insufficiency of Fundamental Theology," *Problems and Perspectives of Fundamental Theology*, ed. R. Latourelle and Gerald O'Collins. New York: Paulist Press, 1982.

"Religious Values After the Holocaust: A Catholic View," *Jews and Christians After the Holocaust*, ed. Abraham J. Peck. Philadelphia, PA: Fortress Press, 1982.

"Editorial," *The Challenge of Psychology to Faith. (Concillium* 156), ed. with Steven Kepnes. New York: Seabury Press, 1982.

"Some Reflections of Christianity in China," *Criterion* 21 (1982) 19-20.

"The Enigma of Pope John Paul II," *The Christian Century* 99 (January 27, 1982) 96-101.

"Theoria and Praxis: A Partial Response [to E. Farley and R.W. Lynn]," *Theological Education* 17 (1981) 167-174.

"Defending the Public Character of Theology: How My Mind Has Changed," *The Christian Century* 98 (April 1, 1981) 350-356. Also published in James Wall, editor, *Theologians in Transition*, New York: Crossroad, 1981.

"Author's Response," In "Review Symposium of David Tracy's *The Analogical Imagination*," *Horizons* 8 (1981) 329-339.

"Theology of Praxis," *Creativity and Method, Essays in Honor of Bernard Lonergan*, ed. Matthew Lamb. Milwaukee, WI: Marquette University Press, 1981.

"Theological Models: An Exercise in Dialectics," *Lonergan Workshop.* Vol. 2, ed. Fred Lawrence. Chico, CA: Scholars Press, 1981.

"The Question of Pluralism in Contemporary Theology," *The Chicago Theological Seminary Register* 71 (1981) 29-38.

"Introduction," *The Challenge of Liberation Theology, A First World Response*, ed. Brian Mahan and L. Dale Richesin. Maryknoll, NY: Orbis, 1981.

"Foreword," *The Tremendum: A Theological Interpretation of the Holocaust*. By Arthur A. Cohen. New York: Crossroad, 1981.

Parish, Priest and People: New Leadership for the Local Church. David Tracy, Andrew Greeley, Mary Durkin, John Shea and William McCready. Chicago, IL: Thomas More, 1981. Tracy made major contributions to chapter 4, "Systematic Theology of the Local Community," chapter 8, "Theological Reflection on Local Religious Leadership," and chapter 11, "Local Religious Leadership and Social Justice."

"Particular Questions within General Consensus [reply to H. Küng and E. Schillebeeckx]," *Journal of Ecumenical Studies* 17 (Winter 1980) 33-39. Also published in *Consensus in Theology? A Dialogue with Hans Küng and Edward Schillebeeckx*, ed. L. Swindler. Philadelphia, PA: Westminster, 1980.

"Reflections on John Dominic Crossan's *Cliffs of Fall*: Paradox and Polyvalence in the Parables of Jesus" *Society of Biblical Literature: Seminar Papers* no. 19 (1980) 69-74.

"Narrative and Symbol: Key to New Testament Spiritualities," *Scripture Today*, ed. Durstan R. McDonald. Eleventh national Conference of the Trinity Institution, 1980.

"Books: Critics' Christmas Choices," *Commonweal* 107 (Dec. 5, 1980) 703.

"Editorial," *What is Religion? An Inquiry for Theology*. Edited with Mircea Eliade. (*Concillium* 136) New York: Seabury Press, 1980.

"Grace and the Search for the Human: the Sense of the Uncanny," *Catholic Theological Society of America Proceedings* 34 (1980) 64-77.

"The Catholic Model of Caritas: Self-Transcendence and Transformation," *The Family in Crisis or Transition.* (*Concillium* 121), ed. A. Greeley. New York: Seabury Press, 1979.

"Theological Pluralism and Analogy," *Thought* 54 (1979) 24-37.

"The Particularity and Universality of Christian Revelation," *Revelation and Experience.* (*Concillium* 113), ed. E. Schillebeeckx and Bas Van Iersel. New York: Seabury Press, 1979.

"Metaphor and Religion," *On Metaphor*, ed. Sheldon Sacks. Chicago, IL: University of Chicago Press, 1979. Publication of *Critical Inquiry* 5 (1978).

"A Catholic Answer," In *Why Did God Make Me?* (*Concillium* 108), ed. Hans Küng and Jürgen Moltmann. New York: Seabury Press, 1978.

"Theological Response to 'Kingdom and Community' [J. G. Gager]," *Zygon* 13 (June 1978) 131-135.

"Responses to Peter Berger (with Langdon Gilkey and Schubert Ogden)," *Theological Studies* 39 (September 1978) 486-507.

"Introductory Essay and Preface," *Toward Vatican III: The Work That Needs To Be Done*. New York: Seabury Press, 1978.

"Christian Faith and Radical Equality," *Theology Today* 34 (January, 1978) 370-377.

"The Public Character of Systematic Theology," *Theological Digest* 26 (1978) 400-411.

"Introduction," *Celebrating the Medieval Heritage*, ed. David Tracy. Chicago, IL: University of Chicago Press, 1978. Originally published as *Journal of Religion* 58 (Supplement, 1978).

"The Catholic Theological Imagination [Presidential Address]," *Catholic Theological Society of America Proceedings* 32 (1977) 234-244.

"Modes of Theological Argument," *Theology Today* 33 (January 1977) 387-395.

"Reflections on the Challenge of Marxism," *New Catholic World* 220 (May 1977) 116-17.

"Ethnic Pluralism and Systematic Theology: Reflections," *Ethnicity*. (*Concillium* 101.) Edited by A. Greeley and Gregory Baum. New York: Seabury Press, 1977.

"John Cobb's Theological Method: Interpretation and Reflections," *John Cobb's Theology in Process*, ed. David Ray Griffin and Thomas J. J. Altizer. Philadelphia, PA: Westminster Press, 1977.

"Sin Against God, Man: Moral Choices in Contemporary Society," *National Catholic Reporter* 13 (May 6, 1977) 14.

"Theological Classics in Contemporary Theology," *Theological Digest* 25 (1977) 347-355.

"On Galatians 3:28," *Criterion* 16 (Autumn 1977) 10-12.

"Revisionist Practical Theology and the Meaning of Public Discourse," *Pastoral Psychology* 26 (Winter 1977) 83-94.

"We Still Have Some Unresolved Theological Differences," Symposium with Martin Marty, David Burrell, and Avery Dulles. *National Catholic Reporter* 14 (November 4, 1977) 9-10.

"A Theological Brief," *American Academy of Religion, Philosophy of Religion and Theology Proceedings*. University of Montana: Scholars Press, 1976: 197-200.

"Analogical Vision: Some Reflections on the American Roman Catholic Bicentennial Social Justice Program," *Criterion* 15 (Autumn 1976) 10-16.

"Editors Bookshelf: Contemporary Theology and Philosophy of Religion," *Journal of Religion* 55 (October 1975) 489-492.

"Theology as Public Discourse," *The Christian Century* 92 (March 19, 1975) 280-284.

"Whatever Happened to Theology? (Symposium)," *Christianity and Crisis* 35 (May 12, 1975) 119-120.

"Tradition and Innovation: the Medieval Religious Heritage Lectures," *Criterion* 14 (Winter 1975) 20-22.

"Eschatological Perspectives on Aging," *Pastoral Psychology* 24 (Winter 1975) 119-134.

"A Response and Commentary on Heidegger and Theology," *Listening* 10 (Winter 1975) 73-77.

"Task of Fundamental Theology," *Journal of Religion* 54 (January 1974) 13-34.

"Two Cheers for Thomas Aquinas," *The Christian Century* 91 (March 6, 1974) 260-262.

"St. Thomas Aquinas and the Religious Dimension of Experience: the Doctrine of Sin," *Proceedings of the American Catholic Philosophical Association* 48 (1974) 166-176.

"Bernard Lonergan as Interpreter of St. Thomas Aquinas," *Listening* 9 (Winter-Spring 1974) 173-177.

"Religious Language as Limit Language," *Theological Digest* 22 (1974) 291-307.

"The Religious Dimension of Science," *The Persistence of Religion*. (*Concillium* 81), ed. Andrew Greeley and Gregory Baum. New York: Herder and Herder, 1973.

"Catholic Presence in the Divinity School," *Criterion* 11 (Winter 1972) 29-31.

"God's Reality: The Most Important Issue," *National Catholic Reporter* 8 (June 23, 1972) 10-11. Also published in *Anglican Theological Review* 55 (April 1973) 218-224.

"Response to Dr. Ogden," *Thesis Theological Cassettes* 3 no. 9 (October 1972).

"Foundational Theology as Contemporary Possibility," *The Dunwoodie Review* 12 (1972) 3-20.

"Lonergan's Foundational Theology: An Interpretation and a Critique," *Foundations of Theology: Papers from the International Lonergan Conference*, 1970, ed. Phillip McShane. Dublin: Gill and MacMillan, 1971.

"Method as Foundation for Theology: Bernard Lonergan's Option," *The Journal of Religion* 50 (July 1970) 78-110.

"Why Orthodoxy in a Personalist Age," *Catholic Theological Society of America Proceedings* 25 (1970) 78-110.

Lonergan's Interpretation of St. Thomas Aquinas: The Intellectualist Nature of Speculative Theology, dissertation excerpt for the Theological Faculty of the Gregorian University, Rome, 1969.

"Prolegomena to a Foundation for Theology," *Criterion* 9 (Autumn 1969) 12-14.

"Review: *Jesus, God and Man*, and *Revelation as History*, both by Wolfhart Pannenberg," *Catholic Biblical Quarterly* 31 (April 1969) 285-288.

"Horizon Analysis and Eschatology," *Continuum* 6 (1968) 166-179.

"Holy Spirit as Philosophical Problem," *Commonweal* 89 (Nov. 8, 1968) 205-213. Reprinted in D. Callahan, editor. *God, Jesus and Spirit*, New York: Herder, 1969.

The Oneness of God, ed. Jerome F. Filteau, et. al. Prepared by Theological College Class 1971 at Catholic University of America School of Theology. Based on notes from the lectures of David Tracy during Spring, 1968. Published privately by Theological College Publications.

Selected Interviews

Kendig Brubaker Cully. "Interview with David Tracy," *The Review of Books and Religion* 10 (Mid-January 1982) 6.

Eugene Kennedy. "A Dissenting Voice, Catholic theologian David Tracy," *The New York Times Magazine* (Nov. 9, 1986).

Cullen Murphy. "Who Do Men Say That I Am?" *The Atlantic Monthly* 258 (Dec. 1986). Includes an interview with Tracy.

Kenneth L. Woodward. "David Tracy, Theologian," *Newsweek*, August 24, 1981: 73.

Scott Holland, "This Side of God: A Conversation with David Tracy," *Cross Currents* 52 (Spring 2002) 54-59.

INDEX

19 not merely a churchly Theologian vs
   Theology for the church = Imbelli

20 - Theology of mediation + !

23 - Public character of theology

24 - quote - nature of Theology = public = correlational

27 - Public square = source of theology

29 - Imbelli! Thrown like a stone

33 - How I changed my mind * +

35 - conversation overcomes circularity

41 - cognitive claims v. action

45 - theological claims argued on public grounds

53 - mode of being in text

54 - religious language = logically odd !

55 - classic Thomism not coherent

63 - Theology must be conversational

66 - live in time of fundamental pluralism — Taylor

74 - Barthian, pure narrative confessionalism

80 - Placher essay

81 - experiential - expressionist

83 - Tracy finds sacred presence in many places

90 - "buzzing, bloomy" James

93 - pluralism danger = collapse other into
   generic humanism

98 - quote - summary of Yale School

101 - quote — "no innocent texts"